D1056528

FROM
Stress
TO
Success

Xandria Williams, M.Sc., DIC, ARCS, ND, DBM, MRN
Naturopath, Nutritionist, Herbalist, Homoeopath, NLP and Reiki
practitioner

Xandria Williams obtained her chemistry degrees from Imperial College, London and began her career as a geochemist. She then turned to biochemistry, human metabolism and nutrition. She trained as a naturopath, nutritionist, herbalist and homoeopath and subsequently in NLP, psychotherapy and personal development techniques. She is currently in private practice in central London and near Dublin, Ireland.

Xandria has lectured extensively on biochemistry, nutrition, the natural therapies and physical, mental and emotional health care, both in undergraduate courses and to graduates and special interest groups. She has presented many seminars on personal development and stress management, written over 350 articles and 14 books and has appeared frequently on radio and television.

Her unique skills in explaining complex concepts in simple, straightforward terms and in showing people the direct and personally-applicable steps by which they can achieve the desired results have been developed over more than two decades in private practice. Her ability to make all this knowledge practical and accessible has enabled her to help many thousands of people to a happier and healthier life, both through her writing and her clinical work with patients.

Xandria can be contacted for consultations, books or products in London on (44) 020-7824-8153 or in Ireland on (353) 0405-31191 email to xkw@bigfoot.com
www.xandriawilliams.com

FROM
Stress
TO
Success

10 Steps to a Relaxed
and Happy Life

Xandria Williams

Thorsons

Thorsons
An imprint of HarperCollins*Publishers*
77–85 Fulham Palace Road
Hammersmith, London W6 8JB

The Thorsons website address is
www.thorsons.com

First published in 1993 by Charles Letts & Co Ltd
Revised edition published by Thorsons 2001

1 3 5 7 9 10 8 6 4 2

© Xandria Williams 2001

Xandria Williams asserts the moral right to
be identified as the author of this work

A catalogue record for this book
is available from the British Library

ISBN 0 00 711791 4

Printed and bound in Great Britain by
Martins the Printers Limited, Berwick upon Tweed

All rights reserved. No part of this publication may be
reproduced, stored in a retrieval system, or transmitted,
in any form or by any means, electronic, mechanical,
photocopying, recording or otherwise, without the prior
permission of the publishers.

Dedication

To Shelagh Riall, my aunt, my friend,
my guide and my inspiration,
in loving memory and positive anticipation

To friends, patients and workshop participants,
for their trust in me and for giving freely of themselves,
thereby offering the examples that are shared here
with you, the reader

While the author of this work has made every effort to ensure that the information contained in this book is as accurate and up-to-date as possible at the time of publication, medical and pharmaceutical knowledge is constantly changing and the application of it to particular circumstances depends on many factors. Therefore it is recommended that readers always consult a qualified naturopathic or medical specialist for individual advice. This book should not be used an as alternative to seeking professional advice which should be sought before any action is taken. The author and publishers cannot be held responsible for any errors and omissions that may be found in the text, or any actions that may be taken by a reader as a result of any reliance on the information contained in the text, which is taken entirely at the reader's own risk.

Contents

Part II: The Physical Aspects of Stress

Preface

This is a book about choices. Stress is not necessary; it can be eliminated. It is yours if you choose to experience it; equally, by the choices you make, you can avoid and eliminate stress from your experience.

You are only stressed if you think you are. You are only helpless if you think you are. You are only trapped in a situation from which you cannot escape if you think you are. By altering the way you think, your attitudes and your expectations you can choose to have a stress-free existence. In this book you will learn how to accomplish this. The changes you make in your life as a result will enable you to change the way you think and feel and will also bring about unexpected changes in the people and events around you.

There is no such entity as a stress, out there, waiting to get you. What stresses you depends on your response and says more about you than about the external factors that trigger your stress response. Learn about yourself. By developing a better understanding of yourself and your reactions, by being willing to take control of your life and your thoughts, by coming to terms with yourself and by giving yourself the respect, trust and love that you give to other people you can turn a stressful and worrying existence into days of peace and pleasure.

The aim of this book is to empower you to re-create your life. The future is yours: it can be similar to the present with its anxieties, fears and stresses, or it can be positive and peaceful.

Stress or peace, the choice is yours. This book will give you the tools and help you to make the choice and create the peace.

The following concepts and strategies are covered in Part I:

1 Stress is your own experience. It is personal to you and generated by you. It is not directly to do with things outside yourself; they are only the triggers to a response from within you, a response that is individual to you.

2 Feeling stressed is your choice and you can choose to continue or to stop. There is no such thing as a universal stress.

3 You can use the awareness of what stresses you to learn more about yourself and then use this knowledge for change (of yourself).

4 Be willing to change what you are doing – if what you have been doing has not been working, be willing to do something different.

5 You are responsible for, and have had some input into, all that happens, and has happened, in your life. Be willing to assume that you are in total control. Be willing to give up victim status.

6 Get clear on your outcome – what are you really trying to achieve? Are you trying to prove someone else wrong, to force someone else to be different, to have something to complain about, to get sympathy or attention? Do you really want to reduce your stress?

7 Know you can cope. Avoid the stress caused by fear of the unknown. Imagine the worst possible scenario. Find out how you would deal with it. Then get on with handling the present.

8 Believe in a positive future, that whatever happens is, and will be, for the best, but do this without ceasing to care and without developing a laissez-faire attitude.

9 Much stress is caused by your fear of other people's opinions of you and your deeds. Decide who you are and who you want to be. Get a clear statement of purpose, develop your own Life Plan. Keep this plan clearly in your mind, live by it and many of your stresses will dissipate.

10 You are terrific. Most stress comes from your feelings of inadequacy. Develop full confidence in yourself, be willing to like, love and approve of yourself. If you don't, who will?

Introduction

Since this is a book about stress it is important, from the start, to establish what we mean by stress. Many people discuss stress as if it is some
sort of external agent or event that has attacked them. In fact, stress is
not something external that you can define, identify and measure.
Stress is the disturbance created within you by your response to a situation or activity, be it internal or external.

Stresses can be pleasant, such as the excitement caused by an anticipated pleasurable event. They can also be unpleasant and cause you
distress. It is these unpleasant stressful responses to situations that we
will be discussing and dealing with here.

This book will show you how to handle these unpleasant stresses in
your life by a new and positive method, one that helps you to get to the
real heart of the problem and solve it. In this way you can rid yourself of
all your responses to situations and people that currently cause you to
feel worried, anxious, fearful, angry, resentful, guilty, dominated, out of
control and many other unpleasant emotions.

You will learn how to eliminate the stress from your life, once and for all.
You will learn how to discover the real causes of the way you feel and how
to change so that your life is stress-free and positive. You will still have
challenges but they will be of your own choosing and will not distress you.
Stress in itself is not bad; it is part of the challenge and excitement of life. It
is the stresses that cause distress that we are aiming to eliminate.

To eliminate this stress you will not be taught first aid techniques for
handling it. Techniques such as deep breathing, relaxation, meditation,

learning to count to ten and so forth may indeed help you to handle the stresses you have now, provided you practise them consistently, but they will not eliminate your stresses. They may even work against you. I recently spoke with someone who said they did their relaxation techniques so well before an exam that when it was time for them to write the paper they were too relaxed to put a lot of energy into it and as a result they failed.

The ideas described here are not designed to help you cope with stress. They are designed to reduce and even eliminate the times you feel stressed, the times you feel an unpleasant response to a situation.

Identifying the problem

Most people have problems and most people put these problems down to stress. The trouble with this is that it is not specific. The statement 'I am stressed' does not identify the problem and so it does not lead to the finding of a solution to the situation.

Over the years countless patients have come into my practice saying that they are suffering from stress, with no details as to precisely what they mean by that, as if the term alone explained everything. It sometimes even seems that they think of it as some sort of bug they have caught, for which they are not responsible. As they might expect, inappropriately, an antibiotic from a doctor for a cold, they seem to expect a few vitamin pills or herbs from a naturopath to give them the calm they desire.

The really troublesome aspect of their approach is that their argument seems to go like this:

My life is not working at the moment, there are problems. I have too much to do, too little money, too many responsibilities, too little time. I'm not loved enough by people I love, my friends let me down, the boss is impossible, the children are a worry, the news is always bad, times are tough. If only the recession would lift, the children would behave, the boss would retire, my marriage could be the way it was in the beginning, people would expect less of me, then I would be happy.

In other words, if those outside situations changed then they would be happy. There is rarely a recognition that they could change and thus improve the situation.

There are always many seemingly rational explanations for the fact that your life is not exactly the way you want it to be. It is all too easy to assume that the solution lies outside yourself, in the world at large. The problem is that you cannot force all these external factors to change in the way you would like them to. The next assumption is that since you cannot change these external factors, you are helpless to improve your situation.

The comforting thing about this assumption and this attitude is that the problems are not your responsibility, they are not of your own making and you cannot be blamed for them. The trouble with this view is that since, for things to get better in your life, things outside your direct control have to change, you are helpless and the best you can do is to try to make the best of things and learn tolerance and acceptance.

This attitude means that the solution to your present stress must come from improving your ability to handle your present, apparently unchangeable, stresses. Thus you do relaxation exercises, deep-breathing exercises and go to classes on other stress-handling techniques, all aimed at increasing your ability to cope. Sadly, these are largely quick fixes and rarely work on a long-term and permanent basis to make your life happier and more stress-free.

The alternative method is to believe that you are indeed, in some way, responsible for the way you feel. You may not be able to control the recession, but you can control your own finances and the way you think about them. You may not be able to force the children to behave differently, but you can change the way you treat them and the way in which you respond to their behaviour. You can assume that a way does exist to create a more comfortable relationship with your boss and you can then work on discovering it.

While this approach takes away the comfort of blaming outside factors for your situation and stops you being a victim who deserves sympathy, it does give you a powerful tool in return. It encourages you to make the positive changes that will indeed lower the amount of stress you experience. So let's explore this approach further.

The concept of stress

Stress is not a new or rare concept. Almost everyone, at some time or another, thinks they are stressed. The overworked, overworried, unhappy person knows they are stressed all the time. Worse still, they will claim their problem is (non-specific) stress rather than concern over a specific issue. Even the happiest of people will almost certainly claim to feel stressed occasionally. There are few people who have not, at one time or another, said they were stressed. Most people feel stressed, and say so, at some point. People you know do. You do, don't you? Otherwise you wouldn't be reading this book.

It may surprise you to know that stress, as an entity, is a new concept, a concept of the past 40 or so years. Our grandparents did not grow up with stress as a familiar word. They might have said they were worried, afraid, tired or had too much to do, but they probably didn't lump it all together and call it stress. Today, however, everyone is familiar with the concept of stress. You probably think of stress as anything difficult, troublesome, painful, challenging or harmful in your life. You may blame stress for the way you feel and the way you behave. You probably blame stress for everything that goes wrong in your life, much that goes wrong with your body and most of the things with which you cannot cope. You may then blame these problems, in turn, for making you feel even more stressed. You may even think that if you had a totally stress-free existence your life would be perfect.

If you read the papers, magazines and books and listen to the media, you will have realized that you are constantly being exposed to the idea that you should reduce the stress in your life, you should learn to cope with stress, you should overcome stress and not let it get you down. You may indeed have tried the old and hackneyed so-called remedies for stress, but the stress and your feelings of tension and diminished health have continued. You may even be feeling more stressed by your inability to profit from the books on relaxation and meditation and your inability to conquer your stress.

All too often the problem of stress can become overwhelming. When you are under great strain it is easy to lose the ability to view yourself and the situation from a realistic perspective. You may then make a number of rash decisions, based on erroneous premises and create more stress for yourself, thus generating a vicious circle.

The pace of life is faster in the 21st century than it has ever been before. In the past we spoke to our friends face to face or wrote letters; later we used the phone; now we are supposed to be able to master computers, mobile communications, the internet, IT, WAP and a multitude of technologies. In the past we walked from place to place; now we are supposed to be able to handle with equanimity crowded trains on unreliable timetables, road chaos and traffic jams or near misses in the sky. In the past we lived close to the earth with space to move and breathe freely, space to be alone or with friends; now we live in crowded towns and cities, rarely exposed to the peace of the open countryside. When some of us grew up we had a full expectation of getting a job and finding full employment for our whole working life; that is no longer the case. We used to live in a relatively unpolluted world; now we consume or are exposed to thousands of toxins, many of which affect our emotional state and mental clarity. No wonder so many people feel that stress is on the increase.

Where other books on stress tell people how to relax, how to meditate, how to do deep breathing exercises, in this book you will be taken back to the ultimate source of your stress and given assistance in identifying the specific problem. 'Stress', as a word on its own, is, as we have seen, too vague and non-specific. It is an amorphous monster waiting to attack and forever evading defeat. If you say you are stressed, there may seem to be little you can do about it. On the other hand, if you say you are frightened, you can identify the object of your fear and deal with it. If you say you are angry, you can identify the cause of your anger and do something about it. If you say you feel guilty, you can identify the cause of your guilt and do what is appropriate to assuage it. In phrasing the problem you also identify the area of your life with which you have to deal. By putting the problem into a large miscellaneous basket labelled 'stress', it loses its identity and becomes some overwhelming ogre that you cannot fight.

There are, however, several levels in this self-exploration. At the first level you may say you feel stressed. At the second level you may identify the major problem in your life as worries about money. In turn this may worry you because it may mean you cannot provide for those you love. At an even deeper level you may fear that if you cannot provide for them they will leave you, or they will think badly of you. Thus you will, in time, get down to the ultimate problem, your own insecurity about yourself.

You can deal with specific emotions more easily than with unidentified 'stress'. Finding the root cause of the problem will enable you to solve the problem rather than just deal with it. Here we will be working together to find the specific cause of your feelings of stress and then to resolve the issues involved.

Once you have done this you no longer have to deal with stress, you no longer need to feel stressed, and it is easy. The solution, once you have grasped it, is not something that you have to work at remembering to do. You do not have to be disciplined and force yourself to deal with the problems in the new way. The new way, once you fully grasp it, becomes the obvious, easy and most satisfactory way of dealing with the challenges in your life. It is like walking through a peaceful and newly discovered mountain pass rather than having to struggle to climb the rugged and dangerous mountain. Just as you do not have to discipline yourself not to struggle over the rugged mountain to get to the next valley, once you have discovered the easy pass, so it is with this new way of dealing with the situations that arise in your life. It is much easier than the old approach.

This book is divided into two parts involving respectively your emotions and your physical health. Before you start on your journey it is important for you to consider whether or not there is a physical basis for any of the stress you are feeling. A number of physical health problems can lead to you feeling stressed, uptight, easily irritated, depressed or anxious.

The first, and major, part of the book covers your own internal emotional and intellectual responses to situations and the ways in which these can be changed. The second part covers the physical health problems that can generate feelings of stress. If you think there is a physical health problem to be solved then take a quick look at Part II. After all, there is little point in working through Part I and searching for problems in your apparently happy childhood when the real cause of your present situation is the tension caused by consuming a food to which you are allergic, the jitters caused by hypoglycaemia or the emotional disturbances resulting from an excess of *Candida albicans* in your system.

You may indeed have unresolved issues resulting from your parents' divorce or your feelings of being second best as a child, but focusing on these will be of only partial help if you neglect your nutrition and suffer physical ill-health as a result. Most people will find that both parts of the book are important and helpful.

Do not be misled by the fact that the second part is the shorter of the two. It is meant as a guideline, to point you in the direction in which you need to go for better physical health. The first part is the longer of the two, as here we explore the emotional aspects of stress in greater detail than the physical ones. It offers some new concepts on ways to deal with stress, concepts that have been used extensively with patients and workshop participants and produced exciting results, concepts that, therefore, warrant a more extensive explanation and discussion.

It is now time to outline the various components of the book in greater detail.

Part I: The emotional aspects of stress

Your first challenge starts right here. The following 10 points are fundamental to the method of dealing with stress presented in this book. Read these 10 points before you read the rest of the book and as you do so, become aware of your own reactions to them and, more importantly, write these down.

You will almost certainly feel like arguing with some, if not most, of the points listed. You may want to claim that things are not your fault, that you cannot change things but are stuck in a highly stressful situation. You may argue that there is nothing to be done about the stresses in your life or that if there is then someone else should be doing it. You may insist that things are so bad there is no way out and the future can only be worse. Write these thoughts down.

You may protest that the ideas expressed are familiar to you, that you have read or heard them before, that you have done the things that are suggested and yet you still feel stressed. Write these comments down.

Keep these notes handy. Read the book and do the (mental) exercises suggested. Make the changes that seem appropriate to you. Then, when you have completed the book, read this section again with your original notes beside you and discover how much you have changed.

Once you have done this you will realize fully how much less stressed you are, how much better you are at handling your life and how much more in control and happy you are.

Having said all that, it is worth pointing out that, like the instruction to write down your goals, 95 per cent of you won't do it, 5 per cent of you will. If you do you will get far more out of this book than if you don't. I am assuming that you are one of the five per cent who will.

There is one further task for you to do before you start. Make a list now of all the things that stress you in your life and the reasons why you find these things stressful. Include all the big stresses in your life but also all the small stresses, the little things that cause you problems. Some of them may seem too small to mention but write them all down now. You will then be able to use this list as you go through the book. Any time you have an insight into one of your stresses you will be able to check it off as something you can now deal with in a different and more peaceful and productive way.

Stop reading now. Follow the above suggestions. Write this list down before you read on. This is essentially a practical book, not a book to be read through fast and taken in passively. The method works, if you do. Make your list and then read on.

You are in for an exciting journey in personal growth and development. If you follow through with the things you will read about you will also find that life is a lot less stressful for you in the future.

Dealing with external stressors

- If you can change the external stressors in your life then do so. If you feel cold, put on more clothes. If you hate your house and can move, do so. If a divorce is really essential then get on with it.
- If you cannot change the external stressors, then working with the following points will help you to reduce your feelings of stress. Even if you can change the external factors, working with the following points will help you to create a stress-free future faster than you could otherwise do.

Here we go.

1 **Stress is your own experience; it is personal to you and generated by you. It is not directly to do with things outside yourself; they are only the triggers to a response from within you, a response that is individual to you. There is no such thing as a universal stress.**

This covers a controversial and, at the same time, exciting approach to stress. The controversial hypothesis presented here is that there is no such thing as stress. There is only your own, individual, response to situations. This may set you thinking and even protesting. Yet we will persist with the idea. According to this hypothesis there is no such thing as a universal stress 'out there' that comes to 'get you'. There is only you as an individual and your response to a situation.

Most people find speaking in public to be a highly traumatic experience. A few people love doing it and thrive on it. Many people find a cocktail party or a similar social gathering to be a high point in their social calendar. Some people find this a highly stressful experience. They are frightened of what people will think, unsure of what they will say or do and delighted when the evening is over. Most people love a chance to lie on a sunny beach and soak up the sun as they let the tensions ooze out of their life. A few people find this a highly stressful situation, feeling frustrated at the lack of things to do and accomplish. Most people hate wars and fighting. A few people look for wars and are only happy when in highly dangerous situations. Some people find routine jobs boring and stressful, other people love them for their predictability and their routine. Some people feel stressed by challenge. Others respond to and thrive on it.

There is no single thing that is a universal stress. There is only your response to the outside world and the situations it provides. These you will either enjoy and respond to positively or will dread and fear. When you fully understand this you have made the first step in recognizing and then reducing the stress in your life. The next step is up to you.

2 **Feeling stressed is your choice and you can choose to continue or to stop. It is up to you to make the changes.**

Since stress is an individual thing experienced by you in response to both external factors and your own inner interpretation of them, you can be in control. If you are willing to change your response you can reduce or eliminate your feelings of stress.

Will you continue on your present path or are you willing to learn more about yourself? Are you willing to change yourself so that you do not respond to the outside events with all the reactions that you now group together under the heading of stress?

Your immediate answer may well be, yes, of course I am willing to change, I do not want to go on feeling stressed. However, a surprising number of people are not willing to be the ones to change. They think other people should change first. Others insist they are willing to change yet they do not do so. Others change a little and then stop. Perhaps they think that other people should now change too. Perhaps they think that there has not been sufficient benefit from the changes they have made. Just a few people are willing to change, and keep on changing and developing, until their life is just the way they want it and their stress is negligible.

3 **You can use the awareness of what stresses you to learn more about yourself and then use this knowledge for change.**

Finding out what causes you to feel stressed tells you more about yourself than about the stress. Some people like responsibility, some don't. Your response says more about you than about the responsibility. Some people like solitude, other people don't. Your response says more about you than about solitude.

The next step is for you to find out why a perceived stress in your life is indeed stressful for you, and why it makes you feel uncomfortable. The causes behind your response almost certainly lie somewhere in your past. After all, they can hardly come from the future, and the present is but a fleeting moment. You may have to search back to infancy and childhood. You may only have to go back to times in your earlier adult life.

One woman, Rosemary H., felt stressed every time her queue in the supermarket was not the fastest. By using various techniques that are described later in this book, she came to realize that this reaction stemmed from a feeling that if she was served last she was not getting the attention she deserved, and this in turn meant that she was not good or important enough. This came from a childhood where she was the youngest of four and her older siblings were always calling her stupid simply because she, being three years younger than the youngest of them, could not keep up.

When she understood this and realized how many things she had achieved in her life, she was able to develop the assurance she needed to be ready to drop the belief that she was not good enough. Her feelings of stress in queues then evaporated. Instead she spent the time usefully in thought and contemplation, or took something to read with her so the time in the queue wasn't wasted.

Another woman felt stressed every time she thought about the fact that her husband, a senior executive laid off in the recession, was no longer supporting her. The money was not the issue – they had reserve assets and his golden handshake. Her problem was a subconscious belief that if he didn't make the effort to go out and look for another job, hard to get at his age, and if he didn't actively work to support her, he didn't care, if he didn't care then he didn't love her, if he didn't love her she was no longer part of the loving and nurturing relationship that she craved.

Her stress came from the underlying fear of not being loved and nurtured, not from the more obvious cause of having a non-working husband. The stress she felt both caused her direct distress and led to overeating. This increased her weight which in turn made her feel more stressed, inadequate and unlovable. Once she identified the real problem she was able to discuss it with her husband.

The solution was not for him to go out and work again but rather for him to show her how much he loved her. Even more importantly, she had to develop her own sense of self-worth since, without that, all the loving he gave her would be insufficient for her to feel secure in that love. Resolving her beliefs about being inadequate and unlovable helped her to deal with the situation and reduce her experience of stress. She was then able to enjoy the free time her husband had and they started to share a number of hobbies. In the long run her recognition of the underlying problem brought them closer together.

Learning how to look at the subconscious beliefs that make you respond to outside events and experiences in a manner that you label 'feeling stressed' can lead you to a number of positive results. Provided you act on what you learn, are willing to change and to put the information to good use, it can take the stress out of your life, increase your self-respect and self-confidence, increase your positive plans and improve the outlook for the future.

4 **Be willing to change what you are doing if what you are doing is not working and has not been generating the desired result.**

Have you ever seen anyone beating their head against a brick wall? Unless they are mentally ill, if they beat their head against a brick wall and it hurts they will soon stop doing it. Yet at the emotional level this is what many people do for much of their lives and it leads to enormous stress. They continue in behaviour patterns that result in rows, in disappointment, in irritation and frustration, in boredom, in being let down. Sometimes they even realize what they are doing yet refuse to change; more often they don't.

Harold sat across from me telling me about his ulcers and how stressed he felt every day. He ran a small retail business, a delicatessen and a take-away food bar with lunch-time catering. He was very successful but at great cost to his health. The work was intense all morning as the staff got the food bar ready for the lunch-time crowd and for the regular orders to be delivered to nearby offices. Then came the lunch-hour rush when everyone wanted their sandwiches or take-away food in a hurry. Once or twice a week there would be a sudden phone call during the morning for a rush order of 50 sandwiches to be delivered by one o'clock to an office that was not on the regular list, or for a double order to be delivered to one of the regular customers. This upset Harold's routine and caused him enormous stress. So much so that he blamed the stress of his job for everything else that went wrong in his life and for his ulcer.

'There is nothing I can do. How can I stop feeling stressed? I shout at the staff and tell them to work harder but they won't. They don't seem to care, and it all comes back to me.'

Was he willing to put on more staff? No, that cost too much money. Was he willing to look for better staff? No, that took too much time, he worked non-stop as it was. Was he willing to tell people their orders had to be in by nine o'clock? No, he might lose customers. Was he willing to sell up and find a more routine business? No, this was not the time to sell. He had just built the business up and started to make good money.

Harold was not willing to change. As I asked him to consider other options all he could focus on was the reasons why there was no alternative to his present actions.

Stop beating your head against a brick wall and be willing to change. If you are not, then you must ask yourself why you are not, what benefit you are getting from your present course of action. Harold was not willing to change. Ultimately that is an individual's right, but it does not lead to a reduction in stress.

Christina's problems were with her boss and her family and the demands that, she felt, they each made on her time. Her boss kept giving her work to do at the end of the day with the result that she stayed back to complete it, missed her express bus home and got in too late to cook dinner for a tired and irate husband who had arrived home an hour earlier and for two teenage children who were no help around the house. She told me that her job was stressful, so was the boss, so was the travelling, so was her husband who expected her to do all the housework as well as her job and so were the children who wouldn't help. She had plenty to say, to me, to her boss, to her husband, to the children and to anyone who would listen about the problems they and other people caused in her life. But what she was saying and what she

∽

was doing weren't working. Her words and her deeds did not change the amount of stress she experienced.

She had told her boss repeatedly that she had to have the last letters before three o'clock so she could get them typed and finished and get the express bus home. She had told her husband she couldn't help being late, it was the boss's fault. She had told the children over and over again that it was time they did some of the chores round the house. She kept talking. It wasn't working. But she kept doing it.

What she really wanted was for them to change. The real solution was for her to change. She could either change her job or change her reactions or change the way she handled things. If she didn't she could continue as she was and complain and feel stressed. Until she was ready to change she would feel stressed, no matter what changes occurred externally. Like Harold, she had to be willing to change. In addition, she had to be willing to take responsibility for the way things were and not to blame everything on the other people involved.

We will follow Harold and Christina's stories as we move to the next point.

5 **You are responsible for all that happens, and has happened, in your life. Be willing to assume that you are in total control. Be willing to give up victim status.**

There is a definite pleasure, for many people, in being badly done by, in having something to complain about and in getting sympathy for their hard lot in life. You may prefer getting sympathy to relying on people liking you for yourself. You may feel that other people will be more tolerant, more kindly, more generous if you yourself have something to complain about and are deserving of sympathy. You may feel ashamed or guilty if everything in your own life is going smoothly.

Does this apply to you? If the answer is yes then congratulations for recognizing a behaviour pattern that you can now change to your advantage. If you think this does not apply to you then ask yourself when did you last tell someone about something bad that happened to you. What was your motive in telling them? Were you seeking attention, sympathy, a ready ear? What was your goal? Why did you want to be seen as a victim?

Harold enjoyed being a victim. He, in some perverse way, enjoyed having things to complain about. Later on I spoke with his wife who worked with him and she said he seemed to thrive in the mornings. If things were going wrong he could complain of the terrible time he was having. If things were going smoothly and all the work was getting done he complained at the lack of orders and what that would do to their income. She also told me that Harold's father had been the same and that he had, ultimately, been a successful man.

'I really think that Harold feels he can only be successful if he is worked off his feet. Also,' she said with rare insight, 'I think he feels guilty at how well we are doing and how much money he is making and only feels he has deserved it if he has suffered to get it.'

Until Harold is willing to make changes in his attitude and give up the need for victim status he will continue to feel stressed and continue to have and get ulcers, whatever medication, drug-based or natural, he takes to help him in the short term.

Christina's response was different. Initially she complained that it was not her fault that she felt stressed. It was the fault of her boss and the way he did his work, the fault of the children who would not help to prepare dinner and the fault of her husband who did not earn enough so that she could work less. She was a victim and relished the complaining this allowed her, the sympathy it earned her and the limelight that fell on her.

When she decided to accept that she was responsible she also learnt that she did have the ability to change things and to control the situation. After some sessions during which we explored her options and her fears, she was ready to change. She talked with her boss and explained the situation to him and told him that from the following Monday she would leave on time, no matter what work he gave her to do late in the afternoon. She told the children that they would have to take care of their own rooms and their own clothes and her husband that, if he wanted her to work full time, he would have to help with dinner or they wouldn't eat.

The results surprised her. Her boss did not sack her. After two days of letters not sent on time he reprogrammed his work so she could have them typed and completed by the time she was supposed to leave. After a week of having no clean or ironed clothes to wear, the children got the hang of putting their dirty clothes in the washing machine and after only one evening with bread and cheese for dinner her husband started to prepare the vegetables and have things ready for when she got home. Since she was now able to catch the express bus, they finished up cooking dinner together and having that time to share their news of the day.

She admitted to feeling a little uncomfortable at having nothing to complain of but soon got used to the new regime and, as she said, it was amazing the way everybody was benefiting from the changes.

6 Get clear on your outcome – what are you really trying to achieve? Are you trying to prove someone else wrong, to force someone else to change to the way you want them to be, to have something to complain about – or do you really want to reduce your stress?

Let's continue with Christina's story. After these changes had come about she was able to acknowledge that they had been relatively easy. When asked why she hadn't made them before she came to understand that what she had really wanted was to prove everyone else was wrong. She had wanted to prove what a thoughtless boss she had, how unhelpful her children were and what an inconsiderate man her husband

was, expecting her to work full time and be a housewife as well. She
was looking for sympathy for her hard lot in life. When she got clear on
her goal of having a relaxed and stress-free time both at home and in
the office, it was much easier for her to let go of her grudges, change
the situation and reduce her stress.

7 **Know you can cope. Avoid the stress caused by fear of the
   unknown. Imagine the worst possible scenario. Find out how
   you would deal with it. Then get on with handling the present.**

A lot of stress comes from your fear of the future. You worry that this
will happen, you're afraid that that won't happen. This in itself is stressful. It also reduces your ability to deal with the present and your ability
to prevent this unwanted future. Further, since this bad future may
never happen, you may be experiencing the stress needlessly.

The solution is to allow yourself to imagine the unimaginable. Create
the worst possible scenario that could occur, the worst possible outcome
that would result if all your fears were realized. Then plan what you
would do. You would cope. Somehow or other, with the exception of
the few people who opt for suicide, we all do cope. Recognize in detail
just exactly what you would do and how you would cope. Then look for
the benefits, even small ones, in this scenario, for there certainly will be
some once you learn how to look for them.

Once you know that you can cope, no matter what happens, then
you can free yourself from the crippling effects of your fear. If the outcome is bad but only half bad or two thirds bad then you are better off
than you might have been.

You can either view a glass of water as half full or half empty. It won't
change the amount you have to drink; it will change your level of stress. If
you have recognized what you will do if it becomes empty then you can
enjoy the half you have rather than fret over the half you haven't got.

This will give you an enormous increase in peace of mind and free
your energies so you can focus on achieving the best possible outcome
and deriving maximum enjoyment of the present.

8 **Believe in a positive future, that whatever happens will be for the best, but do this without ceasing to care and without developing a laissez-faire attitude.**

A lot of stress comes about from the belief that something bad will or could happen. The stress of public speaking is based on a fear that you will make a fool of yourself or that people will think badly of you. If you were totally convinced you would be a roaring success, you could look forward to the event with equanimity. The stress of an argument with your spouse may be due to an underlying fear that they are being un-faithful or are considering a divorce. If you knew that you were going to remain happily together then the argument could be an interesting difference of opinion. The stress at work could stem, not from the work itself but from a fear of losing your job. If you knew you were about to be promoted, the work could be an enjoyable challenge.

Thus a further aspect of minimizing the experience of stress is to believe in a positive future. Choosing to believe that the future will be good can take a lot of stress out of the present. Choosing to believe that any apparent setback is merely a move to allow something better to occur can reduce your experience of stress. These beliefs can also put you in a positive frame of mind such that you deal with current situa-tions more productively and more peacefully than you would when afraid of negative outcomes.

Perhaps you are looking for a house and see the one of your dreams, one that is ideal and covers all your requirements. If you decide that you absolutely must have it and that no other house will do, you put yourself under enormous pressure. You will put in an offer and start bit-ing your nails with the fear that someone else will offer more or that something will happen to jeopardize your purchase. If on the other hand, you work hard to get it but choose to believe that if you do you will be thrilled and if you don't it is because you are about to find an even better one, you can save yourself a lot of stress.

There are two aspects to this. Firstly the belief helps you to proceed with a minimum of stress. Secondly it leaves you in a frame of mind in which you can negotiate the price from a position of strength. If fearing you won't get the house and believing it is the only possible one, you get anxious, you are likely to offer a higher price than necessary and the owner will recognize your desperation and hold out for an even better price. If on the other hand, you choose to believe that if this purchase doesn't come off you will find an even better house, you are more likely to base your offer on what you truly believe the house is worth rather than on how much you want it.

A word of warning here. If you translate this to mean that you don't care if you get it or not, on a 'laissez-faire', 'she'll be right' basis, this is a cop-out and you are missing the point. Stay positive and do go for your target but don't live as if your life depended on it or as if another even better option isn't possible.

9 **Much stress is caused by your fear of other people's opinions of you and your deeds. Decide who you are and who you want to be. Get a clear statement of purpose, develop your own Life Plan. Keep this clearly in your mind, live by it and many of your stresses will dissipate.**

Much stress occurs simply because you don't know who you want to be or what you want to achieve. Thus you are tossed around in a sea of other people's opinions with no firm anchor.

If you are too timid the go-getters and positive people will call you a wimp. If you are too strong the nervous and the under-achievers will call you aggressive. If you are too noisy and outgoing the timid will call you brash. If you are too quiet and retiring the extroverts will call you dull. If you do too much for other people the selfish will call you a door-mat. If you do too little for others the generous will call you unhelpful.

Too timid, too strong, too noisy, too quiet, too helpful or selfish for whom? For them? For you? By what standards are you judged? By what standards are you willing to be judged?

Create your own standards. Decide who you are and what you want to be. Once you have decided this and are happy with your description of your ideal self then live by it. If someone criticizes you, check it out against your own standards. If you have done the right thing according to them then relax. If you have not then use this as a learning experience and plan how you can change in future.

When you are behaving according to your own standards it is not possible for you to feel stressed by the opinions and criticisms of others. If you find repeatedly that you still feel stressed, even when you are doing what you think is right, it may be time for you to reassess your own standards. If they need to be changed, change them. If they don't then find out what the underlying problem is, why you are still feeling stressed. There are many ways described throughout the book for doing this.

In the same way set out the plan for your life. Be very clear on your goals. Once you have done this, work towards them. Recognize the things you will have to avoid and omit if you are to reach them. Recognize the things you will have to do if you are to reach them. Once you are happy with this then get on with your life, head in this direction, clear in the knowledge of where you want to go.

Many stresses will then fall away. The stress or anxiety of not having a fixed income will be lessened when you recognize you are doing the appropriate study to reach your goal. The anxiety or discomfort of being pregnant will be reduced when you keep in mind the large family you want. The stress of not being invited to a party is reduced when you know your career is of prime importance to you.

Having a clear idea as to exactly who you are, who you want to be and the type of life you want to have leaves you much less vulnerable to other people's opinions and criticisms than when your goal is to please everybody else at all times, an impossible task, and when their opinion is of paramount importance to you.

10 **You are terrific. Most stress comes from your feelings of inadequacy. Develop full confidence in yourself, be willing to like, love and approve of yourself. If you don't, who will?**

You grew up in a world where, under the disguise of modesty, you were taught to put yourself down. You were taught, under the guise of generosity and caring for others, to put other people first, to put others ahead of you, to give them the biggest slice of the cake, to let them go first, to praise them before praising yourself.

This is fine as far as it goes, but sadly it is all too easy for it to have negative repercussions. For most people, having been taught, as children, to put other people first has resulted in a diminished respect for themselves and their own achievements. In clinic work, in workshops and in life in general I have found that most people have a poor opinion of themselves. Even the boasts and bombasts, under all the external cover-up, have, deep down, the fear that they are not good enough, not clever enough, not loving enough, not helpful enough, not successful enough, not sufficiently worthwhile.

Learning to love yourself, like yourself, approve of yourself and be comfortable with yourself and the way you are is a major way to reduce the stress in your life. This does not mean you should be aggressively telling everyone else how wonderful you are, boasting, hogging the limelight or telling everyone else you are better than them. It does mean having the inner certainty that you are OK. You are perfect just the way you are, for this moment in time.

This attitude does not mean that you do not recognize things about yourself that you wish to change. We are, hopefully, all on a path of growth, change and development. It does mean becoming content with yourself, being willing to give yourself the unconditional love and acceptance that you give to other people to whom you are close.

It is a sad comment on the way we bring up our children and that you were probably brought up as a child, that for most people this is one of the hardest steps to make in reducing stress. Learning to give yourself full love and approval may be the most difficult step to take; at the same time it is also one of the most powerful.

These and many other similar concepts are discussed in detail with practical examples throughout the first part of this book. These ideas follow on from the ideas developed in two earlier books, *Choosing Health Intentionally* and *Choosing Weight Intentionally*. In these, attention was focused on the way that thoughts, emotions and past experiences affect an individual's health and weight. Here these ideas have been developed further and applied, specifically, to the stresses in your life.

There are other topics covered in the first part. You are given tools that will help you to understand yourself better and to learn more about past problems and past experiences that you are letting, often subconsciously, contribute to your present stresses. You are given tools with which you can unearth some of the subconscious reasons why particular situations stress you. One such technique is Running a Phrase. You are told how to go back into the past in ways that will help you to unearth buried memories, memories that may have been suppressed yet may be the cause of much of your stress. You are shown how to take the remembered trauma out of past stressful situations and to reduce the impact of these situations on your present stress. You are encouraged, and shown how, to have positive beliefs about yourself instead of being self-critical.

In these and other ways you will be able to understand and remove the stresses in your life. Having recognized old triggers and old sensitivities, you can reassess present situations and will, almost certainly, decide to view them in a new light.

You will learn to be proactive and to create your own life, just the way you want it, rather than being reactively jerked around on the strings of other people's opinions and emotions. You will spend time assessing just exactly who you are and who you want to be, which values are important to you and which aren't, and therefore which criticisms are relevant and may assist in your growth and which aren't. You will learn a lot of wonderful things about yourself that, so far, may have gone unrecognized.

You will also be encouraged to use the amazing power of your mind to change both the events and the situations in your life and your attitude to them and to yourself. By the end, if you go through the processes with real conviction and serious intent, you will be able to relegate stress to the position of a negligible problem in your life. Things that once stressed you will become positive challenges and learning experiences to help you develop further.

You will find one or more of the 10 points that we have discussed at the beginning of some of the chapters that follow. This is meant as a guide only. Many aspects of the 10 points itemized above will come up more than once throughout the book, to a greater or lesser degree. Having the major concept of the chapter at its head will help you to incorporate it into your thinking. Repetition, often in a different disguise, will help you to become familiar with these ideas and techniques and to make use of them more readily.

Part II: The physical aspects of stress

While most stress comes about as a result of your mental and emotional states there can also be physical contributing factors or causes. Thus it is wise to make sure that there are no physical health reasons for your feelings of stress. These physical factors may seem to be a direct and prime cause of your stress. Alternatively they may seem to be contributing factors that decrease your ability to handle the other stresses in your life. Either way you will need to deal both with the physical factors and with the emotional ones that result from them and may also have contributed to them.

It is the old chicken and the egg question. Which came first? The emotional stress which caused you to make excessive demands on your body and give it diminished care or the physical problem which led to your emotional stress and worry and which in turn led to the physical problem? The nice thing about chicken and egg situations is that you can begin to change things by working with both the chicken and the egg. So do both.

Clearly any physical health problem can cause you to feel stressed. Anything from a toothache to the knowledge that you have a fatal disease will stress you. However, there are some physical health problems that can, as part of their symptom picture, generate nervous, irritable and stressed emotional states. These include such health problems as allergies, candidiasis, hypoglycaemia, poor nutrition, poor immune function and the effect of toxins. If these problems are part of your experience then you can, by doing what is necessary to your lifestyle to improve your physical health, greatly reduce your stress at all levels, physical, emotional and mental.

Be warned, though, that it is all too easy to blame these possible physical causes exclusively for your stress and thus to avoid making the mental and emotional changes discussed in Part I. This is a mistake and leads you back into victim status, this time a victim to your body.

If you are not willing to make the necessary changes in your diet and lifestyle described in Part II you may at some subconscious level be showing your preference for hanging on to the physical problems as useful excuses for your emotional stress rather than facing up to the emotional and mental changes that are necessary. If this is the case then working through Part I is even more important for you.

It's time now to focus attention on some of the physical health problems that may affect your ability to handle the outside (perceived) stressful events in your life. Some examples are outlined below and you may find it useful to consider if they could be affecting you in some way.

If you suffer from hypoglycaemia, a condition characterized by low blood-sugar levels, you will not feel relaxed and comfortable. Instead, following a large meal or an intake of sugar-rich foods, your blood-sugar level will first rise and then fall to disastrously low levels. When the level is low you will feel anxious, irritable, uptight, frightened and out of control. Under these circumstances any outside pressure at all is likely to have you complaining that you feel stressed. The slightest thing that happens will trigger off an emotional response and you will complain about the level of stress in your life.

It is not of paramount importance that you reduce the outside events that are perceived as stressful, nor is it of primary importance that you learn relaxation techniques and do deep breathing exercises. The answer is to deal with the physical problem of your hypoglycaemia. The way to do this is discussed in the relevant section in Part II.

Alternatively you may suffer from allergies. Eating certain foods may make you feel anxious or irritable. It is unlikely that you can recognize these foods yourself; they are usually masked food allergies. Fortunately, tests are available by which you can identify them. If allergies are part of your stress problem the answer is not to learn to relax but to have the appropriate tests done and change your diet accordingly.

You may suffer from a variety of infections, possibly only minor ones, that leave you feeling vulnerable and anxious. Again, the answer is not to learn to relax and deal with the stress, it is to take better care of your diet, take nutrient supplements if necessary and improve your immune function.

You may be suffering from vitamin or mineral deficiencies, or candidiasis or lacticacidosis (*see Part II, pp. 319–22, 341*). In all these situations and in many like them you will have a reduced tolerance for outside stresses. In addition, the physical health problem can generate its own stresses. Yet again, the answer is not for you to do deep breathing exercises, learn relaxation techniques, meditate or listen to tranquillizing music and sounds. The answer comes from dealing with the physiological problem that is stressing your body to such an extent that you have reduced emotional balance and reduced tolerance for external and perceived stresses.

Thus the first part of the book deals with your individual reaction to an outside event based on your past mental and emotional experiences and on what that event means to you at a subconscious level. It also includes the necessary background to the way you use your thoughts or the way in which you are at the mercy of your thoughts and how to control or change them to your own benefit. Techniques are included that will help you unravel your past and be more relaxed about the present and future.

The second part deals with any physical problems you may have that will reduce your tolerance to outside events and explains how these physiological problems can be remedied.

When you use the two approaches together you will have the tools needed to reduce your perceived stress levels to near zero.

Overall

In the course of researching this book I have asked a large number of people the same question, namely 'What do you find stressful?'. The one outstanding result from this has been that no two people find the same things stressful. Things that stress one person are no bother to another. In fact, things that stress one individual may even be a positive pleasure to another. The conclusion from all this has been to bear out the hypothesis that there is no such thing as an independent entity called 'a stress' on which everyone can agree.

Rosemary H., already mentioned, found standing in supermarket queues thoroughly frustrating and she would mutter and fume at the slowness of the check-out girl and the customers in front of her. Another woman thought long queues were wonderful: they gave her time to stand quietly and think, an oasis of time in a busy day that seemed to be all rush and go.

One man, Peter L., felt very stressed when family members depended on him to know what to do and how to do it in any emergency. Tom D., on the other hand, loved being asked for help and thrived on the challenge of an emergency; but when nothing was happening and no-one needed him he then felt anxious and unwanted.

Denise H. could only complete a task when she had a definite deadline and knew it simply had to be done by then. Once she knew or set the deadline she could settle down and get on with the job. With no deadline she would potter around, getting nothing done, and feel thoroughly dissatisfied and stressed at the end of the day as a result of having achieved so little. In contrast Charles T. hated to be rushed or have deadlines. He accomplished most when he could get on quietly at his own speed. Knowing he had to have a job done by a certain time or date could freeze him into immobility and diminish his output.

What does all this mean? It means that each individual responds to outside events in a way peculiar to them. If you experience the outside events as pleasurable, fun, satisfying, challenging, exciting, positive, etc. you are unlikely to call them stresses. If you respond to them as worrying, frightening, threatening, unsettling, disturbing etc. you are likely to call them stresses.

Stress rating scale

A patient once said to me 'I wish there was a pain scale so I could measure my pain on it and tell you I have pain at level 4, or whatever, just as there is the Richter scale for earthquakes. Then you would know what I am feeling.'

This is an understandable wish yet impractical because the pain of a cut finger can be nearly intolerable to one person and barely noticeable to another, or it can be unbearably painful when you are bored and thinking about it and of little consequence when you are absorbed in something exciting that you are doing. Pain is a subjective experience, so is stress.

Many efforts have been made to quantify stress and then measure the effect of a given number of units of stress on the body. They have failed. One such scale was quoted in *Choosing Health Intentionally* (X. K. Williams, Letts, 1992). This scale ranged from death of a spouse at 100 points, through being fired from work at 47 points to minor violation of the law at 11 points. In the original study it was found that 49 per cent of the people who scored more than 300 in a twelve-month period developed serious health problems.

However, this also means that 51 per cent of people who scored over 300 points did *not* develop serious health problems. Either their bodies were more robust or their experience of stress was much milder. In fact this is fairly obvious. The death of a spouse is going to be a far greater stress for a devoted partner who depended on the one who died than for a partner who was already contemplating divorce. Travel is a major stress for people who like a structured life with a steady routine whereas for those who are easily bored and like constant excitement it is a delight, and so forth.

It all comes back to the basic premise that is worth repeating over and over. There is nothing that is inherently stressful. It is your subjective assessment of the situation that determines whether or not it will be a stress.

This is a good time to consider the dictionary definition of stress. According to the *Concise Oxford Dictionary* it is: (i) a constraining or impelling force; (ii) effort, demand upon energy; (iii) emphasis or; (iv) force exerted between contiguous bodies or parts of a body. Another way stress is described is as some outside factor that impacts on you the object. In these definitions there is no suggestion that a stress is either good or bad. The stress of the wind on the yacht's sails is what keeps the yacht moving once the helmsman masters the art of harnessing this stressor.

Pleasures may also be stresses. Anything that takes you outside your routine may involve a stress. Going on holiday involves the stress of deciding what to pack. Having a party involves the stress of extra cooking. A new and exciting job involves the stress of leaving old friends. There are stresses that you welcome and enjoy and call excitement and there are stresses that offer no pleasure.

Life without stress or challenge would be very dull and boring indeed. To avoid this and to avoid the pain of unwanted stress you need to convert all the unpleasant stresses into challenges, non-events or pleasant stresses.

It is time to start. If you think your problems are purely physical you may want to have a quick look at Part II and attend to whatever you feel needs attention. However, I strongly encourage you to work with Part I in depth. If you can sort out your reasons for thinking of things as stresses and learn to respond differently to them you may not only solve your emotional problems, you may also start to treat your body differently. The physical problems of Part II may disappear and thus their consequences may cease to be perceived as stress.

In other words you could be in a catch-22 situation. The thoughts and emotions you find unpleasantly stressful could be causing you to do things that are contributing to your health problems which in turn could be reducing your capacity to deal with situations in a non-stressful way.

Finally

Most of the contents of this book apply to most people but certainly all of the book does not apply to all people. As has already been said, it is common to find that something you thrive on worries someone else and things that other people take in their stride cause you considerable anxiety.

For this reason there may be times when you want to put the book down or skip a section, insisting it is not relevant in your case. This may be true but beware. If you feel irritated, impatient or uncomfortable with a section it may well be that it is in some way making you nervous by triggering off an emotion or concept that you have managed to bury. This may be the very section from which you can benefit the most.

The ideas expressed here have been developed over many years in clinical practice and in workshops. During this time thousands of people have, directly and indirectly, contributed their experiences and their response to this approach to dealing with stress. Very few ideas are original. Much of what any one person creates is a combination of many inputs that are then gathered together and developed further by the individual concerned. So it is here.

Many different techniques have been included in this work. Some have been successful; others less so. Over the years these have been distilled into my own particular way of working. I owe grateful acknowledgement to many sources often now long-forgotten. Most of all I owe thanks to the many thousands of people who have entrusted me with their confidence and shown a willingness to explore their innermost thoughts and experiences, out of which has come, hopefully, their opportunity to create a happier and much less stressful future.

Overall it can be said that the results, achieved largely through the efforts of the individuals concerned, have been impressive. Some people have made major gains, others have been willing to take only small steps. The most unexpected people have shown a willingness to make huge changes in their lives, to push their fears to the limit and to face up to and explore their inner anxieties, their uncertainties and past traumas. They have had the courage to take a good look at their past and their own attitudes and out of what they have learnt in this way to create a new and independent future, largely free from stress. You too can do this.

I have learnt many things during these years. I have learnt never to second guess what is bothering someone. The moment I do we get off track. Only you know what you feel. Only you know what is right for you. Only you can make the changes. I have also learnt that, by using the methods described in this book, people have been able to deal with a wide variety of stresses and come through smiling. The more willing you are to work with these ideas and explore them fully, the more successful you can be and the better your life can be in the future.

Finally, I have learnt to have great respect for every single person, not to judge them but to value them just as they are. Each individual is a single and valuable entity. Each individual is perfect, just as they are, for their present step on the pathway of their own chosen growth and development. This is true however much they plan to change and grow in the future, both immediate and distant. You too are perfect, however much you want to grow and change, and as soon as you can value yourself in this way you can have a happy and stress-free life.

One further point is worth emphasizing. The object of this book is to enable you to be in control of your life, your emotions and your responses to situations, to give you a clear base from which to enjoy your life and its relationships. It is you who can alter and improve your life, no-one else. For this reason you are not encouraged to lean on anyone or anything, including this book. At no time will you be told that it is all right in this particular situation to blame someone else, to depend on someone else rather than yourself for support and succour, to lie back and say that this time, just this time, the stress is too much and you cannot cope. You will always be encouraged to find your own way out, to rely on your own inner strengths. By all means relate to other people, share your emotions with them and welcome their concern for your welfare. But what happens if you are depending on them and they are not there for you? If you are relying on them and they don't help, you have yet another stress with which to deal.

By not relying on others you are not becoming heartless or cut off. By being independently strong, centred and focused in such a way that you do not have stresses in your life you are not cutting yourself off from the normal interplays of emotions and relationships. On the contrary, when you are self-sufficient and centred you have much more to offer to other people. You no longer relate to them in a way that involves blame or guilt, strength or weakness. You will no longer try to manipulate situations, emotions or people, nor will people be able to manipulate you. Your relationships will be much more clear, honest and harmonious.

There may be times when the approach may seem to be heartless. It is not, nor is this the intent. There is a fine line between empowering you and seeming to be uncaring. The aim at all times is to empower you. I care too much to want to deprive you of your ultimate resource – yourself and your own strength.

This is a very practical book. You will be given a lot to think about and a lot to do. The result should excite you. Start reading – and enjoy.

Running a Phrase

Often in this book you will see the term 'running a phrase'. Running a phrase is a very useful way to discover what is going on in your subconscious so let's find out what happens.

The phrase you are told to run may be simple; it is usually short and you are told to complete the sentence over and over again. We will start with a simple and appropriate phrase, one you have probably said to yourself many times: 'I feel stressed because ...' Say it once, complete it and write down the completion, or the second part. Then do this again. Repeat the process until your responses become repetitive but don't give up. Continue for a while. There may well be some very valuable bits of information your subconscious is just getting ready to release.

There is a certain hypnotic power about the first part, the phrase itself. It's as if it occupies your conscious mind and takes its attention away from monitoring what you are going to say next. Your subconscious is then free to let out little whispers of underlying truth.
The results may look like this:

- 🐾 I feel stressed because – I have too much to do
- 🐾 I feel stressed because – I may not get everything done
- 🐾 I feel stressed because – things are getting on top of me
- 🐾 I feel stressed because – if I get behind I will be in trouble
- 🐾 I feel stressed because – I'm not able to do everything I have to
- 🐾 I feel stressed because – they'll think I'm stupid
- 🐾 I feel stressed because – I am stupid, I can't cope

It is important that the completion is short and carries no explanation. If, after the first one, '… I have too much to do', you had continued with '… there's all the housework, and the children all seem to think I should do everything for them, and my husband does so much business entertaining and wants me with him…' you would have lost the benefit of the process. You would have gone into justification, into logic, into the conscious brain's ingrained pattern of justifying everything you do intellectually.

By returning to the starting phrase each time you will find you get much more interesting and useful information. You will get a truer window into your subconscious and into some of your hidden and buried memories.

Consider the above completions. This was the list Jennifer got by doing the process above, by running the phrase 'I feel stressed because…'. At first they were logical and commonplace completions. They were the reasons many people give for feeling stressed. Many people feel they have too much to do. They worry that they will not get their various tasks done in the time available and that if this happens things will get on top of them and they won't be able to cope. However, as Jennifer relaxed into the process, her subconscious came up with the last two, 'They'll think I'm stupid' and 'I am stupid, I can't cope'.

When you get something useful and interesting like that it is worth exploring it. Jennifer was told to run the phrase 'Being stupid means…'. When she did she came up again with several everyday things at the start such as not being clever, not being bright, not being able to do things. Then she found herself saying '… my husband won't love me'.

As she said this she looked first surprised, and then as if the pennies were beginning to drop. During the discussion that ensued it soon became clear to her that she was afraid she would lose her husband if she could not keep up with him. He had started in a junior position in the company for which he worked but had been promoted several times and had a lot of responsibility. His work now involved some international travel and the responsibility of entertaining a number of clients. Jennifer felt he had had the chance to grow and expand his horizons while she had been cooped up at home with three children. If she couldn't do all the tasks allotted to her then, how, she wondered subconsciously, could he expect her to go on being worthy of being his wife? Once she realized this she had the start in her plan to deal with the situation.

None of this had come up during logical discussion. It took this technique to unearth the deeper fear. Now you see what a useful tool this 'running a phrase' can be.

You may find you get several different bits of information. Keep going with the one phrase until you have a large number of responses. Then choose the one that seems a little disconnected, as we did above, shape a phrase around that and run it. You may then take one of these responses and run a third phrase, and so on.

When that is complete go back to another of the original completions. In Jennifer's case we ran 'Being stupid means...' until we had milked it dry. We then followed up on '... I'll be in trouble' by running the phrase 'Being in trouble means...' and got a variety of phrases and then '... my husband will leave me'.

Clearly this was a major fear for Jennifer and dominated much of her thinking. She was encouraged to talk it over with him. When she did she found this was far from his thinking, that in fact he found his home with its quiet domesticity and basic values a relief and haven after corporate life.

One thing I can guarantee, provided that you relax completely into the process and allow your subconscious to speak, when you run a phrase you will be surprised at the results. They will certainly help you in your bid to become more relaxed and calm. They will almost certainly change your life for the better in other ways too as you learn more about yourself and your reactions.

We will consider another example. James was at university and finding the whole situation stressful. He ran the phrase 'A reason university is stressful is ...' and got a number of completions such as '... there's lots of new stuff I have to learn', '... there are all those tests I have to swot for', '... the other boys speak better than I do and they laugh at me'. All these were fairly standard reasons for feeling stressed. Then he came up with '... Dad resents me'.

He then ran the phrase 'Dad resents me because ...' and got completions that included '... I'm not working', '... he has to support me', '... he thinks I'm not good enough'. It was this last one that really hit home. He said that he thought his father was proud of him going to university and impressed that he had got a place. Yet deep down there was this fear that his father thought he was not good enough, not good enough to pass his exams and obtain a degree. Eventually he recognized that this was, in fact, his Ultimate Negative Belief, discussed in the chapter on Affirmations.

Here is a clear example of the way your mind works. If you try to analyse the situation logically to find out why you are stressed you will almost certainly run into all the logical and practical reasons, the obvious ones. When you let the subconscious mind throw up the information it has you can learn a lot more.

Use this technique of running a phrase whenever you are asked to in this book. You can also use it at other times, times of your choice and under any circumstance. For instance, if you are getting angry in a particular situation run 'The reason I'm angry is …', 'Another reason I'm angry is…'. Note the slight change in wording for the second and subsequent repeats of the original phrase.

Or you may be sitting around with friends enjoying a chat, then feel yourself getting anxious. Run the phrase 'A reason I'm getting anxious is …', 'Another reason I'm getting anxious is …'.

Remember, as a wonderful book called the *Course of Miracles* (Foundation for Inner Peace, 1975) says 'You are never upset for the reason you think'. This technique of running a phrase is an excellent way of finding out the real reason you are upset. Use it at every possible opportunity.

PART I

THE
Emotional
Aspects of Stress

CHAPTER ONE

Creative Thought

Your feelings of stress are a product of the way you think. When you think things are going to be bad, difficult and stressful then you experience fear, worry and stress. When you think they are going to be good, exciting and fruitful you feel happy, expectant and fortunate. These diametrically opposite results are the consequence of diametrically opposite ways of thinking. So let's consider the way you think.

The title of this section, creative thought, may seem to imply that there is non-creative thought as well as creative thought – not so. All your thoughts are creative, one way or another, and your thoughts create your reality.

People think in different ways. Some people think only, or largely, in words, some people think only, or mainly, in pictures and others think only with their feelings. Most of us, however, think in all three modes, even if one mode does predominate, and the combination of all three gives you your total 'thought'. For our present purposes we will use 'thought' to cover all three modes of experience.

If your thoughts create your reality and part of your reality is the experience of stress then it should be possible to change the experience of stress by changing your thoughts. This is the concept we are going to explore.

Good and bad days

Consider some of the good and bad days you have had. On a bad day you might wake up late, you trip getting out of bed, run the cold instead of the hot tap in the shower, burn the toast, find the milk is sour and mutter to yourself that this is going to be an awful day. After that it probably will be.

On a good day you may find everything goes right. The clothes you want to wear are all clean, the sun shines, you catch your bus and get to work exactly on time and decide that this is going to be a great day. And it probably will be.

How does this come about? There are two possibilities. Either you focus your attention on the things that fall within your expectations and, consciously and subconsciously, ignore or filter out those that don't, or, by your focus of attention and expectation, by the subtle messages you give out, maybe even by the sheer power of your thoughts, you actually change the way things happen.

Filtering

The first of these two possibilities involves filtering the input you receive from the world around you and the events happening in your life. In this way if you expect it to be a good day you will focus your attention on the good and positive things that happen; if you expect it to be a bad day you will focus on the problems and setbacks that occur.

You may insist you do not filter, that you see the world rationally and objectively, as it is. However, if you are willing to open your mind and see past your normal mode of thinking you may be in for some surprises.

You filter the world in which you live in a number of ways and the ways in which you do this can have a great bearing on the amount of stress you experience.

Species filters

As human beings we filter out much that is going on around us. We have ears to hear, it is true, yet they can only hear certain sounds. Dog whistles are tuned to a frequency that can be heard by a dog yet is outside the range of the human ear. Many other animals hear at a frequency that is inaudible to human beings. The same is true of vision. Some animals can see in the dark while we as human beings are blind. Our sense of smell is minimal when compared to that of many animals, and thus we filter out many major olfactory experiences that are part of the daily life of other species. We filter out the radio waves that pass through us and our environment every day, likewise the television waves, the electrical and magnetic frequencies and so forth. All these things pass us by because we do not have the sense organs to perceive them; they are filtered out by the details of our make-up as a species.

This means that you are only consciously aware of part of your environment. It also demonstrates that something doesn't fail to exist simply because it is not detected by your senses, a point that is well worth bearing in mind.

This filtering also means that there could be a number of stressful things happening but because you are not aware of them you do not feel stressed. For instance, sounds that fall outside your auditory range will not frighten you, smells that your nose doesn't detect will not trouble you.

Cultural filters

Secondly you learn to filter as part of your upbringing. Some things stress you because they are not what you are used to or what you consider to be normal. These same things that you find stressful could leave someone else totally calm because they fit in normally with their expectations as to the way their life would be.

Consider, for instance, the wearing of the correct clothes and shoes. John and Susan were going to visit Susan's parents. John, who had met and lived with Susan in Australia, hadn't yet met her parents who lived in central London and this first meeting was to be at a dinner party in their honour. Since it was the middle of a summer heatwave and they had been told that the occasion was not formal John wore a beautiful Batik shirt, smart light-coloured linen trousers and beautifully tooled leather sandals, an outfit that would have been perfect at a similar dinner had it occurred in the Australian township where he grew up.

Susan's parents were mortified when he appeared in sandals and without socks on. They considered the evening ruined and endured it in an embarrassment of wondering what their friends would think of him. John, unaware of the social rules he was flouting, had a wonderful evening and expressed himself delighted with them as he drove home with Susan. Susan, used to John's choices of clothing, was unsure of the reasons for her parents' distress yet felt stressed by the tension in the air all evening. As her mother said afterwards, the shirt and light trousers were bad enough, but no-one, absolutely no-one, went to a dinner party in sandals.

Consider, however, what would have been happening had Susan been Japanese and taken John home to visit her Japanese parents. They would have felt stressed and mortified if he had worn shoes at all.

Many times when you feel stressed it is the result of things and events that are occurring in a way that does not fit in with your upbringing and expectations. If you can change these filters, change the way you view things, you can change your experience of stress.

Had Susan's parents acknowledged that the man was more important than his clothes and had they assumed that their friends would have understood that what he wore was correct within John's world and that he was not belittling them by dressing down, they need not have felt stressed and could have had a wonderful evening.

A western woman of conventional upbringing, used to covering her breasts at all times, could feel highly stressed when taken to a topless beach by her latest boyfriend. Yet had she been brought up in any one of many other cultures where it was perfectly natural for her to bare her breasts, such exposure could have seemed perfectly normal to her.

If events fall within your expectations of what is right, normal and safe, based on your culture and your upbringing, they probably don't stress you. If they fall outside those expectations you probably do find them stressful.

Individual filters

The third type of filtering is done on an individual basis and there are at least three sub-filters in this group, namely, generalization, deletion and distortion.

Generalizing

The filters you apply through generalizing involve taking one experience that is bad and assuming that all such similar experiences will be bad. This then causes you to feel stressed.

Martha was a strong woman who helped her husband in the hardware store they owned. Her delight in the evenings was to take their large and strong labrador, Chappie, for a walk. When her city-bred sister, Jennifer, came to stay there was more work to be done so she asked Jennifer to walk the dog. All went well for the first week. Then on the eighth day Chappie found a smell that excited him and he took off with the lightly-built Jennifer clinging to his lead and desperately trying to keep up. Eventually she had to let go and returned home, after searching high and low, shaken and embarrassed, without him. Chappie, needless to say, was waiting quietly at the front door. From then on Jennifer refused to walk him at all saying: 'He always runs away when I take him, I'm not strong enough to hold him.'

In this way she generalized from the one event that stressed her, ignoring the previous seven successful walks, to create a feeling of stress whenever she was faced with a large dog.

Jim was frequently called on to present material to the board of directors of the company for which he worked. All went well for his first year in the job. Then at one meeting he got confused by the questions being thrown at him and got his figures muddled up. In a lather of embarrassment he extricated himself as well as he could and went back to his office. From then on he felt thoroughly stressed and developed tension headaches during the days prior to a board meeting knowing that he 'always got his figures muddled at board meetings'.

Deletion

Deletion is the second kind of individual filtering. In this you ignore certain things that happen and focus on others. You may ignore the good things and then feel stressed because you are aware of their absence.

Mrs G. had come to my office several times complaining of many health problems, all of which she attributed to stress, and largely to the stress of her marriage.

'My husband no longer cares,' she said. 'He doesn't care how I'm feeling and he thinks I'm stupid. He either ignores me or contradicts what I say and argues with me. I can't cope with the children, he undermines my authority and I can't keep going this way.'

Eventually I decided I needed to see them both together so she brought Mr G. in with her on her next visit. He sat in a chair beside her and rested his arm along the back of hers in a protective gesture. As he introduced himself he explained that he was worried about his wife's health and willing to do anything he could to help.

For the first 10 minutes she spoke and I asked questions. Mr G. remained quiet but observed her and me closely with obvious concern for her showing on his face. Eventually Mrs G. said, 'And I've had a headache every single day with the stress of it all.'

'No, dear, you didn't have a headache at the weekend, remember, we remarked on it.'

'There you are,' she said angrily, leaning towards me, 'see what I mean, he doesn't care and he contradicts me all the time.'

One look at Mr G.'s face showed his progression from happy optimism that she had been headache-free for the weekend to resignation at her outburst.

She had followed her habit of filtering out the care he was expressing by his body language and the 10 minutes during which he had listened to every word she said without a contradiction. Her filtering and her expectations were leading her to have the type of experience she expected to have. It was going to be another bad day.

Distortions

Distortions are probably the easiest type of filtering to describe. Your boss gives you a bunch of flowers, delighted with the work you have done and you think 'what does he want from me now'. Or the children come home from school with a present for you and you wonder what crime they have committed. Perhaps you are invited to a party and think 'they've only asked me because they feel they must'. Or perhaps you are not invited because they have only asked their friends who are interested in music. You're not, and yet you choose to assume they don't like you enough to want you.

There are more ways of distorting situations, remarks, looks and so forth than there are people. We all do it all the time; it is impossible not to. No-one can be totally objective; we are all biased by our past experiences.

Good and bad days 2

Think back to the good day and the bad day that started this section and we will see how filters could apply to them.

On the bad day you have woken up late, you've tripped getting out of bed, run the cold instead of the hot tap in the shower, burnt the toast and discovered the milk was sour. Expecting the rest of the day to be full of problems, you filtered out of your mind the green traffic lights through which you sailed and focused on the red ones that stopped you. You ignored the smiles on the faces of the happy people you met and focused on the people who were cross. You hurried past the friendly check-out girls in the first two shops and then were stressed when you were kept waiting by the slow girl in the shoe shop who was new at the job. The pleasant 'good morning, have you time to come in for a coffee?' from a usually quiet neighbour could have set you wondering what she wanted to complain about when all she wanted was to cheer you up a bit. You could then have gone home safe in the knowledge that the day had been as awful as you had known it would be from the start and spent the evening complaining of the stress you were under, saying: 'I knew it was going to be a bad day from the start. All the traffic lights were red [generalization from a few], no-one smiled at me [deletion], the shop assistants were hopeless [deletion] and the neighbour probably wants me to baby-sit [distortion].'

On the other hand, consider the good day. The clothes you wanted to wear were all clean, the sun shone, you caught your bus and got to work exactly on time and decided that this was going to be a great day. In this case you would have ignored the office cross-patch [deletion] and enjoyed the humour of the new junior. You would have focused on all the things that went right [deletion of the problems] and been sufficiently relaxed that when the boss complained of errors in your work you showed your concern for the extra pressure he was under to make him so touchy [a distortion in your favour].

Coming home you could have described the pleasant day you'd had and anticipated the chat you would have with the neighbour who had asked you to drop in, not realizing that she felt guilty for not including you in her recent dinner party [a distortion, again in your favour].

The person having the bad day would have been aware of all the problems in the office of the second, happy, person and the second person would have been aware of all the green traffic lights and smiling assistants in the day of the first, unhappy person. Same day, different people, different experiences, the final result depending on your expectations as to how the day would be. Your stress level depended on your expectations and on your filtering.

Your reality

In these examples several things are clear. The day doesn't exist independently of you. Objectively it is neither a good nor a bad day. The day, in these examples, was what the person involved chose to make of it. The first person focused on so many of the things that weren't perfect that she created for herself a great deal of stress and aggravation. No matter what happened during the day, good or bad, she had focused on the bad and was feeling thoroughly stressed and unhappy. Her neck muscles were tense and sore, the spasms in her blood vessels had created a headache and when she sat down to dinner she was so uptight she got indigestion. All these problems she put down to the stress in her life. When a friend told her to take up yoga or go to relaxation classes she glowered at him muttering that it was all very well for him, he didn't have to deal with the stresses she had.

When a colleague phoned the woman who'd had the good day and talked about the office cross-patch and the boss who was never satisfied she would have been surprised to find that her friend had hardly noticed these and that she was still happy and relaxed and looking forward to a good dinner and an enjoyable evening.

Filters exist. If you can make them work in your favour rather than against you, you can have a happy and relaxed day instead of a tense and stressful day. It is your choice.

A friend who I'll call Sara is a perenially happy optimist. Living in a different city I see her only occasionally but speak to her on the phone
often. On one of our Christmas get-togethers she mentioned what a
wonderful year it had been for her. I stared at her in surprise. She had
her own business, a pleasant daytime restaurant, and it had suffered a
major fire as a result of the faulty wiring about which she had several
times complained to the landlord. Later burglars had broken into
her house and stolen her TV, video machine and a lot of clothing. Her
boyfriend of several years had left her and a car crash had left her unable to compete in the dancing competition for which she had been
training.

Interested to see her reaction I listed all these things for her. She
looked a little surprised and then reluctantly admitted that all those
things had happened.

'However,' she said, 'I felt good most of the year and lots of good
things came out of it.'

'Like what?'

'Well, look at the restaurant now. I may have lost three months of
business but at least I had a bit of a holiday in that time. It is now
newly decorated and looks fantastic and business is picking up again. I
got insurance money for the things that were stolen so I now have a
new model TV and video, and you know how I love to buy clothes and
keep complaining that I have no room for them in the wardrobes. I miss
Bob but I must admit I'm enjoying the freedom after five years with
him and look at my lovely new car.'

'What about the dancing that you had to give up?'

Here she had the grace to look a bit sheepish.

'I think I was really glad of the excuse not to compete. I only really
took it up for fun, then I got talked into competing. I suppose I was
glad of the excuse to give it up, and look at all the free time it has
given me for my painting.'

Can't you just hear how someone else might have described the
year? It could have gone something like this;

> 'This has been a dreadful year, thank goodness it's over. It's been one stress after another. I lost a lot of money while the restaurant was closed, I had no money coming in and now it's barely paying its way. Burglaries are so stressful, you feel as if you've been violated. All those lovely clothes I lost, I could never replace them. And as for Bob, it just shows, you can't trust men, some little thing and they up and leave you. As for that idiot in the other car, because of him I'm scared every time I drive and I've missed out on dancing. I'll bet I could have won the competition too, and now my social life is nothing at all.'

It was, or would have been, the same year for both people. The events didn't change but the interpretation and focus did and so did the experience of stress. Whatever happens around you, your personal experience depends totally on the filters you apply and the attitude you choose to take through that day or year and into the next. This is what determines your level and feeling of stress.

Creating

Now, let's go back to the beginning of this chapter. I suggested there were two possible reasons why an anticipated good day would follow expectations and an anticipated bad one would do the same. We have discussed the first possibility, the possibility of filtering, the possibility that you filter out all events that don't fit in with your expectations of the way the day will be.

The second possibility is that, by the very conviction of your expectations, you somehow actually create the type of day you expect to have. Let's assume both days were your days.

On the anticipated bad day you were already in a bad mood when you left home. When you scowl at shop assistants they tend to scowl back at you. When you show a newcomer to the job that you are cross and impatient they are likely to get more confused and take even longer to get their job done. By the time you stomped into your neighbour's house for coffee you could have been such poor company that her behaviour to you would have been affected and she might indeed have brought up the problem of the noise your children were making just to show you that she too had stresses to deal with.

On the anticipated good day you would have smiled at everyone you met, been pleasant to the people in the office and generally created good humour around you. Even a cross boss responds positively to a happy smiling member of his staff and is likely to have been less cross than he would have been had you been grumbling about the stresses in your life.

Martin is a typical example of the way your attitude can create your outcome. He had a good position in the city, in the head office of the company. Then he was asked to go to an industrial area and head up a section of the company that was in trouble. He hated it. The position was beneath him, he missed the acknowledgement of his peers, the whole organization was sluggish, his staff were suspicious of him, corning in from outside with new ideas, and they took his appointment as a criticism from head office.

As a result Martin started to complain of the stress he was under. He became cross in the office and barked at the staff when they were too slow. Although excellent in his technical area he had trouble motivating the people in the plant and the outside contractors. Each day he was met with resistance.

'It's no good,' Martin thought. 'None of them like me, and I don't like them much.' So he settled down to endure and make the best of it, getting an ulcer in the process.

Then he noticed a new man in administration. Each time they met the man smiled at him and hoped he was having a good day. Tentatively Martin started to smile back. Then he started to smile at other people, and they smiled back. Gradually he became more optimistic about the future until one day he realized how much more supportive his staff were and how much more relaxed he felt.

As his own behaviour and expectations had changed so had the world around him. He had significantly lowered his experience of stress by his change of attitude and the results this change had produced. Again he is an example of the way your thoughts and your attitudes can change your experience and thereby change your stress level.

Can your thoughts change the world?

For the adventurous, who like to explore further, there is yet another possibility to consider. Your thoughts may, as we have seen, influence other people and events by the way you look, speak and behave and the impact this has on others. It is also possible that there are other more subtle effects. We talk of vibes. You can probably think of a time when you picked up on what someone else was thinking. Perhaps you were about to phone them when they rang you. Perhaps you were about to invite them to stay when they phoned and said they were coming to town and could you spare a room for the night. Perhaps, with your thoughts, you can actually change the world, change your experiences and thus further create or reduce the stress in your life.

Before you retort that this is a bit far-fetched consider the following. Many of today's atomic physicists and related scientists are coming to the belief that thought has an effect on the way sub-atomic particles function (e.g. Fritjof Capra in *The Turning Point*, Flamingo, 1983). If this is so then thought also has an effect on atoms and the way they function. These in turn affect the way whole molecules function and molecules can affect the way your tissue and thus your body, including your brain, functions. Therefore it is possible that your thoughts can affect the physical substances of your body, other people's bodies and the objects in the world around you.

This in turn means it is possible that your thoughts can indeed affect objects as well as people and, by your thoughts, you can change what occurs in your life and therefore your stress levels. Indeed some atomic physicists have suggested that matter is the lowest form of consciousness.

Remember too that, with the work of Einstein, we know that energy and matter are interchangeable. If this is taken to its logical conclusion then it is indeed possible that by the energy of your thoughts you can affect physical matter and the way it behaves. As far back as 1935 this seemingly modern concept was expressed thus by Dr Alexis Carrel in his book *Man, The Unknown*. 'The mind is hidden within the living matter … completely neglected by physiologists and economists, almost unnoticed by physicians. Yet it is the most colossal power of this world.' He also wrote 'Each state of consciousness probably has a corresponding organic expression … Thought can generate organic lesions …'

James Jeans in *The Mysterious Universe* (Macmillan, 1930) said 'Today there is a wide measure of agreement … that the stream of knowledge is heading towards a non-mechanical reality; the universe begins to look more like a great thought than a great machine.'

In these quotations we have the concept that different thoughts, or experiences of stress, can generate specific health problems, and the concept that you can use the power of your mind to alter the world around you, as well as your perception of that world, and thus your experience of stress.

This is not a necessary belief to have. You don't have to believe that your mind has the power to change matter to be able to reduce your stress or to handle the ideas in the rest of the book. But if you are willing to consider the idea that your thoughts can have a physical effect it is worth considering the possibility of this way of reducing the stress you experience and it gives you another powerful tool with which to work.

Your thoughts are enormously powerful. Use this creative power to create a stress-free life rather than a stressful life.

CHAPTER TWO

More Thoughts

In the last chapter we considered the possibility that you create for your-self the type of life and experience that you expect to have. It was suggested that you may do this by the way you view what happens in your life and the ways in which you filter it by generalizations, deletions and distortions. We also considered the possibility that, by your words and actions, you influence the people and events around you as your words and deeds impact on them. Further, for the more adventurous, it was suggested that you may, by thought power alone, actually influence events.

These are interesting ideas and can have a lot to do with the way you manage stress. Let's consider now some ways in which they can be put into practice.

What to do

If you consider the above ideas as theories but do nothing with them, they won't help you to reduce your stress levels. You may say you believe in the ideas but that in your case there is nothing you can do. Your stresses are different, they are real, and all you can do is endure them. I have found, while seeing patients, that it takes courage to face these possibilities, the possibility that you are, in some way, contribut-ing to your experience of stress. At the same time, I have found that when people do make the necessary changes, their lives can become exciting, wonderful and stress-free.

If you claim to believe and accept all that is said, yet say that your case is different and that the ideas wouldn't work for you, it will be easy for you to do nothing, or to do so little that you remain stressed, thus further proving that these ideas do not and will not work for you. They do, they will and they can, but you must remain open-minded. You must also put the ideas into practice as actively and consistently as you can.

I recall a seminar in which I was to give the second of four two-hour talks on the power of thought in relation to health to a group of about 300 people who all had cancer. They were all well-read in the ideas that I was about to present regarding the ability of human beings to use the power of their minds to change their physical health. Furthermore, the previous speaker had given an excellent compilation of the many times in the medical health literature in which positive health outcomes had occurred in people with cancer who had a positive mental attitude and vice versa.

As I started I wondered how I could make my session interesting and not leave them feeling bored and claiming that they had heard all I had to say many times before and that I had given them nothing new or useful. Finally I decided to ask a few questions.

My question 'Wasn't the last speaker excellent?' produced claps, cheers and positive acknowledgements.

My next question 'How many of you believe the information he gave and do believe that by your own mental attitude you can change your life?' brought such a huge show of hands that I asked the opposite question.

'How many of you do not believe that your thoughts can make any difference?' This brought a show of about three hands only.

My next question was 'How many of you are currently leading a life that is exactly the way you want it?' No hands went up. This was not surprising since they all had cancer or were accompanying someone with cancer.

I had made sure that everyone looked around at the responses to each question so it was easy to make my concluding remark.

'I don't believe you.'

After a suitable pause, during which time no-one said a word, I continued. 'Either your life *is* the way you want it to be or you do *not* really believe that you can change your life and your state of health by the way that you think and behave.' This had the effect of shaking them up. Some protested, others started to ask questions. It is certain that they listened to the talk with a more active and open mind than they would have done otherwise. I ask you to read the rest of this book in a similar way.

You may well be saying, at this point, that it is all very well for other people to be happy optimists, but you just don't feel like that and you do feel stressed, and the world is a tough place, and indeed you cannot cope, nor can you change the way things are by plastering a false smile on your face. After all, if it was that easy you probably wouldn't be reading this book at all. If this is what you feel then I suggest you should be willing to suspend your disbelief and come along with us to see where we're going. After all, nothing else has worked for you, has it?

If you do not change the directions in which you are headed, you will land up where you are going.

Taking control of your life

It is now time to take a leap forward. Be willing to accept the following assumptions and come with me as we find out where they lead. You owe it to yourself don't you? You've been feeling stressed for a long time. What if, just possibly, these ideas could be the basis by which you can find ways of eliminating stress from your life? Let's go. Here are the assumptions.

1 **By your thoughts you have created the experience you have each day.**

You have generated the assumptions that lead you to believe people do
or don't like you, that your employees do or don't respect you, that you
can or can't trust people, that your family does or doesn't appreciate you
or that you are a success or a failure.

2 **What you choose to think about yourself becomes the truth. Your
truth is your world view. It has little to do with an (impossible)
objective reality.**

If you dress up and feel terrific you go to the party and have a ball,
feeling glamorous and admired. Even if you go home and realize your
petticoat was showing and you had a ladder in your tights it didn't spoil
the fun you had at the time.

On the other hand, if you were convinced that your white underclothes
were showing through your black dress in the strobe lighting you would
have had a ghastly time, even if, afterwards, you realized they weren't. I'm
sure you can think of examples of such situations in your life.

3 **Your present situation is the result of your own thoughts and
actions and the decisions you have made in the past. You are the
creator of your present situation.**

You may argue that much that has happened to you has been outside
your control. Maybe that seems true. However, at every step you did
have other options. They may have been totally unacceptable options,
but you did have them. You may have wanted one career but bowed
to parental pressures and gone into another one. You may have wanted
to travel but been unwilling to give up your job. You may not have
wanted to move to the country when your husband was transferred but
preferred to go rather than separate. You may not have wanted to marry
your girlfriend when she got pregnant but preferred to do so than to
incur your parents' wrath. Whatever the situation there were other options. The one you followed was, ultimately, your choice.

If you hold to this belief it leaves you in a position of power. It leaves you secure in the belief that you have control of your life, you had control in the past and, best of all, you have control of your future. In turn it leaves you in control of your stresses and tells you quite clearly that you can alter them.

Having said this, you may still be unconvinced and want to argue that you are not in control so let me ask you a question. Can you be absolutely sure that you are not in control of your life? Can you be certain that, no matter what you do, the good and bad things that are going to happen to you will happen anyway?

If you are not sure either way, not sure that you are in control and yet not absolutely sure that you are not in control, you have a decision to make. If you cannot be sure either way you could be wrong whichever option you choose. For most people, believing that they do have control of their lives is a positive belief system, believing that they don't have control is a negative belief system and leaves them powerless. Wouldn't it be better to be wrong in choosing a positive belief than to be wrong in choosing a negative belief system?

If indeed we are not in total control of our lives then you can either believe that, in which case the outlook for positive change to your stress levels is indeed grim, or you can disbelieve it. If you refuse to believe that you are not in control you will at least feel more positive and optimistic as you try to take charge of things and mould them your way.

On the other hand, if you are in fact in control and you believe this you can act positively, whereas if you choose not to believe it you will miss out on a lot of positive changes you could have made.

Since this may be a little complicated to grasp let me put it another way. There are four options:

1 If the truth is that you are not in control and you believe it then there is little you can do to change your stress levels and you might as well give up right now.

2 If the truth is that you are in control and you believe this then you
   can change your stress levels, starting right now. It is the two other
   options that are important.
3 If you are not in control but choose to believe you are, you are in a
   much better situation than either 1 or 4 (below).
4 If you choose to believe that you are not in control when in fact
   you are, you will as a result miss out on a lot of the positive
   decisions you could have made and benefits you could have
   achieved.

In other words, the most *useful* belief system is the one that says you are,
in fact, in control of your life, of your thoughts, of all that occurs
around you and of the amount of stress that you choose to experience.
Since this is the most useful belief system to have, let's hold to it and
work with it, particularly since there is much evidence to support it.

If you feel you cannot do this I suggest you be willing to work with
the ideas for the duration of this book and act 'as if' it were true and see
where this leads you. The alternative is to give up at this point, stop
reading and say that you can do nothing about the amount of stress you
are experiencing.

Limiting thoughts

Everyone has some negative thoughts about themselves, at least some of
the time. You may believe you are not good enough, not attractive
enough, not unselfish enough. You may think you are too tall, too fat,
too stupid, too slow, too impatient. You may think you can't sing, can't
draw, aren't artistic, aren't intelligent, aren't capable. You may think you
handle money badly, handle people badly, make decisions badly and so
forth.

Underlying all these surface negative beliefs that you have about
yourself there will be one that is the biggest, worst and most painful to
contemplate. We will call this your Ultimate Negative Belief or UNB.

The irony is that this Ultimate Negative Belief you have is never true. It is a belief that you have built for yourself based on past experiences, yet in an outward objective sense it is not true. Isn't that nice to know? After many years of working with patients in this way I have not yet found one whose UNB was based on fact. They have all been based on inappropriate but understandable interpretations made by people in response to situations that arose earlier in their life.

One of your tasks, in reducing the stress in your life, is to identify your own UNB. We will do this fully a little later on. For now consider what limiting or negative beliefs you have. They may be thoughts about yourself, they may be thoughts about other people, outside events, objects or the world around you. Stop reading right now, find a pen and paper and make a list of all the limiting or negative thoughts you have about yourself and about your life. They may include any or all of the following:

- I'm not good enough.
- People always let me down.
- I could never do so and so.
- Other people have all the luck.
- I'm no good at numbers.
- I can't sing in tune.
- For the next 10 years I'll have to deal with the mortgage.
- I'm a poor parent.
- Things always get on top of me.

Write your own list now.

Simply having these limiting thoughts can be stressful. The consequences of thinking them, day after day, can be even more stressful.

Mr T. came to see me because of the stress he experienced both at home and at work. In time we came round to the concept of limiting beliefs and, on his next visit, he produced the following list:

- I've reached the top of my profession.
- I'll never earn more money than I do now.
- I can't leave this job, I'm too old to get another.
- My new boss doesn't like me.
- My colleagues don't respect me the way they did.
- The children have gone their separate ways, you can't expect them to stay close.
- The other grandparents have more to offer the grandchildren than we do.
- My wife and I don't communicate any more. She keeps spending money we haven't got.
- I'm getting angina like my father, I'm likely to have a heart attack.
- We're too old to move to the country.
- We can't afford to travel.
- I'm too old to do many of the things I had planned but haven't yet done.
- When I retire, we'll have to learn to manage on the pension. This means that life will be very restricted when I retire.

Is it any wonder Mr T. felt stressed? With all these Limiting Beliefs he was facing one perceived stress after another. I suggested that he change them.

'I can't change them,' he said, 'they're true. I **have** reached the top of the profession, we **don't** have enough money, I **am** too old to do many of the things I would have liked to do.'

'Only if you think so,' I said and then kept quiet while he let that sink in.

'You mean if I think differently then things might change?'

'What do you think?'

'I don't know. It seems too easy.'

I suggested we take the beliefs one at a time. With regard to his profession, was there more he could do? He agreed he could in fact go higher, his equal-ranked colleague had just been promoted.

'But they don't need two senior executives,' he said.

'How do you know? They might expand, they might want you somewhere else.'

He still looked thoughtful, so I continued, 'If you are convinced there is no future there for you, you will feel stressed; if you choose to believe there are good things ahead, (a) you will look for them, (b) you may even create them, and (c) you will feel good in the process.'

I decided to leave work and focus on his home life.

'You and your wife don't communicate any more?'

'No. She's not interested in what I do and she's all involved with her bowls and her women friends. We have nothing to say to each other in the evenings.'

'When did you last share the things you do at work with her?'

'She wouldn't be interested.'

'How do you know?'

'Well...'

'How about giving it a try?'

He agreed that he could, and that he would also try to take an interest in what she did.

We went through the other restrictions he was placing on himself.

When he came back a fortnight later he reported that having talked things over with his wife he had found she had been growing depressed because he didn't share things with her any more and that she felt this was because he had lost interest in her. She was delighted when he started sharing again. At work he had suggested a new project and his ideas were being considered.

The real point here is that if you decide to limit your horizons with these thoughts then they are limits, and therefore stresses. If you choose not to believe in them, if you choose to believe you can change things any way you want, you will feel more positive and optimistic. After all, you can't be absolutely sure you can't change things, so why choose to believe it? Choose to believe that you can and '.... thinking can make it so'. Your subconscious has a way of making your thoughts come true, not your goals and dreams necessarily, especially if they are vague hopes rather than definite aims, but your deeper thoughts and beliefs.

One of my Limiting Beliefs was that I couldn't sing in tune. When I started running the workshops, which involved group singing, I found I had to sing out to lead the way or no-one else would so I prefaced the song with a self-defensive 'Come on everyone, sing, it doesn't matter if you're in tune or not. If I hit the right note it is purely by accident so if I'm prepared to sing out you'd better be too, and for your own sakes you'd better drown my voice out.'

Not only did everyone feel a lot more comfortable but after a while I found I actually was hitting the right note more often than not. Relaxing does wonderful things for your vocal cords.

Some of your Limiting Beliefs may not involve you directly. They may include

- 'men don't cry',
- 'women are paid less than men',
- 'single parents are social misfits',
- 'there are more single women around than single men',
- 'you can't make a living as an artist',
- 'you can't rely on other people',
- 'if you haven't been to university you can't expect to get a good job',
- 'it's impossible to get a job in the current economic climate'.

Again, thinking will make it so. Men *do* cry, I've seen them and so, probably, have you. There *are* some very well-paid women; there could be more if they believed sufficiently in themselves. You *can* be a well-paid artist under the right circumstances. There *are* jobs to be had, even in a depression. These things may happen less often than you would like but they do happen. The point is that while you have these Limiting Beliefs your deeds and actions are likely to contribute to them. Further, these Limiting Beliefs are putting restrictions on your life and you are feeling stressed by them. If you weren't stressed by them, they wouldn't come in the Limiting category. A belief like women aren't violent' may be stressful if you are a woman and feel like hitting out but think you have to suppress this. But if it makes you feel safe rather than stressed, it is a useful belief to have and not limiting.

Your ultimate negative belief

Your Ultimate Negative Belief has already been referred to. It is the biggie. It is the major stumbling block on your road to a happy and stress-free life. We will discuss it further, but later. If you want to pursue it now, turn to the chapter on Affirmations. There you will learn both how to find your Ultimate Negative Belief and how to antidote it with a Positive Alternative Belief.

Conscious and subconscious

We have talked about conscious thoughts. We have also talked about and alluded to deeper thoughts, thoughts that you perhaps haven't brought to consciousness for many long years. It's now time to take a closer look at the conscious and the subconscious minds and to consider their similarities and, more importantly, their differences.

Your conscious mind is where you do all your rational thinking. You plan, you consider, you analyse. You make decisions and you assess their results. With your conscious mind you keep yourself in line with reality, you try to be objective. Most people like to think they are rational human beings who can think and reason logically and act accordingly.

Your subconscious mind is subjective rather than objective. It relates to you personally. It is creative and intuitive. You can think of your subconscious as an entity that has your best interests, as it sees them, at heart, that is responsive to your logical thoughts and that assists you in creating a reality that conforms to your expectations.

If you think you're going to be late for an appointment you will have the thought going round and round in your mind, 'I'm going to be late'. Your subconscious picks this up and interprets it, not as a fear but as a statement of fact. Since it has your best interests at heart it then does all it can to make sure that reality works out the way you expect it to be and it makes you late. It may encourage you to do just one more task before leaving home or allow your mind to focus elsewhere so you forget something and have to go back for it, or it may take your conscious mind off where you're going so you take a wrong turning. All or any of these things can make you late and your subconscious has done its job in making sure that your conscious prediction came true.

If your conscious mind keeps repeating that you're unpopular and no-one loves you and your friends don't really want you then your subconscious will make sure that you focus on the events and situations that conform with this view, thus again supporting your conscious mind with its view of reality.

Your subconscious mind will also make you behave in such a way that the outcome conforms to your world view. If you think you are unpopular you are likely to withdraw in social situations and keep to yourself, thus encouraging other people to leave you alone and proving, to you at least, your unpopularity.

The subconscious has little sense of humour. It is also very literal. Be careful of such phases as 'I'll die if I don't get that job'. You just might.

Little Johnnie had just learnt to walk when granny came to stay. He insisted on carrying a plate of cakes to her at teatime. All was going well until granny saw what he was doing and said, in an endeavour to make him more careful, 'Watch it, Johnnie, you'll fall.' He did just that. He watched it and then, as instructed, he fell.

Spend a few days listening to all the messages you feed into your subconscious. Are they serving you? Are they positive? Do you tell yourself you are happy or sad, successful or a failure, liked or disliked, good-looking or a mess, wealthy or poor, healthy or sick? The first step is to become aware of these messages, then to analyse them and then to change them as appropriate.

If you have a spotty face but lovely glossy hair you can either gaze into the mirror and say 'what a mess' or 'how pretty/handsome'. If your subconscious gets the 'mess' message you are likely to do a lot of things in the day that will contribute to making you more of a mess. You may slouch, spill things, be careless with things that make your clothes and hands dirty or do a number of other things to increase your look of dishevelment. If, on the other hand, your subconscious gets the 'pretty/handsome' message it is likely to encourage you to act more cleanly and do things in such a way that you are neater and more elegant and generally contribute to your overall feeling of looking good.

It is not simply a question of focusing on the more positive aspects of your appearance, although this is a powerful tool in decreasing the stress you might otherwise feel about it. It is also important to encourage the unconscious actions and decisions you make that contribute to the desired end result of looking good rather than the unconscious actions that make you look dowdy.

It is valuable to know that the power of this subconscious mind, which is enormous, is yours for the asking. You don't have to plead with it, pray to it, or bully and cajole it into doing what you want. All you have to do is recognize its capacity and programme it correctly and you will get the desired result.

The limiting factor in all this is yourself. If you choose to you can use the power of your subconscious to your own advantage. Equally, if you choose, you can use the power of your subconscious to keep you where you are and encourage all the things you fear. Which course will have you less stressed? Obviously the former course is the one that will lead to less stress. It is sad that so few people choose to use it. I repeat, the limiting factor is yourself. It is up to you what you choose to do and how you choose to think.

Fear of failure

So many people behave as if it is easier to predict failure and make that come true than to predict success and bring that about. The very notion of 'touching wood' tells us that we're afraid our successes will be taken away from us, we're afraid we'll fail. There is a common fear that if you predict that something good is going to happen you are jeopardizing the positive outcome by even mentioning it; 'touching wood' is, in some way, supposed to undo the harm that could be caused by making the prediction.

It seems that in our society it is thought better not to predict success or a good time for yourself than to predict it and then not get it. It is more acceptable to predict that you have failed an exam and then be bashfully grateful when you have passed than to predict success. Many have a fear that if they predict and expect something good to happen and it doesn't, people will think much less of them than if they had predicted a poor outcome initially. The saying 'Pride goes before a fall' says it all. Why not be proud? Why not be positive and hopeful?

Betty told me that she was always afraid of doing badly in the exams at school even though she was a good scholar and usually came in the top third of the class. While some of her close friends, who were also in the top third, were saying the work was easy and that they felt they'd done enough study, she couldn't admit to them, or to herself, that she had done enough or that she was confident. Her greatest fear was appearing confident and then finding the result was worse than she had anticipated.

Even at the times when she felt she did know her work well she still couldn't leave her books alone, fearing she'd overlooked something. She'd get into last-minute panics and rush back to check on facts. She'd create in her mind exam questions that she couldn't answer and she'd get very stressed and tense in the days leading up to the exams. Even afterwards she would focus on all the things she hadn't included in her answer. She hated hanging around with people discussing the papers and hearing the things they had put in and that she had omitted or done differently, fearing that they were right and she was wrong. She'd then tell people she was sure she'd failed. The results, when they finally came out, were an anticlimax. Invariably she had done well.

Her mother had brought her in to see me because Betty's major school exams were looming at the end of the following year and she was afraid that the stress would be too much for her. I pointed out to Betty that it was fine to study hard. It was indeed silly to assume she knew everything she needed to know and to stop studying too early, but that it was also counter-productive to get over-stressed by focusing on the things she didn't know.

During the tests and exams of the coming year she was to work just as hard as ever at her books, but she was gradually to start focusing on all the things she did know and to start assuring herself she could learn all her work in time and that she would do well in the exams as a result of her diligent efforts. In the few hours before each test or exam, when further study was impossible, she was told to start affirming to herself that she knew all she needed to know, that she had done her work well and that she would do well in the exam.

Note that she was not told simply to assume she had done enough work and that all would be well. She was not told to stop trying. The aim was to create a situation where she did study hard but where the extra, non-productive stress was removed from the situation.

The results were interesting. Both she and her mother reported that she was indeed less stressed. There were two added benefits that she had not foreseen. Firstly, she told me, study was becoming easier as she kept telling herself she was capable of learning and understanding all she needed. Secondly, she said that when it came to the actual exam she was able to answer the questions better both because she remembered more and because she was less stressed and was able to relax and think more clearly and formulate her answers better.

The period between doing the exams and getting the results had always been a trial for all the family. They were tense because Betty was tense; they were also tense because they kept hearing her say she had done badly. She was told to start affirming to herself, from the moment that she walked out of the exam room, that she had done well.

'But what if I haven't, what if I'm wrong?' Her greatest fear raised its head again.

'Then at least you'll have spent the intervening time feeling happy rather than stressed,' was my answer.

'That's like living in a fool's paradise,' she said anxiously.

'Better than living in a fool's hell as you do now, worrying when you have no need to.' With this she agreed, albeit reluctantly.

As a result of harnessing her subconscious, by programming it for success rather than failure, she was not only less stressed but more

> successful too. She still found it hard to tell people she was sure she
> had done well, but at least she was able to stop bewailing how badly
> she had done.

It is worth repeating one important aspect of this. Notice one very important thing about the way Betty reprogrammed her subconscious. She did not go into the study period saying 'I know enough. I know I'll pass and do well.' She included in all her affirmations both the concept that she was working hard and well and the concept that *as a result* she would do well in the exams.

In this she was in sharp contrast to Edward.

> Edward had gone to a new and progressive university where the students were encouraged to set their own study patterns. He had been at a strict school and the new freedom was going to his head. Further, he had joined friends who were familiar with affirmations and their use and who spoke glibly about the power of the subconscious without really understanding it. He decided to copy them. His affirmations included 'the work is easy', 'I am good and will pass all my exams', 'I'm tops, I'm successful and I'm competent', and 'when I need to remember what we did in class it will all come back to me simply and easily'.
>
> On the face of it these are all very positive and empowering affirmations. Perhaps, when the power of his mind becomes strong enough, they will become sufficient to see him through the challenges of his life. However, in this instance they took the form of being relatively trivial thoughts and became an excuse not to study. He was surprised when he failed badly at the end of the first term, but he had learnt a valuable lesson about the subconscious.

Use the power of positive thoughts and your subconscious mind in combination with your conscious endeavours. Don't dump the responsibility on to your subconscious and mess around.

CHAPTER THREE

Past Programming

If you were placed on the Earth for the very first time at this moment how would you feel? Would you know what was safe and what threatened you? Would you know you should be wary of snakes or could rejoice in a sunset? Would you worry about money if you had not heard of it before? Would you know what sort of person you could trust and who you could ask for help? Of course you would not. You only know these things when you have had a previous experience on which to base your judgement.

These past experiences may be helpful in the way you form your new judgement or they may be a hindrance. If you grew up in England and knew you could ask a policeman for help any time you were in trouble you might get a surprise when you approached the armed officer of some country in which the police were feared. If, as a woman, you were used to the considerate behaviour of men you might not be sufficiently careful in a situation where any lone woman was at risk. If you come from a warm and loving home you may be inappropriately trusting in other similar situations.

It can work the other way too. If a dog that seemed friendly suddenly turned and bit you some time in the past you are unlikely to trust dogs in the future. If you have always been beaten when things went wrong you may still cringe and feel stressed anytime a voice is raised, even if it is not in anger. If your mother died or left home when you were young and your first girlfriend walks out on you, you may never learn to relax and trust your wife, fearing at any slight or possible sign of her interest in another man, however casual, that she is about to leave you.

Your view of the world and your expectations of the future, immediate or distant, are based on your experiences in the past. It is on the basis of these past experiences that you make your decisions of today. This, at one level, is so obvious that it may seem unnecessary to stress the fact. Yet few people take in the full implications of this. For it means that if you came to inappropriate conclusions in the past your whole assessment of the present may be equally inaccurate or inappropriate. It also means that if you once learnt to filter, to delete, to generalize or to distort in the past, you are likely to continue developing this habit. It is by exploring the past and assessing the relevance to the present of the conclusions you reached then, that you can significantly reduce many of the stresses of the present and the future.

Early experiences

The major conclusions you come to are usually based on your earliest experiences. This means that the nature of your first few hours and of your early and formative years is likely to have a major impact on the way you assess events and situations. However, new learning experiences throughout childhood and into adulthood can also influence how you interpret future situations. They are likely to be less important, however, as you develop an increasing perspective with the years. If you were left on your own (abandoned) for 10 minutes after birth when everything was new and strange to you, this would have been much more traumatic than if you were left alone for an hour when you were five years old. By the age of five you have learnt that Mummy comes back to wake you after your nap; at a few minutes old you do not have such memories to call upon.

If in your teens you had some good friends who were slim, short-haired and had nice smiles you are likely to trust such people in the future, even though they may turn out to be first-class crooks. If your previous two bosses stole your ideas you will probably find it difficult to trust the third one. If close friends have always stood by you, you are likely to feel you can depend on them in the future. The way you assess your world and your position in it today is based on your experiences of the past.

Keep in mind, however, that it is the furthest past that is usually the most powerful, no matter how relevant you think recent experiences are. If you were frightened by a spider as a very young child you may never get over your fear of spiders even though you have been told they are not dangerous. The earliest conclusions are often difficult to dislodge.

Some people are willing to look back into their past for the basis of their belief systems, their fears, their attitudes and their stresses. Other people are not. Which are you? If you are willing to explore further then do so. You will learn much of value and be able to put what you have learnt about yourself to good use in reducing your stress levels. If you are unwilling to delve into your past then you would be wise to question your reasons. Is it fear of what you might find? Was your past unhappy? Does it stress you to think about it? If, on this basis, you refuse to un-ravel your present attitudes and belief systems it is a bit like doing the ostrich trick and burying your head in the sand. The more you refuse to explore the past the more likely it is that there are some valuable clues there as to the basis for your present stresses.

This is true, however seemingly logical and valid your reasons or excuses are. You may claim to be unsentimental, you may say that there are such obvious causes for your present stress that the past is an unnec-essary irrelevance. You may say you haven't the time. You may insist that your childhood was such a happy one that going back will produce nothing useful. Commonly the real and underlying reason is based on the disquiet, apprehension or fear that is brought up by the thought of doing this. They may not even be conscious fears. There may simply be a subconscious feeling of discomfort when you contemplate the general idea. The fact remains that, in my experience, the past has enormously valuable clues to help you unravel your present reactions, emotions and stresses, whether you thought it was a happy past or an unhappy one.

Mr J. insisted his childhood had been happy and that he had always had a wonderful relationship with his parents, especially with his father. Yet he refused to go back and explore his childhood as a means of determining the basis for his present insecurities and stress. It was obviously essential to his self-esteem and his concept of himself to maintain this image of family solidarity and integrity. In time I met his brother, older than him by 10 years, and learnt that in fact Mr J. had been relegated to the background as second son and been bitterly hurt by this. It was only when the elder brother left home that Mr J. got the attention he craved and the happy childhood myth had become established.

If you fear to go back to the past with the keen perception of your present maturity there may be something there that you know about but think is too traumatic for you to face. Sexual interference, which is, tragically, much more common than we acknowledge, violence, an alcoholic parent, the death of a parent, or some other trauma may be an acknowledged memory, but something you refuse to think about. Or there may be something there of which you are aware at some subconscious level, but that you do not want to acknowledge, even to yourself. There may also be past stresses which you have buried so deeply that they have been totally forgotten. Yet even so they, or the conclusions you drew from them at the time, do play into the present and exert their effect.

Miss P. was a perfect and surprising example of this. She was in her late 40s and unmarried. She told me that she'd had a happy life. She enjoyed her work and had lots of friends. From time to time she'd had a variety of boyfriends but had shied away from any serious relationships and had turned down two proposals when she was in her 20s. Now a man, considerably older than her, wanted to marry her. She cared deeply for him, felt comfortable with him and also recognized that if she again

said no she could well remain single for good. Yet every time she considered agreeing to his proposal she got very upset, felt enormously
stressed and returned to the belief that she should stay single.

She came to see me looking for help in her dilemma. When we
discussed her childhood she insisted that it had been a happy one. She
came from a well-off family, had lived in a pleasant town, gone to a good
school and, seemingly, been given every advantage. She loved her parents
and brother and the family was still close. There were no problems there
she insisted. When asked if she had ever been jilted by a boyfriend, let
down by people she loved or had any sexual problems or harassment that
could have led to her fear of sex and a close relationship she searched her
memory thoroughly and said no. I had every reason to believe her; there
were none of the unconscious signs that indicated she was covering up.

She agreed to go back into her childhood and was amazed when she
discovered that she had indeed buried some traumatic memories so
deeply that, even though she had been 16 at the time the events
occurred, she had no conscious memory of them until we unravelled
them in my office.

At 16 she had become pregnant. This was in the early 1950s and at
a level of society where she was expected to be a virgin when she
married, when abortion was illegal and an unmarried mother a pariah.
Her frightened 16-year-old boyfriend had taken her to a back-street
abortionist who had done a very bad job. Her boyfriend had then taken
her, bleeding and in pain, to the home of a schoolfriend whose parents
were away for the weekend. After that he had denied any responsibility and disappeared from her life. She had struggled home on the
Monday and managed to keep everything a secret.

Certainly, going back to this past event was distressing for Miss P.
but the glow on her face when she realized that this had been the basis
for her distrust of men and marriage and that there was no need for
her to feel the same way about the man who wanted to marry her now,
made it all the more worthwhile. Later she reported not only on a
happy marriage but on an inner peace and quiet in many little ways
and the loss of minor stresses that she hadn't recognized previously.

The experience of delving back is rarely, on balance, painful. Whenever I have taken any client back into past experiences, no matter how traumatic they were at the time, we have only found that, by the end of the session, the experiences could be released so that they were no longer stressful, either in memory or in the way they affect the person's life in the present. We have also found that many positive changes are possible and that they start happening almost immediately.

To go back fully in the way Miss P. did you will need some professional assistance but there is much you can do on your own to explore your past programming and we will discuss ways of doing this later. If you refuse to look back you will lose a major tool in reducing the basis of the stresses in your life. If having read this far, you still don't want to explore the past you will have to rely on the other tools given in this book and do the best you can.

'I'm over-stressed and don't know how to cope,' said a smart business executive in his early 30s. 'I know I do a good job but I often worry that I won't live up to people's expectations. All it takes in a big company is one failure and you can kiss your chances of promotion goodbye. If I fail, my marriage will be on the rocks. I have nightmares at night, I'm snapping at my friends and if I don't do something soon I will have a nervous breakdown.'

We discussed his diet and his lifestyle and ascertained that there were no serious health problems. I then suggested we should explore other reasons why he felt so stressed and why he felt he had to be the best at everything, to which his first reaction was 'Fine, I'm willing to explore my attitudes but none of this exploring the past. I don't want to go delving back into my childhood, that's just so much sentimental and emotional wallowing.'

Unfortunately he stuck by that view and so there was little we could achieve. He tried visualizations and relaxation and deep-breathing techniques, but not surprisingly these helped little.

Years later his wife came to see me, after their divorce, and told me that as a boy his father had beaten him when he didn't come in the top five in his class and the whole family had taunted him with not being as good at school as his older sister. When he had failed one subject at school his father had refused to help him any further in his education. If he had been able to understand that he was using these experiences to expect, quite inappropriately, the same type of treatment from his peers and colleagues he could have lessened his stresses considerably, enjoyed his work more and saved his marriage.

All that you think and do today is thought and done against the background of your past experiences. If you are having trouble today, if certain things stress you today, then there is a good chance that the underlying reason for this stress derives at least in part from previous experiences. If you can discover these experiences and reassess them you may well find that your current fears and stresses are unwarranted or inappropriate.

We will now explore some more of the many possible situations that could have occurred in your life, or in anyone's life. My purpose in giving you these examples is two-fold. Firstly, the examples, all taken from patient files, suitably disguised, will help you to appreciate the experiential basis on which my conclusions and recommendations are based. Secondly, the ideas and examples may help you to trigger recognition of some of your own situations. If, as mentioned above, you want to explore this further for yourself then the ideas elsewhere in the book will help you. Alternatively, or additionally, you may find enormous benefit from going to someone who is qualified to help you.

Back to the beginning

Where to start? For most people their first conscious memory is somewhere between two and four years old. One friend told me they could remember their mother's pendant swinging as she stood over the pram when they were less than a year old. Another told me they could remember nothing before they were seven years old, but these seem to be exceptions.

If you truly search your memory you may be surprised to find just how much you can remember. You will almost certainly find that you can remember more than you thought you could and that you can remember further back than you thought you could. Think about the time you forgot something you know well such as a person's name, their phone number or their address. You've forgotten it, it has gone completely out of your mind, then suddenly you recall it again. You forgot what you did on your last birthday, then something happens to trigger your memory and the whole occasion comes into focus.

What happens to these memories, to these thoughts, that you can have them, lose them and then have them again? Where do they go? It has been suggested that all our memories are there still inside us, locked away somewhere, somehow, waiting to be accessed when we find the key to them. Certainly this is what I have found in my practice, with patients. From the years I have spent working with people and researching their past as a way of helping them with their present and their future it seems clear to me that it is possible for us all to remember right back to our earliest moments, not only to the moment of birth but even back to the time in the womb.

Under the appropriate circumstances patients have gone back to the very beginning of their life and been able to recount experiences that throw a lot of light on their present situation. When I first tell them this will be possible most people are sceptical. You may be too. I find the best way round this is to recount some examples from my own experience and so I will do that now.

Examples

The major stresses in Mr A.'s life came from the fact that he always felt he was unwanted, that no-one really cared about him, that other people were more popular, more successful, more in demand, more efficient and that he was not good enough. He always worried about future events and feared that he would not be included. When he was included in invitations or events he worried that people had asked him simply to be polite. If a working committee was formed and he was not co-opted he knew it was because he was not good enough. The same was true when he was not asked on to the parents' committee at his children's school or to be involved with a certain project at work or invited to social events. All these situations caused him enormous worry and anxiety and thoroughly irritated his wife who had tried hard over the years to rationalize the situations that he took as comments on his unworthiness and for which she could see many other more logical explanations.

He was willing to go back in time and the results were surprising, interesting, enlightening and very helpful. He was one of twins and had been born half an hour before his sister. When he regressed back and experienced how it had felt when he first found himself in the womb with her, the two of them were together and surrounded and protected by mother. Then he found he was being pushed, pushed out of the only place he had ever known. Not only that, but his sister wasn't being ejected. His first conclusion was 'Mother doesn't want me, she does want to keep my sister. I'm not good enough, I'm second best.'

After birth he was quickly put in a cradle and left while the staff attended to the mother who was in distress with the second twin. His second conclusion was 'These new people don't want me either, I'm not good enough.'

When his sister was born it took the midwife some time to get her breathing and instead of being put down as he had been she received a lot of attention. His third conclusion was 'They do want her, she is better or more desirable than I am, I'm not wanted, I'm second best.'

His mother, by then, was asking for the babies and the girl, being closest, was given to mother first, then he was picked up and given to mother also. His fourth conclusion was similar to the others: 'I'm not good enough, I'm second best.'

It is surprising, perhaps, that he and his twin were such good friends and very close. However, every time anything went wrong in his life, anytime others were invited to something and he wasn't, he fell back , unconsciously, on these early conclusions. When his sister was invited to a party and he was not he immediately thought 'It's no wonder really, of course I'm not wanted, I'm not good enough, I'm second best.' He didn't stop to think that it was a girls-only party.

Once he realized the source of these ideas he became willing to re-evaluate all the situations in which he found himself falling back on them. It was difficult at first. He kept having his automatic response of thinking he was not good enough when not included in some activity, but, as he'd agreed to do, he practised looking for some other reason, and was usually able to find one. He still felt he was kidding himself but he kept working on these changes.

The results, he told me a month later, were amazing. When not invited to go away fishing with some of his friends one weekend he was able to recognize that they knew very well he didn't like fishing and not to feel that he wasn't wanted. When he didn't get asked to help with a project at work he was able to recognize that it was not his particular area of expertise and to appreciate the time it gave him to get on with other tasks. In one instance he was not asked to help at the school sports and with his renewed confidence and encouraged by his wife he was able to offer his services. Imagine his surprise when they said they had wanted his help but felt that he was too busy and they had no right to ask him.

In another case a particular event during birth caused one man to get enormously stressed during traffic jams or in a train if it stopped for no apparent reason. When he went back and repeated his birth he found that he had been half born, half in and half out, when suddenly everything had stopped. His mother had stopped pushing, nothing was

happening and he felt trapped, caught, helpless and extremely frightened. His big worry had been 'Everything's stopped, what's happening,
I'm not in control and I don't know what's going on.'

Even while one part of his mind was reliving the past experience of
his birth another part was able to say out loud and with surprise and
excitement, 'Now I know why I feel so terrified when my train stops on
the way to work. How silly, I don't need to worry any more.' From then
on he was able to deal with unexpected delays in a relaxed way.

Remember our goals in doing this exercise. I am endeavouring to show
you ways in which your past and long-forgotten memories can be
adding to your present stresses and thus to show you ways to reduce the
stress you experience in your life. I am not endeavouring to establish
the validity or otherwise of these purported early experiences. Maybe
these 'memories' are indeed real memories and as such they may indeed
be the cause of your present anxieties. On the other hand perhaps they
are not real memories, perhaps they are fabrications of the subconscious. Then to me the remarkable thing is how well they have all served
the individual concerned and enabled them to solve the stress or problem at hand. The subconscious must be very wise.

If this was a book about exploring your past and discovering whether
or not you can really remember back to the beginnings of time then we
would tackle the subject in a different way. For the moment you can
take comfort that there is a way, provided you can find someone who is
qualified to help you in the process, of delving back into your past and
discovering some of the reasons why you feel stressed. That on its own is
not enough, however. The full goal is to eliminate or reduce the stress in
your life today. Fortunately the process of recognizing some of the assumptions you made in the past, the faulty premises on which they
were made and the inappropriate generalizations you have made since
as a result of them, often does cause you to reassess some of your current
worries and enable you to drop them, as the above examples show.

Different interpretations

There are many learning experiences that individuals go through in their early years. There are also many different interpretations that are made of these experiences. Two people faced with the same experience may well draw two totally opposite conclusions. Take the case of Mr A. above. Instead of assuming he was not wanted when he was pushed out of the womb first he could have assumed that since he did go first he was the most important. That was the opinion of another patient, one of two female twins. Unfortunately, instead of feeling proud of going first, she felt that she had pushed ahead of her sister unfairly, and that she owed it to her to make up for this during the rest of her life by hanging back and helping her.

We will now take a look at some other specific examples. This time the reason for giving a number of examples is that while several of them may have no direct meaning for you, one or more of them may strike a chord. If this happens then this is an area of your life, of your thoughts and feelings, that you should follow up.

Let the others go first (they're better than you, you're not good enough)

One common experience that all little children go through is that of being told not to push themselves forward, not to demand the largest piece, the biggest toy, the first place in the queue. The adults concerned are doing it in the name of teaching the child manners and consideration for others, but this is rarely the way the message is received by the child, at least at the subconscious level.

Consider the small children you know or have known. They are entirely absorbed with themselves, their experiences and the world around them. They are not self-conscious or self-aware. They do not consider themselves as something separate from other people or the world around them. They do not consider what you may be thinking of them. They are intent on discovering their world, on learning what you are and deciding what they think about you. They have no concept of your experience or your needs. They seek immediate gratification. When they want something they want it at once. They do not want to wait until someone else has had it first, or has had the best part of it. From their point of view it is 'I'm hungry, that looks good, I want to eat it and I want to eat it now.' If that need or desire is not fulfilled at once they are likely to let you know about it in no uncertain terms.

Most babies are fortunate. If they cry loudly enough the adults within range will rush round finding something to keep them happy. They may get a dummy thrust in their mouth, not much fun if what they really wanted was food, but still, attention was paid to them on their demand. They may be given something to play with in the hope that it will keep them quiet. They may be picked up, rocked, chuckled at, tickled. Eventually the adult will find the appropriate response. Baby's needs have been met and peace is restored.

From Baby's point of view the message is clear. When I want something, indicated by crying or some similar signal, the adults rush round finding ways to determine what I want and then give it to me.

Then this changes. Baby becomes Toddler, a few words are learnt and some interaction with other children starts. Suddenly there is competition both for the thing desired and for the adults' attention. Suddenly the favourite toy is being offered to another child. Suddenly, come feeding time, another child is being fed first. Even if Toddler gets to the food first and takes hold of something, an adult may interfere. Accompanied by some (probably unintelligible) words from the adult, such as 'Now now, don't be greedy, you must share this cake with John' the biggest, and certainly the first, piece of cake is given to someone else.

From Toddler's point of view there can be no reason for this except that John is in some way bigger and better than them and deserves to come first and get the best bit. It is easy to interpret this as 'I'm not good enough' or 'I'm second best', or 'Other people are more important than I am'. Indeed, all of these thoughts or beliefs come up frequently as people's Ultimate Negative Belief. From then on, through life, anytime that Toddler, who subsequently becomes Child, then Teenager and then Adult, is in a situation where someone else seems to be favoured over them they all too easily re-experience their Ultimate Negative Belief and get stressed by the thought 'I'm not good enough' etc.

The adults, with the best will in the world, have tried to add a constructive and valuable code of behaviour to Toddler's world, one that will serve Toddler well in the coming years, yet, with the best will in the world, it is also one that has also sown the seed of untold stress in these same coming years.

This is not a book about bringing up children so we will not here delve into the ways of bringing a child up that would lead to a better and less stressful adult life. The aim here is to help you to recognize the sources, or possible sources, of your stress and thus to diminish them.

In this instance you may have a number of childhood beliefs that stem from this type of early experience. If you can get in touch with them, either by thinking back or by regressing, you may come to realize the fallacy of your early conclusions. This is often all it takes for you to be able to drop that particular belief system and thus greatly reduce your stress insofar as it stems from a belief that other people are better or more important than you are.

Failing in one thing doesn't mean being a failure

Many people, in a wide variety of different situations, find themselves enormously stressed when they do not come first. I have described elsewhere the woman who felt very angry and stressed when she picked the slowest, or even one of the slower, queues in situations such as supermarket check-outs or airport check-ins.

In a workshop, where the participants had not yet had time to get to know each other, I got two people to pick teams. They were instructed to pick the best team possible and were told that winning, in the contest into which the two teams were to enter, was vitally important and would affect the rest of their workshop experience, so they should pick the best people first. A sense of urgency was generated and the teams were picked at high speed. No-one appeared to notice that the attributes required for the contest and the nature of the contest itself had not been defined, and indeed I had no idea what the contest would be either.

By the time the last three or four people were left waiting to be chosen and looking thoroughly unwanted, it was clear that the leaders had equated size with ability. The last four people were all tiny. I then quickly devised a game whereby the smallest people would be of the most value to the team and, for about 20 seconds, let them start on the exercise. Then they were told to sit down.

I asked a number of questions.

'How did it feel to be the last people chosen?' The answers included 'terrible', 'unwanted', 'ashamed', 'I wanted to sink through the floor'.

'Was that stressful?' produced a unanimous 'Yes!'.

'Did you realize the leaders had no idea what attributes they were looking for?' This question was followed by much laughter, some of it embarrassed, some of it relieved and, more importantly, some of it enlightened.

'How did it feel at the end, when you realized that, though chosen last, you were actually the most valuable to the team?' This was answered as 'good', 'validated', 'happy'. One person said 'I felt like saying "See, I am good enough, you should have picked me sooner". It would have served them right if the other team had got me.'

Some of the people picked early, particularly the bigger and stronger people, who had been looking pretty cocky, said they had felt embarrassed when their pride in being picked first had been shown to be misplaced.

It was amazing how much stress this game had caused in the minds of the participants for, in the end, reasons based on false premises. How much of your life is like this?

There are many similar situations at school. In every class there is a pecking order. When tests, assignments or exams are set and marked the inevitable list follows. Someone comes top, someone comes bottom, someone comes second, third and so forth. If you come first you are the best, and so on down the line. One of the major problems with virtually all of the assessments at school is that there is one winner and a large group of losers. All the children are, in effect, set in competition, one with the other.

If you do not come top you are not as good as the child who did. The lower down the list you come the more children there are who are better than you. You hear phrases such as 'Well done, Mary, you were the best', 'Top marks, Robert, you did well', or 'Poor old Sally, she's not much good, is she?' and 'Silly old Bill, a real dunce'. All too often the deed and the person are equated. If you are not good at history then you (in general) are not good. Thus a belief sets in early that if you do not do well at something then you yourself are in some way inadequate, not only in that thing but in all ways.

Personally, as mentioned earlier, I was not good at singing at school and found the process of singing, in front of the whole class during choir auditions enormously stressful. In fact I was so bad I was thoroughly laughed at by much of the class. I was mortified. I didn't stop to think that I didn't particularly want to sing in the choir, as I would then have had less time for sport. I let the whole situation stress me and be a reflection of me as a whole, not just one small attribute. How often do you do that?

Consider your life at the moment. Do you feel stressed by certain things that you feel you don't do well and are these things, when you stop and think about it, really important to you?

Mrs R. loathed the various afternoon teas her friends had where each one would bring a plate of food. They would vie with each other to have made the crunchiest biscuits, the lightest cake, the freshest sandwiches. She worried beforehand about what she would take, got a headache in the morning afraid that her latest baking would be a flop. It usually was, and by the time the afternoon came, she was so stressed she couldn't enjoy the company of any of her friends. Had she stopped to think, she would have realized that her skill lay in sewing and that she was frequently in demand by her friends to help them with their own attempts or make things for them. All she knew was the stress she experienced because she didn't come near the top in the cooking stakes and she felt that diminished her as a total person.

I'm not wanted
Adopted

Mrs P. was an elegant woman of 37. She appeared to be very self-confident but this turned out to be only skin-deep. Underneath she often felt insecure and was stressed by any social occasion, feeling that perhaps she was not wanted, that she did not have enough to offer the others and was not sufficiently interesting or exciting to earn her right to be there and to be fully accepted.

She had tried relaxation techniques and she had done what she could to increase her confidence. This had clearly been successful on the surface, but deep down she still felt like a fraud and very uncomfortable.

During our discussions she told me that she had been adopted and had learnt about this early in her childhood. Although she loved her adopted parents dearly and they loved her and had given her a warm and happy home she still, as we discovered during our sessions together, had a feeling, deep down, of rejection. This was based on the assumption that if her real mother had wanted her she would have kept her. The fact that she was put up for adoption, Mrs P. felt, meant that her real mother had not wanted her and therefore that there was some fault in herself. She added more stress to her life by feeling that she was betraying her adopted parents by wondering who her real mother had been.

Regression therapy provided a very interesting answer. On one occasion she went back until she was in the womb and her mother, a 17-year-old girl called Jane, her boyfriend, Simon, and both their sets of parents were together and discussing this unwanted pregnancy. It transpired that both families were well off, but this was the 1950s and socially it was deemed to be much too embarrassing for Jane to have and keep a baby while she was still single. While both the families and Simon and Jane had known each other for years and it was anticipated that Jane and Simon would marry in a year or two, there was no question of them getting married in time for the baby's birth. As a result Mrs P., from her foetal position inside the womb, heard the parents (her genetic grandparents) discussing the arrangements whereby Jane could visit relations overseas, have the baby there, put it up for adoption and then return home.

Jane was totally opposed to this. She absolutely wanted not only to have the child but to keep it. Mrs P., from her foetal position, could feel her mother's unhappiness, her overwhelming desire to keep her, the baby, yet she could also sense the pressures brought to bear on her by Simon and the two sets of parents. Eventually, during the regression, Mrs P. realized just how much her mother wanted to keep her but that the external pressures were too great. She developed sympathy for Jane and began, herself to will Jane to agree to the adoption option, which, of course, is what happened in the end.

The transformation in Mrs P., when she came out of the regression, was amazing and immediate. To have experienced her mother's fierce desire to keep her, she said, made her feel more wanted than she had ever felt and changed her whole view of herself. Interestingly Mrs P. felt no need to discover who her blood mother was in real life; it was sufficient that they had had an affinity during her time in the womb.

Months later she telephoned to confirm that this experience had lasted and that she now had all the confidence in the world in social situations and didn't feel nearly so stressed.

Again you may want to argue that this sort of regression and recall of a past experience is impossible. This book is no place for me to get into an argument on this point. All I will say here is that these are real-life examples and that, whether the regression is real or the creation of the person's subconscious it does, without exception, reduce the person's stress and change their outlook on life for the better. My personal belief at this stage, is, and has been for many years, that the regression is real. My observation of the results is that it is an extremely effective way to help a person reduce their stress levels. Everyone who has been willing to go through this type of work has benefited from it. No-one has reported adverse results.

Another example involves Steven, who was brought in to see me by his parents. He was a lively teenager with lots to say for himself but spoke and behaved very aggressively. His mother explained that he seemed generally unhappy, argued and fought with all the family, even though he seemed to want their attention and approval, and was making very few friends at school. He seemed to be in a state of permanent stress and tension.

After some discussion I learnt that he too had been adopted within hours of his birth. He had been told of this by his parents when he was seven years old. They had done the usual thing of explaining that they loved him even more than other parents and they had gone to the hospital and chosen him especially, over all the other babies there. He had seemed bored with this explanation saying yes, he understood all that and no, it didn't bother him, it was unimportant, and could he please go and play now. Neither parent seemed to feel that the adoption issue could be the cause of the problem.

On their second visit they recalled something that turned out to be helpful. His mother described an afternoon when, soon after his ninth birthday, he had come home from school early, in tears and nearly incoherent.

'Mummy, I did come out of your tummy, didn't I? The other boys are saying I didn't but I did, didn't I?' were the first words she could understand.

'No, we told you, you were adopted.'

'I know, but I did come out of your tummy, didn't I?'

Clearly the full implication of the word adopted hadn't sunk in and he was now feeling the pain. However, because the whole issue had been discussed before, and because he subsequently had not wanted to discuss it and had dismissed it with an airy 'Oh yes, I see, well ...' and gone off to his room insisting that was OK then and that he had studying to do, his parents had decided to let the matter rest.

When I spent time with Steven on his own it gradually became clear that he was angry with his adopted parents for taking him away from

> the hospital where his real mother and father had been. Only after he
> learnt that his mother had died in childbirth and that the father had
> insisted on the adoption was he able to forgive his adopted parents
> and learn to appreciate their love for him. His stress and general
> aggravation declined from then on.

Wrong sex

There are many other ways that a child may get the impression they are
not wanted. Some of them may apply to you. They or you will then
almost certainly take this conclusion, often buried deeply in the subconscious, into the years ahead causing enormous stress in many
different situations for no obvious cause, yet relating back to a belief
involving being unwanted.

Many children are the 'wrong sex'. They may at some stage hear
someone, a parent, relative or friend say something like 'Of course you
were meant to be a boy; most fathers want a boy first and then a girl', or
'Everyone hoped you would be a girl. After two boys your mother was
longing for a little girl to dress up in pretty' clothes.' It is unlikely
but possible that the person saying this means to be unkind. Far more
commonly they are not and they would be horrified to think that the
child had taken them seriously and had suffered as a consequence. Usually it is meant as a joke, an endearment, even as proof of how special
the child is, being loved even though they did turn out to be the 'wrong'
sex. Yet few children have the perspective to understand this and many
children take the concept seriously and to their own disadvantage.

Remember what we said *(pages 66–7)* about the subconscious having
no sense of humour and being very literal. You may even have taken
such comments as a joke at the time, yet at some deeper subconscious
level they may well have raised doubts. These doubts can then work
away inside until they surface when you are feeling insecure. Think how
you felt when someone jokingly said something to you like 'You, oh no,
of course we're not inviting you to the party, why would we want you?
– Don't be silly, of course you're invited', or words to that effect. You

treat it as a joke, of course you do, but is there not a tiny part of you, somewhere hidden inside, that is slightly hurt or vulnerable and would really prefer a full-out declaration of how important you are to the success of their party?

Often the person concerned forgets having heard such comments in their childhood. Or they may recall it yet laugh at it, as if it's a family joke. At the same time, however, it may be doing them harm deep down. It may be part of their inner insecurity that is leading, or contributing to, stress in a wide variety of situations.

Sometimes the wrongness of your sex is underlined by your name. Were you, as a girl, given a boy's name, such as Toni or Jon, or a derivative of a boy's name clearly intended for the desired boy, such as Roberta or Paulette? Perhaps you are a boy and have been given a girl's name or its derivative such as Denis, after your aunt Denise, or a name that applies to either sex, such as Lindsay or Leslie.

Unplanned

Many children discover they were 'unplanned'. Perhaps you did. You may have come too soon, perhaps before your parents had married, or else before they were ready to settle down and start a family. Even more stress can be caused when a child discovers that, because of them, the parents 'had' to get married. This can be especially devastating for the child if he or she thinks or imagines the marriage is an unhappy one. It is rarely possible for other people to gauge the success of a relationship between a married couple. It is even harder for a child to judge this, especially if they are already prepared to feel guilty.

> Mr E. is a typical example. He was a quiet man. He had been a clerk for several years, was still single and lived alone in a small flat. He would have loved to get married, but was far too shy to mix socially with people and told me he always felt as if he was a nuisance, unwanted and in the way.
>
> It transpired that when he was about eight years old he had learnt that he had been a mistake. He had been conceived when his parents

had been going out but had had no plans to marry or even, necessarily, to make this a long-term relationship. Nevertheless, when his mother found she was pregnant the couple had made the decision to marry.

When Mr E. learnt this he spent some time considering their relationship. They were both quiet people. Many evenings they said very little to each other. They would read, watch television or pursue their individual activities but not seem to share much. They never quarrelled, yet Mr E., still a young boy, kept looking for signs that they were unhappy together and felt he discovered them any time they did not show active happiness. In the end he convinced himself that their marriage was a failure and that, having married for his sake, they now stayed together only because of him. Their marriage, and its apparent failure, were all his fault.

As part of the process of helping him to reduce his stress levels he was encouraged to talk the situation over with his parents. Much to his surprise he learnt that they were thoroughly happy together, leading a life of quiet companionship. Far from being unwanted they treasured him as the means of bringing them to the point of marrying. They actually felt grateful to him for existing and pleased at the pregnancy, fearing that without it they might not have expressed their growing love for each other and might have drifted apart, thus missing out on a wonderful and contented marriage.

This knowledge was sufficient for Mr E. to reassess his evaluation of himself and, with some ongoing love and support, gradually increase his self-confidence and reduce his stress.

Being in the way

There are many other ways in which parents, unaware of the possible damage they are causing, can make seemingly casual remarks that can bite deep into a child's mind and severely affect their sense of self-worth and of being wanted and valued.

There are many snippets of conversation you could have heard in your childhood that could make you feel inadequate. Alternatively the same things may have been told to you in no uncertain terms. They may indeed have been real complaints from your parents, now disheartened with the way their own futures had turned out.

- Was it because of you that your parents stayed married?
- Was it because of you they got married?
- Did your mother give up her career when she found she was pregnant?
- Did your father want to go into business for himself but hesitate from taking the risk because of your imminent birth and the responsibilities involved?
- Did they have to move house because of the need of an extra bedroom when you were on the way, and did this mean they couldn't afford other things they had wanted?

One patient was told her father had had to give up his Porsche and settle for a lesser car so he could afford her school fees. Another was told his father turned down an overseas posting because wives with newborn babies were not wanted. Miss K.'s mother told her that, throughout her childhood, she was the cause of her mother not marrying again, that as a young widow she could have remarried but that having a young child had been an impediment. Now it was too late.

A phrase you may have heard in your childhood is, 'If it wasn't for you we could have ...'. All these and many other similar phrases, whether meant seriously by a frustrated, unhappy or angry parent, or jokingly by a loving parent, can have devastating effects on you, the child. In later life you can feel unwanted, inadequate, in the way, a spoilsport or a nuisance. In turn you can develop a number of strategies to deal with the situation. You may become aggressive or defensive. You may withdraw into yourself or you may be exaggeratedly extrovert. You may bury yourself in your career or chase after the opposite sex to prove your worth and wantedness. You may care or cover up. Either way you will feel stressed.

Notice that the stress may have been real or imagined. You may indeed have not been wanted or you may simply have imagined it and been part of a loving and happy family. Either way the resultant stresses, in each new situation in your life, are self-imposed and real.

Whatever your own scenario, notice two things. One is that these early impressions affect your future and can lead to stress in many different situations and the other is that the historical cause on which your feeling of stress is based is often unrelated to the present situation although the present situation may have triggered off the ancient memory that has added to your stress.

In other words, if you are not invited to a party the stress is real, even if you didn't want to go to the party anyway, and it is based on an earlier feeling of being unwanted which is the real reason that it hurts.

If this has seemed like a litany of negative inputs, converting all childhood experiences into ones of self-doubt and pain, it is time to put the whole thing into perspective.

Note that it is not so much what is said or how it is said that can sow the seeds of future stress; it is the interpretation given to it by you, the child, at the time. Because this is a book about stress and the possible causes of it we have focused here on the negative comments and on the negative assumptions the child may have made.

It is true that a child hears 10 times as many negative comments as positive ones *(see page 82)*. This is probably also true of adults. There are no schools for perfect parenting and in any case, parents are individuals too, with their own pre-programming and their own stresses, insecurities and needs. They are simply doing the best they can.

Equally, two children, hearing the same statement, will almost certainly respond differently. Edward and Simon were the youngest two in a family of four. They both heard the rows their parents had over money and the things they had to do without to provide for the boys' education. 'It was you who insisted you wanted sons after the two girls', 'Why do you insist they go to public schools?', 'It's the mortgage for this big house', 'If only we could have holidays like other families', etc. It affected them differently. Simon was determined to show them just how grateful he was and that it was all worthwhile. He studied like mad, went to university and did very well. Edward felt guilty and insisted he didn't want to go to university and that he did want to leave school early and get a job, any sort of job, just so he wasn't a burden on his parents for longer than was absolutely necessary. History does not record if Simon actually wanted a degree or if Edward would have liked to study more.

If you are bad you will not be loved

Earlier on I alluded to the common situation where you and your worth are equated with a deed you perform and its worth. This can lead to enormous stress.

Spend some time listening to parents, teachers and other adults when they are around children. What do you hear? Do you hear phrases such as the following? 'Well done, Charlie, top marks, you are a good boy'. 'Excellent, Becky, you looked after your sisters wonderfully, you are a good girl.' Then there are the negatives such as 'That was a lie, Susan, you know you mustn't tell lies, you are bad', and 'You mustn't hit little girls, David, that's nasty, what a horrid little boy you are.'

Notice that all these comments equate the person with the deed. If you do something bad then you are bad. If you do something good then you are good. This quickly teaches the child, you or any other child, that if they want to be liked and loved then they must do the right thing. If they do the wrong thing then they won't be valued or wanted any more. As an adult this then leaves you feeling that unless you do well, are successful or are approved of you will not be liked, loved or wanted.

What is the alternative? Think of the following ways the four comments above could have been phrased had the parents had more time and understanding.

'That was a lie, Susan, you know you mustn't tell lies, you are bad.' This could have been rephrased. 'That was a lie, Susan. We have told you that it is wrong to tell lies. We love you dearly but do not approve of that behaviour. Please remember in future to tell the truth. We will love you no matter what you have done but you do have to learn the right way to behave.'

'You mustn't hit little girls, David, that's nasty, what a horrid little boy
you are.' This too could have been rephrased. 'You mustn't hit little girls,
David, that is unkind. You are a wonderful boy and able to learn to solve
your frustrations in other ways. Let's see if we can't work out a better way
for you to solve similar situations that may occur in the future.'

In both these examples the adult told the child what was wrong, then
validated the child and then endeavoured to correct the situations or
train the child in a more appropriate behaviour. These outcomes may be
ideal and may not be easy to achieve. After all, remember that the adult
has his or her own problems and frustrations. Keep in mind too, that in
most cases the adult is not setting out to harm the child deliberately.
More often than not they are trying to help them by teaching them
better ways to behave. Unfortunately, however, when their behaviour
is tied in with their sense of self-worth the result is often detrimental to
the child in the long term.

Even when the comments are positive they may have unfortunate
results. Take the first two examples above.

'Well done, Charlie, top marks, you are a good boy.' This clearly tells
Charlie that he is good but it may also imply to him that he is good and
therefore loved and accepted simply because he got good marks. It may
well set up a fear in him that he has to go on excelling to be truly
wanted and appreciated and that if he fails to achieve then he may be
less acceptable. This can lead to obvious stresses as he grows older.

'Excellent, Becky, you looked after your sisters wonderfully, you are a
good girl.' This is similar. It may well tell Becky that she is loved and appreciated simply because of what she does for other people and that if
she doesn't go on helping others she may not receive their love. Many
people in this situation find, subconsciously, that they have to get sick
as a silent way of asking people to care about them for themselves or
their own situation rather than because of what they do for others. [This
is discussed further in *Choosing Health Intentionally* by the same author.]

At this point you may be wondering if it isn't all too complicated. If
you are a parent you may feel you mustn't say a word to your child or
you might damage their lives. You may spend so long assessing the

possible interpretations of what you are about to say that your relationships become stilted. You may then in turn start to increase your own stresses by imagining all you might be doing to others. Relax. Remember that you can only do your best. You know whether or not you are setting out intentionally to help or harm others. If you meant them no harm then recognize that they too have a responsibility in the way they choose to interpret your words and deeds. Do the best you can and then relax.

Equally you may feel that everything in your own life can be blamed back on some fault of your parents, teachers and the other people, adults and children, with whom you associated as a child. There may be a number of consequences of this. You may start to blame them and choose to become a victim. This is useless and unproductive. You may feel that because it is their fault there is nothing you can do about it and you must simply suffer the consequences. This is untrue and inappropriate. After all, the way you choose to interpret the past is *your* responsibility. You may feel it is all so complicated that there is no point in trying to unravel the past situations and their input into your current stressful situation. This is defeatist and will get you nowhere.

Instead you can use these ideas to find positive ways of improving your life. Go back into the past. Be willing to delve back in time and endeavour to find the sources of some of your automatic responses, your belief systems and your stresses. Then do whatever it takes to reassess these in the light of today and to re-evaluate them. Decide whether or not they are belief systems that are working for you and adding to the quality of your life. If they are fine, keep them. If they are not then give thought to changing them for the better. If you decide not to change them then it is time to recognize that your stresses are self-imposed.

Do whatever it takes but gather together all the positive ideas you have derived from this chapter and use them to create a future with less stress than the present. You can do this simply by changing yourself, without necessarily making any changes to outside events and situations. If you can change these too then so much the better, but for you to be less stressed and more relaxed this is not always necessary. It is your own attitude that matters most.

CHAPTER FOUR

Regression, Finding Your Past

In the last chapter we discussed some of the results of an individual being willing to explore their past. Much, though not all, of this was based on their willingness to be regressed into times that were deeply buried within their memory bank.

Obviously you can go a long way back into your past when you have someone who is working with you and guiding you. However, there are certain things you can do on your own to learn more about your past. You can also do the following with a friend who will guide you and keep you on track. Note that this friend need not have any prior training in this.

Re-entering the past

Step 1

Firstly, work out the mid-point in your life to date and go back to about that time. That means if you are 20 years old you will go back to when you were 10, if you are 50 you will go back to when you were 25. The exact year is not important. The aim is to go back to a time of which you have a reasonable memory but which is not often in your thoughts at present.

Next pick a place that you frequented at that time in your life but about which you have not thought for a long time. It might be your school or college. It might be a house you used to live in or visit. It might be a garden or a place in the open air, the countryside or one of your local shops.

Think back to that time now and remember what you can of it. Become familiar with this memory and try to recall as much as you can. Stop reading now and take time to do this. It is important that you do this before reading on.

Step 2

Now that you have a sense of what you can remember it is time for the next step. As a practice run, your next exercise is to do with something closer to the present. Put this book down when you have finished the next paragraph and do the following exercise. Pick a place that you know well and that you have been in during the past few days, possibly your bedroom or your garden. Close your eyes and actually be back in this place and describe it *using the present tense*. This is very important. Do not say 'there is a cupboard beside the bed, the door is on the right hand wall, etc.' Say to yourself instead 'I am lying on the bed, above me I can see the ceiling and to the left I can see...' and so on. This will gradually take you back so that you are in that position where you have lain in the past. In other words it will take you back to the past, albeit a very recent past. Do this now.

If a friend is with you they should ask you questions, also in the present tense, such as 'What can you see on your left? What can you smell? What can you hear?'

Step 3

You are now ready for the next step. Bring to mind the place you chose to recall from halfway back in your life and do the same thing again. If you chose your school it will no longer be 'Yes, I can remember it, my classroom was large, the windows were on the left, the door on the right and the front and back walls could fold away to join it up with the other two classrooms.' Instead get back into your seat at your desk and describe what you can see. 'In front of me is the teacher's desk, the wall on the right has windows all along it, high up. I can see the floorboards running lengthwise, the wastepaper basket in the comer and the door on the right. It opens inwards and the hinges are on the left.'

If you are not sure of something don't think 'Oh, bother, I can't remember any more.' Just keep looking. Everything that you saw in the past is still there somewhere in your memory. It is for you to re-experience it, not to remember it. Keep looking and you will be surprised to find out what you can see. When you are totally familiar with that room again you might like to get up, walk out of it and into the corridor. Look to see which way it goes and what is on each side of you as you walk along it. At all times keep focused on using the present tense, on being the younger version of you all over again. Become aware of the clothes you are wearing, your school clothes, of the way you are thinking and feeling, as a child in your teens, or whatever is appropriate.

Practise this daily and you will be amazed at how much of your past you can re-experience. Do not rely on your visual images alone. While it is true that most people think and recall visually, 30 per cent of people have more pronounced recall with their ears or with their feelings, so use all three faculties. Ask yourself what you can hear, are there other children chattering, what outside noises are there? Then spend some time determining your emotions.

As you do this exercise each day you will become more adept at it and each time you revisit a particular place the more you will be aware of. Each time you will add to your experience of the previous time since the newly recalled past is now much more vivid to you than it was before you started this exercise and you keep with you in your recent memory all the reawakenings.

Step 4

The next step is to compare this re-experience of the old setting, in this example the school classroom, with the memory you had of it when you started the experience. Isn't it a lot more vivid, a lot fuller and more detailed?

Step 5

Once you have done this and while you are still in a relaxed mood, go back further in time. Go back to your earliest memory. It may be only the tiniest snatch of memory but go back to it all the same. Get inside it, describe it to yourself in the present tense and then gradually push back the edges of your vision, hearing and so forth. Don't force this, just relax quietly and let it happen.

If you repeat this several times in the days ahead you will find that your re-experience of this event will grow and you will learn more and more about it. Again, if you want to do this with a friend you can both help each other and the observer can ask you questions. Keep in mind that it is important for the observer to ask questions in the present tense, not 'what else can you remember?' but 'what else can you see?', not 'what happened next?' but 'what is happening now?'.

So far so good, but how does this help you to handle stress? Much of the memory of an early traumatic or stressful situation is tied up in the fear or distress generated at the time. Perhaps you were a child and terrified of an older bully who used to beat you and call you names and tease you because you were no good at your studies. That is what happened to Donald, a nervous young man in his 20s.

Donald was having trouble at work and felt that although he could do his job well he was hampered and making a mess of it because he was afraid he might make a mistake. Initially I had him run a phrase (see p.33) 'Something that will happen if I make a mistake is ...' and he produced completions including 'I will have to do the work again', '... I will feel a fool', '... I will be wasting time'. Then he said '... the boss will beat me'.

Since his boss was unlikely to use physical violence no matter what sort of mistake he made I asked him where he thought this phrase had come from. It was then he recalled being beaten at school by the bully whenever he made a mistake in class. After some discussion he agreed to go back to this time and find out why it had affected him so strongly but it was clear he was agitated at the thought of doing this.

After telling him to sit back, relax, get comfortable and close his eyes I said 'Take your mind back to this time, when the bully was beating you, and tell me what you see. Start at the beginning.'

'I'm standing in the playground.'

'What is in front of you?' I asked.

'Three trees.'

'And behind?'

'The wall of the classroom.'

'And?' (This is a useful prompt if you are working with a friend.)

'The steps down from it. And there are some boys milling around, some are my friends but they are moving away.'

As usually happened, once he had sunk into the experience, fewer and fewer questions were needed to keep his description flowing.

'I can see the bully, he is standing with some other boys and they are laughing ...'

'What is happening now?'

'They are pointing at me, he is coming towards me.'

'What can you hear them saying?'

'He is calling me a dunce, he's saying I'm stupid, he's ...'

'And?'

'He's taking the cap off my head, he's thrown it into the bushes ... he's hitting me ... I'm trying to hit him but I can't.'

'Because?'

'Something's stopping me...'

'And?'

'I can't . . . that's it . . . someone's holding my hands behind me ... I can't move. Oh no, he's torn my shirt, now my nose is bleeding ...

blood's going everywhere ... on to my shirt, oh no, now I'll really be in trouble. Father's going to be furious with me.'

'For . ?'

'For not putting up a better fight ... and mother ... for the mess on my shirt ... I couldn't help it.'

There was more but it was of little importance. When Donald opened his eyes I asked him how much of that he had remembered consciously before we had started. He said he'd only remembered the first part. All the latter part was new to him.

'But that's it,' he said, 'the real stress was knowing that my father thought I was hopeless because I couldn't put up a good fight and defend myself. It wasn't the bully I was afraid of, it was Father. I'd forgotten all about the other boys holding me back.'

'What does this mean to you?'

'It means that I don't need to worry about making a mistake at work or the boss blaming me. If he does ask what's gone wrong I will be able to explain because no-one will be able to hold my hands behind me this time, I'll have a fair chance to put my point of view.'

'And...'

'It also means that I won't have to worry about what my wife thinks of me. Somehow I seem to have equated pleasing her with pleasing my father and I've always been afraid I'd fail. I won't, of course. I only failed then because they were holding my arms.'

When you do this your outcome may be more logical than this or less, it doesn't matter. What you will find, as Donald did, is that when you fully recall a past trauma it is lessened. Donald had hated even to think of his early years at school, even years later as an adult, because when he did so the events came coupled with the emotions he had felt at the time. Once he had done this exercise he was able to put those emotions in a different perspective and release them. Because he understood where his real fears had come from and also that the same causes no longer applied in his work, he was released from much of the stress he experienced at work. He was still worried about doing his job adequately but only sufficiently so to put maximum effort into it and try to achieve the best possible outcome. In the past this concern had been counter-productive, generating fear of an unknown outcome worsened by subconscious triggers from the past.

Diminishing the past

There are other ways of defusing past tensions that affect the present and here is one of them. It involves going back into the past, into a situation that was traumatic, and repeating it but moving the main focus onto other aspects of the situation. You may decide to do this on your own but you may also choose to do it with someone guiding you. I suggest you enrol a friend to help you and that you practise on a situation that was only mildly stressful, not on something major.

We will use Margaret as an example of the technique. She came to see me soon after she first went to university. Her studies were going well but she was not mixing socially, had made very few friends and was not happy. She was too nervous to go to parties and hated entering a room when other people were there, afraid of what would happen.

It transpired that she had an unstable, alcoholic mother and no father. After talking with her and running some phrases, this fear of social occasions clearly came from her fear of going home after school each day and not knowing what she would find. Would her mother be drunk, would she be violent, would she be maudlin, or, wonder of wonders, would she be sober and happy so there was peace? Every day Margaret walked home in fear, delaying her arrival as long as possible yet knowing that this would only create more problems when she did arrive.

Once at university in the city Margaret had stopped going home at all but now her mother was threatening to visit Margaret at her digs unless she did come home from time to time. This was a terrifying thought for Margaret who dreaded her friends learning about the situation. Equally, going home repelled her, yet she also felt she had a duty in that direction, thus creating more stress.

In her teens there had been one particularly bad day when there had been some very drunken violence on her arrival and finally Margaret had fled in fear and spent the night with a girlfriend.

Since she remembered the whole incident clearly she was told to go back to the beginning of her walk home. The first time she went through it, describing it in the present tense, as detailed above, she was obviously distressed.

She was then told to return to the start of the experience and repeat it, focusing her attention fully on every car she could see. When she was finished she was told to return to the start again and repeat the experience, focusing on all the noises she could hear excluding those made by people. Over and over again she was told to repeat the experience, focusing on all she could see at ground level, all she could smell, all she could see that was red, the clothes of all the people she passed. Eventually she got bored and I asked her how she felt.

'Nothing really, it doesn't seem frightening any more. In fact it seems rather silly. Whether she was drunk or not I went to my room and got on with my homework anyway. I can even feel myself getting sorry for her, after all she's not happy.'

The tension had gone out of the experience. Later follow-up elicited the information that she was able to go home once a month without finding the visit too stressful and that she was gradually feeling more and more comfortable in social situations. There was even the chance, she felt, that she might be able to rebuild a somewhat improved relationship with her mother, something she would not even have contemplated a few months before.

Recalling all the peripheral impressions during the dreaded walk home had put the experience into a different perspective. More, it had sufficiently trivialized the experience that the automatic knot of

tension that Margaret experienced every time she thought of it and
of her mother went. Margaret was then able to view the situation in a
more relaxed way and deal with it accordingly.

This technique has worked well for many minor stresses in people's lives
and you may like to try this for yourself You will be able to go much further if you have a friend who guides you by making sure that you focus
your mind on the appropriate peripheral aspects of the experience and
who doesn't let you focus your attention back on the core emotional
stresses.

It works very well for major traumas too, as the above example shows,
but for that you would be wise to find someone with the training and
experience to help guide you properly. For most traumatic memories it
has been possible to release them in one or two one-hour sessions. If you
need much more time than this you are probably letting yourself get too
engrossed in the central emotions associated with the experience or
being allowed to do so by your helper.

Summary

Two ways to release old tensions have been described here. The first is
simply to learn to go back to the past as a present experience and from
that vantage point to remember more, some of which may be relevant
to your understanding of the cause of your present stress.

The second is to go back to a remembered experience and repeat it,
concentrating on peripheral aspects of it. This can be an experience you
recall right now. It can also be one that you recall after doing the first
exercise. In this way you can change the perspective and defuse the situation until it becomes something of a boring memory rather than a
trauma that makes you anxious whenever you think of it.

The two ways can be done separately or combined. They can be used
to learn more about your past and the aspects of it that are, consciously

or subconsciously, causing problems in your life at the moment. They can also be used to release the tensions from old memories and stresses so that their results no longer cause you stress in the present.

Each of them can be done by you on your own or with the help of friends. For the maximum results and for especially traumatic memories I suggest you enlist the guidance of someone trained in this way.

If you do not wish to use these techniques for anything more than increasing your memories of the past that is fine; they will still serve a useful purpose. Using these techniques on your own is not for everybody. The important thing is to find the best way for you to deal with your own stress and there are many other techniques described throughout this book. If, of course, you can find a qualified guide then I cannot recommend these techniques too highly.

CHAPTER FIVE

Addictions and Preferences

Much of the stress in your life comes from the things to which you are addicted. If you can convert these addictions into preferences you can relax.

You may think of addictions in relation to drugs and preferences in relation to shares but we will be using these terms in relation to the things you want in your life. Being addicted to something means it is absolutely essential that you have it; having a preference for something or some situation means you would like it but that if you don't have it your world won't fall apart.

Addictions and preferences are the two ways of relating to things, people and situations that you want in your life. One way leads to pleasure, the other to pain.

Addictions

Let's cover the bad news first. The way that leads to pain is to be addicted to a certain outcome. Being addicted to an outcome means that it is an outcome you absolutely must have. It means that if a certain situation doesn't eventuate you know you will die, you will not be able to cope, you will fall apart. It means that if you do not get something you want or you lose something you value you will feel stressed and upset. You can have major addictions and you can have minor addictions but as long as you have addictions you can never be happy.

Many people have addictions. You probably have several of your own. Think of the times you've said to yourself such things as the following:

- 'If I lost all my money I'd die'.
- 'I don't know how I could go on living if anything happened to my husband/wife/child, etc'.
- 'If so-and-so won't marry me I don't know what I'll do'.
- 'If my partner was unfaithful to me the bottom would drop out of my world'.
- 'If our business goes bankrupt I couldn't cope'.
- 'If I'm not invited to their party I won't be able to face anyone again'.
- 'If I don't pass that exam, win that match, or get that promotion I'll never be able to face the others.'
- 'If I lost this I couldn't bear it'.

If you do not achieve, maintain or keep the things to which you are addicted then clearly life will be hopeless. Just knowing this is enough to make you feel stressed out. You are on tenterhooks until the desired thing happens. You are on tenterhooks in case the undesired situation does develop. But the problem doesn't end there.

What happens when you do achieve something you desire so addictively? Can you then rest easy knowing that your future is assured? You now have the partner of your dreams, the ideal job, the lifestyle you want. Can you relax? No, of course not. Something may occur that will in some way jeopardize your situation and, since you know you cannot live with any other outcome, you have to spend all your time guarding what you have and casting fearful eyes over your shoulder, ever mindful that things could go wrong.

Knowing that you would fall apart if your partner was to be unfaithful to you means you must be ever on the watch for hints that this might be happening. This leads to jealousy, stress and, often, its own destructive activity.

Jenny came in to see me complaining of headaches and stomach upsets. These she said were worse at work and eased up over the
weekend. Was she, she wanted to know, suffering from the effects of
air-conditioning in the office and the effect on her eyes of the
computer terminal? If so, what should she do about it? This seemed an
unlikely explanation as she had been in the same office for five years
and the headaches had only started in the past six months. Further,
they often started on a Sunday evening as she planned for the week
ahead.

We talked about stress and I asked her how she felt about her job.

'I love it, it's exactly what I want to do. I was desperate to get the
job in the first place, I just knew it was the job I had always wanted
and that I simply had to get it. [Addiction]. When I was promoted into
it I could hardly believe my luck.'

Her job as a fashion writer for a magazine was something she had
dreamed of but not really thought possible when she started as a
typist in the pool. Three years later she had been encouraged to submit
some articles. These had been accepted and then she had been promoted to a fully fledged writer and then editor. At first she had been
thrilled. Then she had learnt to accept the position. Finally she had
come to identify with the job. Her social life was built around it and
the status it gave her.

As she spoke there were clear signs of stress as she considered her
work. I used the technique of 'running a phrase' to help her resolve her
problem. The first phrase I ran with her was 'A reason I feel stressed at
work is ...'. At first she denied any stress.

'It's no problem,' she insisted. 'I love my job, I enjoy what I do and the
perks are marvellous. How can I possibly feel stressed when it is what I
have always wanted to do and I've enjoyed doing it ever since I started?'

'A reason I feel stressed at work is ...' I repeated, refusing to enter
into such a discussion.

She acknowledged defeat and came up with a number of completions including '... I have deadlines to meet', '... I have to be careful not

to offend our advertisers', '... I have to be careful not to miss something new' and many more.

As I continued she lost some of her extrovert verve and finally said in a small voice '... I'm afraid of losing my job'.

Even as she said it she looked both horrified and surprised at the same time.

'I'd no idea I felt like that. How amazing, but how stupid, of course I won't lose it.' Yet her eyes were misting over and she was clearly worried.

Obviously what had once been a strong preference (her writing) had rapidly become an addiction. As she thought about it and as we discussed the matter things began to crystalize. She knew that she was courted and feted because of her work. The shops and the fashion houses wanted her approval, her friends admired her for her clothes and her style, and she in turn depended on the clothes she was able to buy at amazing discounts to create her image. She couldn't imagine wearing anything but fashion designs, yet she knew she could not afford them if she had to pay full price for them on her salary as she would have to if she lost this job.

No longer could she relax and enjoy her success. Every new typist in the pool was now a threat. Every new writer was potential competition. She worried that someone else would be found who could do her job better. More and more she was spending time in office politics. More and more she was writing articles with a view to her job security rather than to the inherent worth of fashion and style.

To assess the importance of her job to her we ran two phrases.

'A way I feel about my job is...'. She had plenty to say to this one: '... it's important', '... it gives me status', '... I'm proud of it', '... I love it'.

The second one was 'A way I would feel if I lost my job is...'.

Again the completions came thick and fast. '... devastated', '... I couldn't bear it', '... a failure', '... not me any more', '... unloved', '... unwanted'.

The next phrase was 'A way I would cope if I lost my job is ...' And this time she had little to say except '... I couldn't'.

All of a sudden she found herself wondering who Jenny was, or rather, who she would be if she wasn't Jenny the fashion writer. She wondered who her friends would be and what her social life would be. Her job had become her life, her status, her **raison d'être**. Her job was an addiction.

You can enjoy preferences, not addictions. No wonder she was stressed. No wonder she had headaches. No wonder she had upset stomachs. The solution was not allergy tests for the headache, slippery elm and aloe vera juice for the stomach and relaxation exercises to calm her down. It was not for her to insist on an office without air-conditioning or fluorescent lights or to ban cigarette smoking. All these things would have added to her health but they would not have resolved the deeper issues behind her headaches, namely the stress caused by her addiction. It was time for her to convert her addiction to her job into a preference. Then she would be able to relax and enjoy it and the other problems would vanish.

Preferences

Now for the good news. If something is a preference it means that you have strong dreams and desires, often, seemingly, just as strong as those of a person with an addiction, yet they do not rule your life. Much as you want the desired outcome you know you can live without it, you know that you will survive if you don't achieve it or if you lose it, and that other opportunities lie ahead of you. You can also be happy when you have your preference. You can relax and enjoy it. You do not need to be forever on the lookout for things that can spoil it for you since your survival doesn't depend on it.

A few weeks after Jenny's visit, Rosemary came to me. Rosemary, it transpired, was the art editor for the magazine and had seen the changes taking place in Jenny as her development progressed. She came to see me about her skin problems which were, I thought, clearly related to her appalling diet. Life in the office was hectic, so was her life at home as a sole parent with an elderly mother to care for, a house to look after and her own friends and social life to fit in. As a result she had taken to eating sandwiches when she could and biscuits when she was rushed, both for breakfast on her arrival at the office and for lunch. Once we had discussed her diet and ways in which she could improve it I asked about her work. Was it demanding and did she feel stressed?

'No,' she assured me, 'I love it. I'd hate to do anything else. In fact I don't really know what else I'd enjoy as much.'

With her permission I ran the same phrases with her as I had with Jenny.

'A reason I feel stressed at work ...'. As with Jenny, Rosemary protested somewhat at the start. Then she got into the swing of it and completed with '... my work has to be accurate', '... I have to keep coming up with creative ideas, but usually I have heaps, and anyway the rest of the team is great', '... there are deadlines'.

I ran it to completion but she had little more to offer.

'A way I feel about my job is ...' brought '... I love it', '...it's fun', '... I enjoy it', '... I like the people I work with'.

The next one was 'A way I would feel if I lost my job is...', to which she responded '... disappointed', '... I'd miss the people I work with', '... a bit lost, at least for a while', '... frustrated, I love being creative'.

Notice the different tones of these completions to the ones given by Jenny. At this point I was very interested to get her completions to the fourth phrase, although I had begun to suspect the tone they would take.

'A way I would cope if I lost my job is...' brought a completely different response to the one given by Jenny, namely '... look for another one', '... ask friends in the industry if they knew of any vacancies or opportunities', '... give some thought to doing something maybe a little different'.

Clearly while Rosemary loved her job and had a strong preference for it she was not addicted to it. This meant that she was free to enjoy

> every minute of it, taking the deadlines and the ups and downs in her stride. Because she was not afraid of losing it she was not looking over her shoulder at the rest of her team, afraid someone was trying to replace her. She felt comfortable working with the team, encouraging their efforts and sharing the rewards. She had no need to prove herself and no need to fret over politics.

Do not fall into the trap of thinking that Rosemary didn't really care or that she simply enjoyed her job or wanted it less than Jenny enjoyed or wanted hers. They both loved their jobs, they both wanted them, they both revelled in them. The difference was the degree to which they each would cope if they lost it, the difference between an addiction and preference.

Who had the best time at work? Rosemary. What did Jenny have to do to enjoy her work as much and reduce her stress load? Change her addiction into a preference. Shortly we will see how this can be done.

There are many other situations in which addictions can play a part. They can be small situations or major ones. You can be addicted to your partner in life, addicted to your wealth, addicted to your job, addicted to your family, addicted to certain friends, to social acceptance and so forth. You can also be addicted to routines, addicted to people respecting you, addicted to being served first in shops, addicted to getting your own way, addicted to your secretary jumping to your bidding, addicted to the children behaving in certain ways, addicted to your possessions, your club or your voluntary work.

You can also have preferences for these things and, as such, enjoy them far more and be less stressed.

Your next step is to locate your own addictions and then to change them into preferences. Once you have done this you too will find there is very much less stress in your life.

Finding your addictions

There are many ways to find your addictions. You have to be very careful, however, because they are all too keen to masquerade as preferences. Jenny would have been sure her job was a preference rather than an addiction had I explained the two to her at the start.

None of the ways described below are fool-proof but they all give you a guide and as you put the results together you will gradually get a clear picture as to your own attitudes.

If only

Think of the times you have said 'If only ...':

- 'If only I had a certain job...'.
- 'If only I had the perfect loving partner...'.
- 'If only I had this amount of money...'.
- 'If only I had my own home...'.
- 'If only I was my ideal weight ...'.
- 'If only my skin would clear up ...'.
- 'If only... what?'

The supposition is that if only the above happened then your life would be perfect, or at least in much better order. It's as if you assume that if that one thing was put right then everything else would be all right and you would be more relaxed and less stressed. Implicit in that supposition is that if the 'if only' doesn't come about then you cannot be happy.

> Michael was shy and unhappy. He hated to sit at home alone yet every time he was invited out he went through agonies because of his looks and particularly his acne. 'If only,' he said, 'I didn't have acne... then I could enjoy parties and meeting people and not feel so lonely.'

When he changed his diet, used certain herbs and vitamin supplements, his skin cleared up. Was he happy? No. You are not happy when you have your addiction or when you don't have it. In his case he worried about his skin breaking out again. He also changed his 'if only'. It became 'If only I had the perfect partner ... then I would be happy and relaxed and not feel stressed'.

When he did meet someone he, of course, then worried that he would lose her and he changed his 'if only' yet again. It became 'If only we could afford our own home . . . then we could relax and have fun together. I would feel less stressed'.

Michael's job was to get to the root of his addictions and then change them into preferences. His fundamental problem was his lack of self-confidence. Had he had more of that he would have enjoyed life even if he did have acne. He wouldn't have needed to have the perfect loving partner to validate him or the perfect house to keep the marriage working smoothly.

Anger

Analyse yourself next time you get angry. If you are angry because something isn't going the way you want it to you are probably addicted to that particular desired outcome. If it was a preference rather than an addiction it is unlikely that your response would be anger.

Jeremy, aged nine, was addicted to having a certain toy he saw in the shop one Saturday morning. He wanted it, he asked for it and, when it was denied him, he screamed for it. He insisted he had to have it to play with his friends that afternoon. All the way home he ranted and raved. He stamped around the house and refused to eat his lunch. Eventually he was put in his room and not allowed to play with his friends at all. Was Jeremy stressed? Yes.

What would have happened if he'd had a strong preference for it instead of an addiction? He would probably have made a strong case

> for getting it and then he would have been unhappy at not getting it, but when he realized that was impossible he would have decided on his next best alternative activity for the afternoon with his friends.

Notice that neither way did he get the toy, but when it was a preference rather than an addiction he was much less stressed. Treating something as a preference rather than an addiction does not ensure you get it, although you do increase the odds. It does reduce the stress you feel if you don't.

Anxiety

What things worry you? Do you fret about deadlines, worry about being on time, get anxious when going shopping? Consider the reasons and identify the addiction. Use the method of running a phrase described earlier.

You may find you are addicted to meeting deadlines because you are afraid you may lose your job if you don't, and this in turn may come from a fundamental feeling, an Ultimate Negative Belief, that you are not good enough. You may be addicted to being on time because you are afraid people won't wait for you if you are late, and this in turn may relate back to an Ultimate Negative Belief that you are unlovable. You may get anxious when you go shopping because you are addicted to re-membering everything and getting the best possible buy. Perhaps your Ultimate Negative Belief is that you are stupid and you fear that this will show up if you make a mess of the task.

Other Emotions

Consider all unpleasant emotions. When you are sad, lonely, jealous, afraid, search for the underlying cause. There is almost certainly some-thing to which you are addicted.

The *Course of Miracles* has the statement 'I am never upset for the reason I think'. It is always worth looking underneath the apparent cause of the upset and endeavouring to find the real basis for it, the addiction.

Deborah came in to see me because she felt run down and exhausted. She said she couldn't cope and that she hated the dinner parties and the social entertaining she had to do as part of her husband's work.

'Actually,' she said, 'I love the dinner parties, but only after the guests have gone. I hate the lead-up to them, even though I enjoy cooking. It's the stress.'

'What stress?'

'The stress of having everything ready on time and just right. I know David would be upset if anything went wrong, so would I.'

I started to run phrases right away.

'The reason that would upset me is ...' I said and paused.

Her completions included '... it wouldn't be right', '... I'd have let David down', '... they wouldn't like me.

'The way I'd feel if the food wasn't perfect is ...' was the next phrase I had her run.

She completed with '... devastated', '... a total failure'.

There were more but they all pointed to the same thing. Clearly she was addicted to creating the perfect dinner party as a reflection of her own worth.

As we talked this through she was able to realize that her worth was not dependent on a successful dinner party. It was not the end of the world if the sauce was lumpy or the meal was slightly late. She worked with affirmations both as to her place in David's life and her ability to give good and relaxed dinner parties. In this way she changed the addiction into a preference and was able to enjoy the event both in the preparation and during the occasion knowing that even if it wasn't perfect she would cope perfectly well with the outcome. She was no longer addicted to the outcome as a validation of herself and her marriage. She simply had a preference for a smoothly run dinner party and did her best to achieve this.

~

Manipulations

People with addictions can be manipulated. You can make a casual statement and they will take it as a criticism. You can do something innocuous and they will put a variety of sinister interpretations on it. You can imply that if they don't do something then they will lose your approval. I'm sure you've experienced such situations and observed how they can lead to dreadfully tangled relationships.

Tom coming in from work, 'Is dinner not ready yet?' Addictive response: 'I'm sorry, dear. There was a queue at the supermarket and then when I got home I had to help the children with their homework. I'll hurry things along. I won't keep you waiting long. I'm sorry, I'll be as quick as I can.'

Tom's question could have been a criticism, equally it could have been a simple question as part of his endeavour to find out how much time he had to do something else before it was ready.

This woman was addicted to having things just right, fearful of being thought inadequate and had assumed the question was a criticism. She lived in fear (stress) each day of Tom's arrival home, knowing, in her own mind, that he was bound to find something to criticize.

He in turn knew he could get her to do what he wanted simply by implying disapproval.

Non-addictive response: 'I've just come in. I was playing with the kids in the park.'

This is a plain statement of fact without justification and it is unlikely that the situation causes the woman any stress.

~

Boss: 'This report should be finished tonight. I want to post it to the client in the morning.'

Addictive response: the employee will stay back and get it done, or take it home, even if it means cancelling his wedding anniversary dinner. He will then feel stressed by the work and stressed by the home situation.

Non-addictive response: the employee will work hard, fast and efficiently to get as much as possible done before the end of the day and then point out that the rest can be done in the morning before the post goes. He will not feel stressed, he will not be afraid of criticism, he will not fear reprisals. He is secure in his knowledge of his own self-worth.

The virgin addicted to being popular can be manipulated into sex she doesn't want. People addicted to praise can be manipulated into doing almost anything to get it, thus proving to themselves, at least temporarily, that they are worthwhile people.

I have had many people argue that a preference is a weak thing compared to an addiction. This is true, in a way, but it is only weak in that it can cause you less stress. People have argued that if something is only a preference and not an addiction you can't be serious about it, you don't really care. This is to miss the point.

The words are not meant to indicate the level of desire for a particular thing or outcome. You may want something just as strongly when it is a preference as when it is an addiction. The difference is in the way you handle the situation if you don't get it and in the amount of stress you feel with regard to the outcome, before, during and afterwards.

We will consider a fairly large addiction to demonstrate this. Many people are addicted to their spouse. In a good and close relationship the other person is often pivotal in your life. What happens when they are an addiction and what happens when they are a strong preference?

Henry and Betty had been going out together for several months and were very much in love. They decided to live together and that Henry would move into Betty's flat which was larger and more comfortable than his. One evening soon afterwards Henry said:

'If you ever want your flat to yourself again and want me to leave just tell me and I'll go.'

This upset Betty enormously. She started to wonder if Henry really cared after all.

Several times in the ensuing months Henry made similar comments until she asked him:

'Do you want to leave, are you not happy with us living together?'

'Oh yes, I love it', was his quick reply, 'it's just that I know this is your flat and if you want to end the relationship it might be difficult for you since you couldn't just walk out, as I could. I'd hate it if you wanted me to go, but I'd go.'

Clearly Henry had a strong preference for Betty but equally clearly she was addicted to him. Insofar as it is possible to measure these things they loved each other equally and the relationship blossomed.

In the next few years they had similar discussions from time to time. Gradually Betty came to realize the strength of Henry's feelings for her and she began, tentatively, to relax in the relationship.

Inevitably, however, there were ups and downs, and whenever there was the slightest tension in the relationship Betty fretted that Henry would leave her and she knew that she couldn't cope if he did. She became very anxious when he went away on business trips or spent a lot of time with other women at social events, fearing he might find them more attractive. Any time they talked it over Henry was able to assure Betty that he loved her as much as ever and things settled down for a while. But by the time Betty saw me and explained all this she was a nervous wreck.

Henry's view of the situation was that he had chosen a wonderful woman, one far more intelligent, attractive and popular than himself He told me he almost expected her to leave him at some stage for someone better, more extrovert than himself.

'How would you feel if she did?'

'In many ways I'd be devastated. I hope we will be together for ever, I love her very much and we have a wonderful life together. But if she wanted to leave I'd cope. And if she was going to be happier with someone else that would be better for her.'

'How do you feel when she goes away on business trips with her (male) colleagues. Do you wonder if she has affairs?'

'No, obviously I'd rather she didn't, but I would still love her and feel the same way. Anyway, worrying about it won't change it, only create problems.'

'You know that she's terrified of you having another friendship?'

'Yes, and that's the basis of the few rows we have.'

Four years later I learnt that Betty had left Henry, married someone else and was blooming. She laughed at her fears and the irony of the situation in which she, who had faced the most jealousy and stress, had never had to deal with the anticipated loss of Henry walking out.

'I could have spared myself all that unhappiness,' she said. Henry was indeed devastated when she left but, as he pointed out, he had had the happier time while they were together and he was dealing with his loss.

Needing the other person as an addiction rather than as a preference doesn't necessarily mean that you will be happier or that you will keep them in your life for longer. In fact, the jealousies generated by the addiction may even weaken the relationship. It does mean that you will be more stressed throughout the relationship than if it is a preference, however strong.

Finally

Stop reading now and use what you have learnt from this chapter to identify your addictions. The more addictions you have the more stress you are likely to experience.

Once you have identified the addictions run a variety of phrases to find out the underlying reasons behind them.

Then convert them into preferences. This is usually best done by improving your own sense of self-worth, something we will discuss later.

CHAPTER SIX

Be Willing to Change

If you are currently under stress it means that what you are doing, your present strategy for dealing with your life, is not working. Somehow, somewhere, some way, things could be changed for the better. Either the external parameters could be changed or you could change your attitude or your inner experience. You could change addictions into preferences, you could change the way you view things, the way you interpret things or your anticipations. Yet you don't. You remain the same and you continue to feel stressed.

It is amazing how persistently people will continue doing something even though the outcome is unpleasant or stressful. In the section on Outcomes we will explore some of the possible reasons for this. Here I want to discuss change itself.

A large amount of stress is self-induced and brought about by people refusing to change what they are doing, thinking or feeling. You demand in some way that the other people involved change. You say they should change, that it is they who are making you feel stressed. When they don't change, and what you are doing continues not to work, you rant and rave about your problems, telling the world of their stupidity, the unfairness of your situation and the stresses you endure as a consequence.

Five rats were put, one at a time, outside a maze with a piece of cheese in the centre. Very soon each rat learnt to find the centre of the maze and collect the cheese. Each day they were put at the mouth of the maze and each day they sped into the centre and collected the cheese. Then one morning no cheese was placed in the centre. The rats arrived but there was nothing (except the smell). The same thing happened on the second day. By the third day the rats were reluctant to enter the maze and by the fourth they were definitely not interested.

Five human beings were shown a maze and told there was a cheque for 500 pounds in the centre. Once they had learnt to find it and collect it, it seemed like easy money, 500 pounds a day just for getting to the centre of the maze. Then one day there was no cheque, the second day, no cheque, the third day, no cheque. Even a week later the humans were rushing into the centre ever hopeful.

Be like the rats – learn fast and be willing to change what you are doing if it is not getting the desired result.

Ideas for change

Perhaps you hate your job. Then change it. Even in recessionary times there are jobs available for those determined enough to get them so look for another one if that is the answer. Alternatively change the job itself. Maybe it is some aspect of your job that is bothering you. Consider how this could be changed. If it is your duties then discuss this with the people concerned, rearrange your office, restructure your day. If none of these are possible or successful then change your attitude to the work and the job.

I once took over a business and found that I was thoroughly irritated by one of the staff members I had inherited. It was a major personality clash not helped by her refusal to do things my way. I recognized that she was doing an adequate job, it was just that I thoroughly disliked interacting with her. I went into that business each day in negative anticipation.

I could have sacked her but that might have had unfortunate repercussions. Instead I chose to change my attitude. I used the affirmation technique described later to affirm to myself daily that I liked her, enjoyed working with her and that I valued her input into my business. The result amazed me at the time but would not do so today. Very quickly we became, if not the best of friends, then good working colleagues, and the business improved steadily.

Be willing to change. Much of your stress comes about from things you do repeatedly, even though they don't work for you. Do traffic jams irritate you? Then change your attitude, use the time to listen to tapes, plan your day, dictate messages or correspondence. As long as you have a hands-free microphone you can do wonderful things with your time while your car is in a stationary queue or doing a slow crawl.

Do you get anxious each morning as you try to decide what to wear and get more and more worked up about being late? Lay your clothes out the night before.

Do you worry all the time the grandchildren are with you that they will make a mess? Create a space where they can do no harm or put down covers. Then you can enjoy your grandchildren.

Do you hate queues in the supermarket? Then change your routine. Mrs V. said the worst part of her day was the awful crowds in the shops and then the interminable queues at the checkout. When I suggested she arrive at the shops the minute they opened and be first in and first out she said:

'No, that's not possible. I have to clear up the breakfast things, make the beds, tidy the house. I can't go out leaving it a mess.'

'Why not?'

'Because that would be wrong.'

'Who says?'

'My mother, she always insisted she had to leave the house tidy before she went shopping.'

'How did she feel about the queues?'

'There weren't any then, there weren't any supermarkets. Anyway she liked to chat to her friends and they always went shopping late in the morning, about the time she did ... Oh.'

Suddenly she realized that she had transported her mother's appropriate routine which gave her time to chat to her friends, into her own life where it was causing stress. Even so, she was reluctant to change at first, but eventually became willing to rearrange her day. When she did this and reduced the time spent in irritating queues she announced that it had all been worthwhile. She got far more done and had some time for herself in the afternoon.

Many of the routines we consider to be written in stone can readily be changed. I grew up in a variety of boarding schools where you *had* to make your bed before you went downstairs. It was years before I could change this. Even if it meant being late for breakfast, rushing through it or being late for work, I *had* to leave the bedroom looking immaculate. Much stress was caused in this way. Eventually I learnt to tidy the room at a more appropriate time and so removed the stress.

I have not yet met a stressful situation where some change was not possible that could result in less stress for the people concerned. If external change is not possible, internal change always is.

There are other examples throughout the book. To improve your present experience you have to be willing to change. To feel less stressed than you do now you have to be willing to change the external things in your life and your internal attitude to them.

Many people fear change. It's as if they would rather have the present stress than risk changing their present thoughts and actions in case things got worse. Have faith in yourself. Make the changes, try them out. If you don't like the result then go back or change again.

Be responsible when you initiate these changes. Clearly leaving a marriage, throwing in a job or moving the family half-way round the world are major changes and not to be undertaken lightly. These ones need to be thought out and you may be justified in not making them until you have tried a variety of alternatives. But all too often changes could be made easily; it is simply your moment of inertia or your fear that stops you. Other times, as discussed in the section on Outcomes, it is because you are getting a secondary benefit from the stressful situation and this is something you have to deal with if you want to change your stress.

Pay attention to what is stressing you now and consider, with as open a mind as you can, what changes you could make, internally and externally, that could reduce the stress. If you don't make changes things will stay the same. You may be surprised to find how many situations that you thought were immutable can in fact be changed.

Focus

Focus on what works. A glass with water up to the middle line is either half full or half empty. If you are looking for the stresses in your life you will consider it half empty and fret that you will have nothing to drink when it is gone. If you are willing to reduce the stress in your life then start to focus on the fact that you do have half a glass of water to drink. Either way your thirst will be the same, no more, no less, but with the latter belief you will be less stressed.

It may be difficult for you to change the situation that causes you stress. You may be working on your attitude but finding that difficult to change. Then change your focus. While you are sorting out the stresses focus your mind on the pleasant things in your life.

If you are frightened of your alcoholic husband's return each evening then focus on your wonderful garden. If you are stressed by the gap between income and expenses at the end of each month then focus on the things you do have. If you are frightened your lover is going to leave you focus on your good friends.

In this way we have a third option. Change your stress levels by changing the external situation or changing your own attitude and beliefs. In the meantime change your focus, the centre of your attention, so that you don't dwell on the stress.

Whatever you do, change. If you are not 100 per cent happy with the way your life is right now, then be willing to change.

CHAPTER SEVEN

Get Clear on Your Outcome

As we have just seen, a large amount of stress is self-induced and brought about because you refuse to change, because you keep doing things, even when they don't work. This in turn is often because what you are really demanding is that the other people involved should change instead of you. You may be insisting that they are causing the problem, not you, that the real problem is what they are doing and therefore they should be the ones to make the changes In this way not only are you trying to force them to change but you also want their admission, inherent in their agreeing to change, that the problem was their fault all along.

We will assume that you are intelligent, hopefully even more so than the rats described earlier. They were willing to change what they were doing when their behaviour no longer obtained the desired result. We will assume therefore that if your behaviour was not getting the desired result you would be changing it. This means that, at some level, what you are doing is getting the desired result, or is heading in the direction of the desired result, even if this is not immediately apparent.

Rest assured, it is not uncommon for people to refuse to change what they are doing because their real aim is being achieved by the present stressful situation. Often they want to prove the other person wrong, show themselves up as martyrs, get sympathy or attention or achieve some other hidden goal. If you are, or have been, doing this, don't feel bad. Use this self-awareness to learn more about yourself and then to change.

Having read this you may be resisting the idea but this is the time to be honest with yourself. You may be insisting that it would be a pretty stupid strategy. You may be saying 'Why would I cause myself all that stress and hassle for such a silly goal?'. You may be in for a surprise. Think of the things that stress you, situations where the same stress is repeated over and over. Could you change things if you truly wanted to? Are you willing to change? If not, what is it that you are really trying to prove?

Human beings can be awfully stubborn. It is possible that you are creating your own stress by refusing to adapt to a situation and work for the best possible outcome.

What do you want to change?

It may well be that the hidden factor here, the missing link, is a clear identification of your real goals in the situation. On the surface you may want someone to follow certain simple instructions that you give and you may be getting irritated and stressed when they don't. Yet for some reason you do not change the instructions or the way you give them. So the stress continues. Perhaps the real goal is hidden. Perhaps you are trying to show them up as being stupid, perhaps you find yourself calling them 'silly fools' or 'stupid idiots' under your breath. Perhaps this makes you feel good, superior to them.

This tool in your armoury of ways of reducing your stress is focused totally on your becoming clear on the real, and possibly subconscious, outcome for which you are aiming. The following examples will show you what I mean.

Mrs E. complained that every time she washed the kitchen floor her husband, one of the children or one of the dogs came in and tramped dirt over it. She got thoroughly angry, in fact so angry that just thinking about it caused her to become stressed, before she even started on the job. All the time she was cleaning the floor she muttered to herself about what she would do if they dared to come in and dirty it this time. When someone inevitably did come in and walk over her clean floor she erupted.

'What do you do to stop them coming in?' was an obvious question that I put to her.

'Nothing, they know when I wash the floor, I wash it every Tuesday, they should check and see if it is wet.'

At this point in our discussion I decided there was nothing to be gained by suggesting to her that perhaps it wasn't their responsibility to be aware that she had just washed the floor, that if she wanted a clean floor perhaps she should make a point of reminding them. She would doubtless have produced a variety of reasons why this was impractical (they were out) and further comments along the line of 'they should remember, they know I always wash it on a Tuesday'. So instead I asked her a more pertinent question.

'Is what you are doing now getting the result you want?'

'No, of course not, or I wouldn't get so cross with them.'

'How long has this been happening?'

'Years and years, forever. It's always a battle to get a clean floor in the kitchen.'

'What else could you do to stop them coming in?'

After much resistance she acknowledged that she could lock the kitchen door and make sure they come in by another door until the floor was dry.

'But why should I? I need to use it too. They should be more considerate.'

Clearly there were a number of buried programmes here. We got to the bottom of it when I asked her to run the phrase 'A benefit I get from the present situation is...' and she eventually completed with '... I show them how hard I work' and '... they realize how much I'm doing for them'. The next phrase she ran was 'What I really want is ...' to which she completed '... a clean kitchen floor' '... a tidy house', and other such predictable completions, but then came '... to be appreciated' and '... for the children to help round the house'.

When we worked through to her real goal she was able to admit eventually that she did get satisfaction out of proving the others in the family to be thoughtless and in having something to complain about. It turned out that what she really wanted to complain about was having to do the housework at all, when many of her friends had a housekeeper, yet she recognized that her family didn't have the money for this. When this came up for discussion and some of the work was redistributed between the two elder children everyone was happy and Mrs E. was less stressed.

She still had to wash the floor. However, it was then easier for her to recognize that whether or not her family **should** be more considerate about the kitchen floor she would avoid a lot of stress and aggravation if she locked the door. Once she had got into the habit of doing this there was no more problem with the floorwashing itself.

The desired outcome that was buried here was not the clean floor at all but a recognition of the effort and hard work that she put in. She also wanted greater acknowledgement and appreciation, and assistance so she could relax more.

Patients, when they come into the office, are asked to fill out a questionnaire before their consultation. We used to ask them to come 15 minutes before their appointment time to do this. Usually, however, they assumed that the form would take no time at all and that they really only needed to get to the office with a couple of minutes to spare. As a result they invariably ran late and the day's schedule would be thrown out, much to the irritation of my receptionist. She kept insisting that she **had** told them to come 15 minutes early and complained that they were all stupid for not doing as asked. When I realized this I suggested that, when their appointment was for eleven o'clock, she should simply tell them it was for ten forty-five and only explain about the form when they arrived.

She resisted this until we discovered that her real goal was to show how stupid the patients were so that if there were any mistakes with their records or their accounts it would be assumed it was their fault and not hers. Her need to achieve this goal was based on her own insecurity which was the thing she eventually worked on. She was then willing to change her instructions to patients and the office routine ran smoothly.

If what you are doing is not working, is causing you stress, and you are not willing to change then look for the real outcome for which you are striving.

Mrs M. complained that no-one ever turned up on time for meals. As soon as she had the meal on the table and called them, they all wanted to do just one more thing, go to the toilet, wash their hands, finish a task, etc. By the time she had sat at the table waiting for them and then served a nearly cold meal she felt thoroughly stressed and that all her work in the kitchen was unappreciated.

She had shown no inclination to change what she was doing and chose to insist that if they really loved and appreciated her they would come to meals on time. This then validated her in her thoughts about taking the job she wanted and doing less for them around the house. In other words she chose to see the delay as a direct reflection of their feelings for her instead of understanding that the others were all preoccupied with whatever they were doing at the time. She discussed this endlessly with her own mother and her friends.

After running the phrase 'A benefit I get from this situation is...' we eventually came to '... I can prove I'm being badly treated', and '... I can show that they do not appreciate or need me'. 'A benefit I get from that is...' brought '... it shows how uncaring they are' and '... it means it's all right for me to go out and get a job'.

It transpired that friends thought her husband was wonderful and that she was lucky to have him and such great children. She was

jealous of all the praise he got and felt that she herself was unappreciated. This in turn had led her to want to get a job to show she was
somebody in her own right. Her real goal had been to show everyone else
that her husband and her children were not perfect and then to enjoy
the acknowledgement she would thus get either for putting up with
some of the problems they caused her or for deciding to go out to work.

In the end and once she understood this it was a simple matter to
get her to change. She simply announced one day that in future she
would give them a five-minute warning before a meal. If, when she finally announced the meal, they were not there within one minute they
would get nothing to eat. It only took a few days of missed meals to
have everyone at the table on time.

After that, of course, she had to deal with her real problem, that of
feeling unappreciated and jealous of the reputation the rest of her family
had for being so wonderful. She still felt stressed by this aspect of her
marriage and her own sense of self-worth but by working on these rather
than complaining about late arrivals at meal times at least she was working on the real source of her stress. She could then make a decision about
going out to work on the basis of its own inherent merits.

To unearth your own pattern run a phrase such as 'A benefit I'm getting
from the present situation is...'. Completions could include '... sympathy',
'something to complain about...', 'showing them how little they appreciate me ...', '... I prove them wrong'. When you come to understand the
reasons for which you persist in an unproductive behaviour pattern you
may find it easier to change it.

Anthony was forever in trouble with the teachers at school. He was
bright but kept getting reports with complaints about his behaviour
and being cheeky. When we talked about it he came up with a number
of examples where he said the trouble wasn't his fault, the problem
was caused by the teacher who was stupid.

The teacher, he told me, kept confusing him with another boy who was supposed to get the football out for each game and asking him where the ball was. The conversation would go something like this.

Teacher: 'Where is the ball?'
Anthony: 'I don't know.'
Teacher: 'You're supposed to, go and get it.'
Anthony: 'No I'm not.'
Teacher: 'Don't be so disobedient ...' etc.

As Anthony rightly pointed out, but to me not his teacher, he wasn't supposed to know where it was, it wasn't his job. It was the job of the other boy who looked like him. His 'No I'm not' he argued, logically applied to the first part of the teacher's statement. He hadn't refused to go and get the ball, the assumption inherent in the teacher's final remark.

Clearly Anthony had proved himself right in his own mind. He also boasted of this rightness to the other boys when the teacher's back was turned. He considered the teacher an idiot and so had set out to prove that too. The fact that he got into trouble in the process only made him more angry with the teacher.

He was an extremely intelligent boy being frustrated by the slowness of the rest of the class. It was both his high intelligence and his frustration that were leading to his bad behaviour.

Once he had agreed to work for the best outcome, namely getting the ball rather than proving the teacher wrong, he was prepared to sort out the confusion. This type of change was repeated in several other situations and when Anthony acted on them all he found eventually that he was able to report a week without any detentions. In time he came to realize that he actually felt better inside himself when he focused on what worked instead of trying to achieve some ulterior aim.

His next task, in reducing the stress he felt, was to deal with the lack of stimulus at school. While he was behaving badly, rebelling and doing poorly in exams he had no chance of being moved to a brighter class. Once he modified his behaviour and then talked to his parents about the real problem he was able to achieve his goal. He was moved to a brighter class where his abilities were challenged and he no longer felt the need to demonstrate them by proving someone else an idiot.

If you are stressed by a situation that is repeated then be willing to look for and pay attention to your ulterior motives in not changing what you are doing. You can consider this a wonderful learning opportunity.

CHAPTER EIGHT

Powerful Thought

Thoughts are powerful, yet thoughts are easy to change.

The above sentence embodies the concepts that we will cover in this section. We've already discussed how creative your thoughts can be. You think something and it becomes your truth. You think something else and it in turn becomes a reality. If you think you can you can; if you think you can't then you probably can't.

Beware though. You have to consider your subconscious mind in this as well as your conscious mind. If you tell yourself you can but deep down you don't believe this then it is quite possible that your subconscious negative belief will be borne out. Conversely, if you secretly and deep down think you can do something but keep saying you can't then, if you really do try to do it, you probably can.

For one brief moment in this book you are allowed to be negative. Listen to the following and really let your whole being take in the meaning of the words. 'I'm horrid, I'm miserable, I'm lonely and depressed, I'm angry, I'm poor and stupid, I'm run down and unhealthy, I'm unwanted and unloved, I'm unworthy, I'm helpless, I'm ugly, I'm dull and boring, I'm a failure, I'm selfish, I'm worried and frightened, I'm stressed ...' Stop.

What has happened to your body, your face, your muscles, your stomach, your mood? It is likely that your back has slumped, your head fallen forward, your mouth turned down, your forehead creased and your stomach knotted up. You have become stressed and unhappy.

Now it is time to change the mood. Listen to the following, and again, really take in the meaning of the words. 'I'm happy, I'm loved, I'm popular, I'm successful and good-looking, I'm confident and capable, I'm loving, I'm excited, I'm optimistic and joyous, I'm efficient, I'm wealthy and prosperous, I'm wonderful, well and healthy...' Stop.

Pay attention to your body. It is likely that your back has straightened, your shoulders are back, there is a smile on your face and your chin is up. Internally you are likely to be feeling much happier and less stressed than after the first group of words.

Thoughts are so powerful. Just by the sequencing of letters in the alphabet to make words that have certain implications for you your whole body structure changed, your hormone levels changed, your facial expression changed and so did your mood and your level of stress.

Notice that you yourself didn't change between hearing the first group of words and the second group of words. You didn't suddenly become less stupid or more clever, you didn't suddenly become less ugly or more attractive. You just changed the words you used and hence the meanings you took in.

They were just words. They are just thoughts. Thoughts are powerful. They are also easy to change. Is one group of thoughts more true than the other? No, not necessarily. So use the group that serves you the best. Use the group that reduces your stress levels. Risk living in a fool's paradise; it is better than living in a fool's hell when there is no need.

Take responsibility for your thoughts

There are some interesting repercussions from this. If you recognize that you can change your stress levels by changing your thoughts and that you are the one who decides what your thoughts will be, then you have to take responsibility for your stress levels.

For many people this is frightening. Suddenly, since it is their responsibility, it is their fault that they are stressed. This was Susan's reaction. She was running a negative that said 'I don't deserve to be here [to exist]'. We had already traced this back to hearing, in her early childhood, that she was a 'mistake', a late child of her parents in their early 40s, coming when her two elder brothers were near school-leaving age and her parents were making plans to do a variety of things together, including some travelling holidays.

Her stress came from her extreme shyness and her insecurity in social situations, family gatherings and human relationships, and from her feeling that by her age among a much older family she could be seen for having come at the wrong time and being an intruder. She perpetually felt that she didn't deserve to be part of things, that she was more trouble than she was worth and that if only she wasn't there everyone else could have a lot more fun. Every time something went wrong she felt that in some way it was her fault and that she was to blame.

This happened even though no-one else seemed to feel the same way and even though the other people involved did nothing overtly to tell her she was a nuisance. In other words, her stress came solely from her inner programming and her own expectations.

When it was suggested to her that she had generated a lot of this stress by her own internal feelings, and by her belief that she didn't deserve to be there she immediately felt even worse. She took on guilt as another stress, saying 'I knew it, I really am the cause of it all, I'm to blame'.

In time she came to realize that, while she had created the feelings, no-one was blaming her for them. The real issue was whether or not she wanted to continue having them. If she did, then that was her right of choice. She could continue to feel her presence was inappropriate and to feel stressed. If she did not she could choose to drop the view of herself as a nuisance and start with positive thoughts that she was a wanted and valuable member of her family and community.

This is in fact what she chose to do. It was made easier by discussions she had with her parents during which she came to understand that while they had indeed not planned to have her, and had often, in her early years, jokingly called her 'our little mistake', they had quickly adapted to her existence and been so thrilled to have a girl that they in no way felt that her birth had been undesirable.

This is another example of how misconceptions can arise early in life, misconceptions that can have lasting consequences. Her parents had, from the moment of her birth onwards, been so thrilled to have a daughter that they had felt safe in their gentle joke, 'our little mistake', using it, in their minds, to highlight their delight when she had finally arrived and to laugh at themselves and their fears during the pregnancy. She, on the other hand, for all the love she received had never been quite sure that, deep down, she was wanted and not in the way. Ironically this type of early programming can be just as devastating for a child as the open and overt criticisms.

Accepting that you have, in some way, created your own inner tensions and stresses, can cause you to blame yourself and generate yet another stress. However, it can, and the choice is yours, also give you an enormous feeling of power and resourcefulness. After all, if you created the stresses in your life you can just as easily uncreate them.

Do not then immediately feel guilty about being stressed. Clearly there is no reason to equate blame with responsibility. We will take it for granted that at no time have you consciously tried to harm yourself or to create unnecessary stress for yourself. We will assume that, to date, you have done the best you could for yourself along the way, given what you knew at the time. The difference now is that you know you are responsible for your stress levels and that you can control them. You also know that you have some of the tools to change these stresses. It is up to you to use them.

Just as you are becoming aware of the concepts in this book, the same is true of your friends and other people who are also becoming familiar with these and similar ideas. If they and you know that you are responsible for the way you feel and what occurs in your life, just as they are responsible for what occurs in their lives, then consider this. Do you want to tell them what a bad time you are having (have created for yourself) or what a good time you are having (have created for yourself)? It would seem to be pretty silly to try to create problems for yourself and even sillier to boast of them.

This does not mean that you must simply bottle up your problems and only discuss the good things while all the time feeling miserable inside. It means making a radical change in the way you think and how you focus your mind. It means not only paying lip service to the changes but making them real and internal as well.

It means that when you work with these concepts you will want to start telling people about the good things that do exist in your life, as a demonstration of the good things you can create. It will mean an end to complaining and moaning about some of the things that you are endeavouring to change and the beginning of a more positive communication about the good things that are occurring. As you fully focus on what works your own inner moods and stress level will change.

You will become a happy optimist bringing cheer into your relationships rather than one of the wet blankets, however mild, that pull other people's moods down.

Listen to the people around you. A huge proportion of our communicating time is spent in negative discussion. The same is true of newspapers and the media. When interest rates were high the media told us horror stories of people who couldn't pay their mortgages. When interest rates came down we were told horror stories of people trying to live on the diminishing income from their investments. Rarely are we told the good news.

Listen in to people at parties or other social gatherings. It is all too common to hear a series of stories of complaints or misfortunes in which each narrator tries to tell you of a dreadful time they have had, and one that is worse than the previous speaker's.

Become one of the first to focus on positive things rather than negatives. You will be encouraging your subconscious to create new positive situations for you and thus less stress. If your friends also follow your ex-ample you will be helping them. At a recent painting workshop in which I was a participant there was the usual chat while we worked. At one point I realized that it had comprised a solid half hour of negative stories from all the other people present. Finally I said 'Could we please focus on something positive for a while?'. There was silence while they all wondered what to talk about.

For some people it is difficult to start talking about all the good things in your life. It may even seem like boasting. Perhaps you feel guilty if everything goes right for you, as if others will feel you have taken more than your fair share of the happiness pie. Maybe you feel that by telling others what a rough and stressful time you are having you will not owe anyone anything, nor need to feel guilty when others are having a more stressful time than you. People have an odd preference for feeling stressed and getting sympathy rather than feeling understressed and telling the world about it.

You may be protesting that you do indeed want things to be better, but this may just be your conscious, intellectual mind speaking and making what it thinks are the right noises. The subconscious has often been programmed to expect and feel comfortable in the times of in-creased stress.

You can change this. A valuable tool in achieving this change is being willing to take responsibility for having created your own state of mind. If you feel that your happy and stress-free life is of your own creating there is no need to feel guilty when other people have not created their own peace. It is no longer a slice of some universal happiness pie. This happiness pie is infinite. Your slice is the size you have chosen to make it; it can be as large as you like. Being happy and relaxed now reflects well on your creativity rather than badly on your greed.

Courage

Certainly it takes courage and maturity to do this. It is all too easy to complain of the stresses in your life, to blame outside events for them and to expect sympathy and support in return. It is also easy to look to outside people and events to change your stressful situations for you, to leave it up to them and then be able to blame them when things go wrong.

To reduce the stress levels in your life you have to be willing to grow up. Whether you are five or fifty, growing up can be painful, but the rewards are great. Once you are willing to put these ideas into practice, to take control, and to reprogramme your thinking, you can reduce the stresses in your life by huge percentages.

It is even possible, if you work fully with these ideas, that you can reduce your unpleasant stress level to zero but I do not want to get into an argument on the possibility of zero stress as opposed to a small amount of stress. It will only decrease your focus on the huge gains that can be made. Be happy with reducing your stress level to well within your comfort zone and use any remaining stress as a starting point for learning more, developing new attitudes and taking on new challenges.

Do you have 90 per cent of what you want in life yet spend 90 per cent of your time worrying about the 10 per cent you don't have, and being unhappy as a result? All too many people do this. Focus on what works, and know that these tools given here can help you to reduce your stress level enormously.

If you lack courage and are not willing to take responsibility for your own thoughts and your own stress level it is all too easy to justify your position and to lay blame on other people and outside events. When you find yourself doing this, stop. Recognize the ways in which your own actions have contributed to the situation. Be willing to take responsibility for the present and thus able to grasp control of the future, from the next second onwards, and do whatever it takes to reduce your stress level.

Don't blame others. Equally don't blame yourself. Don't lay blame at all. Look for causes as useful information on which you can base decisions about how to act in the future, not as sticks with which to beat yourself. Stop every time you find yourself using the words 'I should have'.

'I should have done so and so' implies blame.

'I should have remembered to have the car serviced' puts blame and stress on you for forgetting and for having to book it in at a time when it is really inconvenient.

Instead you could say 'I didn't get the car serviced on time. This means I will have to have it done at an inconvenient time. I can learn from this. In future I will make a point of booking it in ahead and making a note in my diary'.

In this way you are using an event to pat yourself on the back. By choosing to learn from it and thus creating a more stress-free future you are affirming that you are in control rather than using the event to increase your feelings of guilt, inadequacy and stress as you rush to repair the situation.

You are indeed responsible for your past and you did many wonderful things in it as well as creating some learning experiences. The exciting thing about that is you now know you can create your future any way you want it. Go to it.

CHAPTER NINE

Affirmations

We hear a lot about affirmations these days. With the increase in the number of various personal development workshops, the publication of numerous books on the subject, and the general awareness of the effect your thoughts can have, many people are saying that all you have to do to get something is to repeat over and over the statement that you have it. This may or may not be true. It may work and be beneficial, it may be too simplistic. It may also be counter-productive if not dangerous. Let us consider the whole idea of affirmations.

What is an affirmation? Take time to consider this. Put the book down and think about it. Try to forget anything you have read or heard about affirmations and consider the real meaning of the word.

One definition, commonly heard among people who have worked with them, is that an affirmation is 'a positive statement that you make and believe to be true'. I suggest the answer is much broader than this.

An affirmation is something you affirm. This, according to the *Concise Oxford Dictionary*, is to 'assert strongly', to 'make formal declaration'. There is nothing here about it being inherently a positive statement.

In fact you are making affirmations to yourself all the time. Each time you form a coherent thought in your head you are making an affirmation. It may be positive, it may be negative. The following are all affirmations and they and thousands like them are ones people make every day to themselves. You may be making some of them yourself.

> 'Silly me, I'm stupid'
> 'I'm afraid I'm going to lose my job'
> 'I'll be late'
> 'They won't ask me to join them, they never do'
> 'My life is full of stress'
> 'There's nothing I can do about it'
> 'I'm never going to meet this deadline'
> 'I know those children will make a noise again'
> 'I'm broke'
> 'I can't do it'
> 'We're going to lose our house/car/furniture'
> 'I'm not good enough'
> 'No-one loves me'
> 'The boss is a monster'
> 'My partner's going to leave me'
> 'I won't ever get this right'

You also hear statements from other people each day that you take in as negative affirmations, such as the following examples:

> 'Not now, I haven't time [for you]'
> 'Hurry up [you're too slow]'
> 'This [job you've done] isn't right'
> 'Don't be [you're] stupid'
> 'Tidy this up [you're untidy]'
> 'You're late'
> 'You're early'
> 'I'll get so and so to do it [you couldn't]', and many more.

These are the sort of statements and affirmations you can hear even when living in a relatively happy and peaceful situation. The negative affirmations you can hear in more stressful situations can be much worse.

- ❧ 'You're hopeless'
- ❧ 'You're stupid'
- ❧ 'You're an ugly old bag'
- ❧ 'You're a drunken sod'
- ❧ 'You'll never be any good'

Scatter in there a few, but only a few, positive comments and you have a fairly typical example of the daily chatter that fills most people's brains.

All these negative affirmations, like drops of water onto a stone, eventually erode your self-confidence and your sense of self-worth. The few positive ones you may get or make to yourself are usually lost in the overwhelming deluge of negative ones.

There is nothing new about affirmations. You are making them and hearing them all day long, and in most people's lives there are at least 10 negative ones for every positive one. This in itself can cause an enormous amount of stress.

Affirmations are ancient. They belong not just to humans but to animals as well. The bellowing of a herd affirms to all the animals in it that there are others of their own kind around and that they are safe. The roar of a lion affirms that it is a winner and the prey should beware. Equally, the rear view of an animal leaving a contest after losing is an affirmation of defeat.

Tribes doing a war dance before going into battle are affirming to themselves and to their comrades that they are strong and powerful and will win the coming encounter. The chants before sports matches are affirmations that the team will win. Watch two playing partners hitting each other's right hand, palm to palm in a silent affirmation that they are the tops.

From this you will see that affirmations do not have to be verbal; they can be auditory in a variety of ways and they can be visual. Even the thumbs up sign is a positive affirmation.

When I was playing competition tennis there was a Japanese pair in one of the opposing teams. If they were doing well and winning all was quiet. But if they were in strife or if the following point was important to them they would, jointly and in unison, emit a loud 'Hah'. This is enormously unnerving to the opposition. It throws you off-balance so you play the next point less well. Further, it tells you that they are affirming to each other that they are going to win the next point – and they usually did.

There are other examples of visual affirmations. Cave paintings of heroic deeds were positive statements of the power of the tribe. Totems too were powerful affirmations. If someone had left a harmful totem in your cave or tent you knew you were in for a tough time.

Yourself

You are making internal affirmations to yourself all the time. They will be positive, negative or neutral. Stop and consider whether or not the particular statements you choose to make to yourself are in your best interests. Are they statements you want to incorporate into your personal belief system, are they serving you and providing positive benefit? Or are they beliefs that are holding you back by adding to your feelings of stress?

It is true to say that for most people the great majority of the affirmations they make to themselves about themselves are negative. Think back to some of the negative affirmations you make about yourself. Can you feel relaxed, happy and, above all, unstressed when your brain is full of such negative and unhappy thoughts? Of course not. Your negative brain chatter is adding to your feeling of inadequacy and stress.

Remember your childhood. If you had a typical childhood you would have heard about 450 adverse comments in the day and about 40 favourable ones, or 11 bad ones for every good one. Is it any wonder you felt stressed as a child? If you continue to do this as an adult, of course you will feel stressed.

The better you feel about yourself the less stressed you will feel. Therefore one way to lessen your stress is to start making positive, helpful and supportive statements (affirmations) to yourself rather than negative ones. Initially you may have trouble doing this. Your upbringing has probably led you to focus on what you can't do. Rather than saying 'I can cope with this situation and I know things will turn out perfectly' you are probably saying 'I'm sure something is going to go wrong'. It's almost like touching wood. You may feel that by taking the positive view you are alerting the gremlins. Yet by taking the negative view you are adding to your stress and handicapping the result.

If you have been saying to yourself 'We're going broke, I know we are' the chances are that you have been creating the very situation that you dread, both by willing it with your thoughts and creating it by the actions these thoughts generate. Try instead saying 'We're going to be all right, we are steadily improving the situation'. At the very least, if you affirm this often enough, you will feel better within yourself and less stressed. In addition, your subconscious will be working for you. We've already seen that it tries to please you, to prove you right, and that it tries to bring about the things you affirm.

However, a word of warning is appropriate. Your subconscious has a mind of its own, so to speak, and little sense of humour, so do be careful how you phrase your affirmations. If you are broke and have no money in the bank and affirm to yourself 'I am wealthy' your subconscious may well sit back and do no more. It may think, in effect, 'that's OK then if that's all s/he wants, if s/he thinks s/he's wealthy now, there's nothing more I need to do'. Things may then stay as they are rather than get better. You may feel less stressed, you may learn to appreciate what you have, but this affirmation is unlikely to help lift you out of your inadequate financial state. Affirm instead something with an ongoing improvement such as 'Day by day my wealth increases'.

At first you may complain that what you are saying to yourself at the moment is indeed the truth, that the negative beliefs you have about all that is wrong with your life and the worries and fears you have *are* true. You *are* under stress, times *are* difficult, you *do* have problems, your life *is* a mess.

But I'm sure you can also think of ways in which these statements are not true, or at least not the whole truth. You may be under stress a lot of the time but there are also times when you relax. Things may be difficult but there are some things that come easily to you, even if they only include cleaning your teeth and talking. You may have lots of problems but there must also be some areas in which there is no problem. After all, the lavatory flushes when you push the button, the stove heats when you switch it on, some things do go right. Focus on these as you make your positive affirmations.

By affirming you are a failure you create failure. By affirming you are a success you create success. By affirming you are stressed you become stressed. By affirming that things are going to work out well you can create a more positive future. Which type of affirmation do you want to make?

Keep in mind that I am not asking you to do anything new, in asking you to make affirmations. You are making affirmations all the time. All I am suggesting is that you make your affirmations (thoughts) more positive than they are at present.

Some people think of affirmations as something they do as part of their daily routine. They will make positive affirmations for 10 minutes a day, then stop, tick it off as having been done for the day and then continue with their old (negative) thinking patterns. Alternatively they may write a positive affirmation out 100 and then consider that done for the day.

No. Positive affirmations should be going on in your head *all* the time. You should always be positively affirming the good things in your life and your own value and worth. Convert isolated positive affirmations into a more positive approach to yourself and your life in general and maintain them all the time.

Do this even when things do go wrong. Don't say 'I'm stupid' but replace it with 'That was not the best possible thing to do but I am learning from it and acknowledge myself for this development'. There is no need, ever, to make negative statements, and there is no point in doing so. They only pull you down and that helps nobody, neither you nor the other people in your life.

Ultimate negative belief

As we have seen, much of your feeling of being stressed comes from the negative affirmations you are making to yourself. The worst and the deepest of these is your Ultimate Negative Belief. This is something you believe about yourself so strongly that, at some level, it is an almost constant (negative) affirmation. We discussed this UNB briefly in Chapter 2, when we were considering Limiting Beliefs. Here we will take it further and endeavour to find out what your own particular UNB is.

You, like everyone else, almost certainly make several negative comments about yourself each day, and hold a variety of negative beliefs about yourself. Even the most positive people do occasionally say something negative about themselves. Since you say more than one negative thing about yourself it is likely that there is one negative belief about yourself that is greater, more important and more painful than the others. It is the one that underlies all the others; it is your Ultimate Negative Belief. This Ultimate Negative Belief runs most people's lives and is the cause of much of their stress. Ironically it is never true. It is simply a belief established very early in life, that the person has come to accept as true.

Here is what you do to find your Ultimate Negative Belief. Make a list of all the negative things you say or think about yourself then work on them by adding the word 'because'.

Here is an example. Perhaps you have listed the following. 'I'm no good, I'm not popular, I look a mess, I can never think of the right thing to say, my skin is a mess'. Then you run the phrase: 'I'm not popular because...' and discover what your subconscious produces as a completion. Do this several times if necessary. Let's say you get 'I'm not popular because ... I'm a mess', '... no-one likes me', '... I'm a failure'.

Then run another one, 'I'm no good because ... I'm stupid', '... I'm a failure'. You can even change the phrase mid-stream. For instance, 'I look a mess because ... I don't take care of myself', 'I don't take care of myself because... I'm not worth it', 'I'm not worth it because ... I'm a failure'.

In this example you can see that they have all come back to a common root, 'I'm a failure'. This is the person's Ultimate Negative Belief. It has its genesis way back in the past and is probably based on something that now, with adult wisdom, you would recognize as a fallacy. For instance, one patient with this Ultimate Negative Belief finally traced it back to not being able to urinate standing up like her two elder brothers and vividly remembers hearing them shout at her 'you're a failure, you're a failure' every time she went to the toilet and had to resort to the indignity of sitting down.

Once you have found your Ultimate Negative Belief you need to create the Positive Alternative, the opposite belief system. In the above situation it could be 'I'm a success'. The first time you make this statement to yourself you may feel it is all wrong and your mind may scream out that it is untrue. Not so.

You may indeed be able to think of many ways in which you are a failure, but you can also think of many ways in which you are a success. You can think of many things you *can* do. You can read, you can write, you can talk, you can walk. You can run a home, hold down a job, get yourself from one place to another, and so forth. These, you may say, are pretty basic things and everyone should be able to do them as a matter of course. Maybe. However, they are areas in which you are a success thus you can, with honesty, affirm 'I'm a success'. This is no more of a lie than the affirmation 'I'm a failure' which flies in the face of the many things at which you have succeeded. It is simply a matter of shifting your focus from the negative to the positive.

Once you start making this positive affirmation you will find a strange thing happens. By affirming that you are a success you will start to focus on the things at which you are successful. This will breed an increasing sense of self-confidence and this in turn will give you the confidence to tackle more things with a sense that you can achieve them and hence with an increased likelihood of achieving success.

In this way you will feel more successful and less stressed both by filtering – filtering out the setbacks and focusing on your achievements – and by achieving – actually bringing about greater success in your endeavours.

Once you convert your UNB into its Positive Alternative you are likely to find that all your stress levels are reduced. This follows because it is likely that all or most of your stresses ultimately stem from this Ultimate Negative Belief.

Derrick is a case in point. Sitting opposite me, slumped in his chair, he told me that life was so stressful he didn't see how he could cope any more. A secondary school teacher in an industrial area of town, he admitted that, although he loved his work as a teacher, he couldn't control the boys in class and he was beginning to dread going to work. He also said that his wife was complaining of their income level since prices were rising and he hadn't had a promotion for several years. He said he was worried and anxious and that he was no longer able to relax at the weekends, even though he continued to play golf and visit friends for bridge in the evenings, things he had always enjoyed.

His younger brother had gone into law instead of teaching and was both more obviously successful than him, and wealthier, a fact that irked Derrick's wife when the two couples met on social occasions. Derrick's Ultimate Negative Belief turned out to be 'I'm not good enough'.

'It's obvious,' he said, after we had worked through to this point. 'Here I am still teaching in the same school at the same salary and doing all the same things I was doing five years ago. Bob, on the other hand, has just been made a partner in his law firm and they can afford to holiday all over Europe whereas we've never been outside England. In fact I'm not even teaching so well. I don't seem to be able to control the classes any more and this worries me. After all, what would I do if I lost this job?'

His troubles had increased as Bob had become more successful. When he added this to his UNB that he was not good enough he generated enormous stress. As Derrick focused increasingly on his lack of material success his concept of himself as being inadequate had seeped into his teaching. His belief in his own failure was contributing to his insecurity in the school-room, hence to his lack of control of the boys and so on. Golf was becoming stressful as he doubted his ability to hold his handicap and the bridge evenings were getting tense as he took each loss or mistake as further confirmation of his growing failure. In fact he was creating the perfect negative spiral for himself.

In this way, UNBs tend to be repeated and reinforced and thus proven, to the willing listener, namely you, to be true.

Derrick was encouraged to start affirming 'I am a success' and focusing on his achievements. Further, it was emphasized that he wasn't just to think the words but was to give them meaning and substance within his emotional experience, to 'live' the idea that he was a success. Within a month he was able to report an improved control of the class and increased pleasure in his work and more relaxed enjoyment of his social times. With his increasing confidence his wife was able to feel more proud of him and insist that his work was important and that the money was not really a problem.

Other common Ultimate Negative Beliefs include:

- 'I'm unlovable'
- 'I'm not wanted'
- 'I'm a failure'
- 'I'm not important'
- 'I don't deserve to be here'
- 'I'm horrid'
- 'I'm stupid'
- 'I'm not worthwhile'.

There are more but, surprisingly, most people's Ultimate Negative Belief comes down to one of just a small group of beliefs that are shared by many people, and the above list includes most of them.

You know you have found your own UNB if saying it hurts or makes you feel exposed. It is relatively easy for you to make casual negative comments about yourself to other people. You are probably doing it all the time. You may claim that you're not good-looking, that you 'look a mess', that you're a dim-wit and so forth. If these things don't matter too much to you, you can probably say them without great discomfort.

Mr J. had no trouble when describing himself as an overweight, beer-drinking version of Henry the Eighth. Secretly, and probably subconsciously, he was proud of his image as a lady's man, he felt his girth showed him up as a well-established and successful businessman and his lack of fitness as a serious man's disdain for the frivolity of sport. When we got down to his Ultimate Negative Belief by running a series of phrases it turned out to be 'I'm not popular'. Having got there in a relatively unguarded moment he immediately felt the need to deny it.

'No, no,' he said, 'of course I'm popular. Look at all the friends I have at work, in the pub, etc.'

He had great difficulty in repeating the statement. It was clear that he immediately felt seriously threatened and that he had a strong desire to deny his lack of popularity and show that this statement wasn't true. It was also immediately clear that this indeed was his Ultimate Negative Belief, that he did indeed fear, deep down, that he wasn't popular, and that he was desperately afraid that other people might discover this or say this to him.

Remember that your Ultimate Negative Belief is never true. It is only a belief based on one or more early experiences and generalized into a belief sufficiently strong that you filter out things that don't endorse it. Remember the twin who believed he was not good enough simply because he was pushed out of the womb first.

With repeated use you strengthen your Ultimate Negative Belief and let it run your life and become the basis of your stress problems.

〜

Your positive alternative

It is now time to counteract your UNB. You must first create your Positive Alternative Belief, the opposite of your UNB. You know you have found it when your toes turn up as you say it. If it makes you feel really uncomfortable and all your senses scream 'but that's not true' then work with this positive statement.

> The moment Mr J. started to say to himself 'I'm popular and well-liked by everyone I know' he started to look uncomfortable. He was not in agreement. Even though this is what he desperately wanted to be, clearly, deep down, he 'knew' or feared that this was a false statement. He had indeed found a powerful Positive Alternative that, if he worked with it, would help him to improve his opinion of himself and reduce his experience of stress.

Be sensible, however. Don't affirm the impossible even though that too makes your toes curl up.

> One timid, small, middle-aged motherly woman with nondescript features believed she was 'not good enough' because she was unattractive and hadn't shown that she could do anything with her life since she didn't have a career. She started to affirm 'I'm a tall attractive extrovert and tough and successful in business', modelling herself on her brother's wife whom she admired. All this did was set up more stress in her since she didn't really want to be any of those things. She loved her role as mother, wife and aunt. Once she changed her affirmation to 'I'm attractive, loved and popular and bring warmth and ease to those I love' she felt more comfortable with it and gradually learnt to build on her own special attributes.

Be careful with the words you choose for your Positive Alternative. If your UNB is 'I'm not good enough' don't choose 'I am good enough' for your Positive Alternative. It is too wimpy. Consider instead how this statement of not being good enough expresses itself in your life. If it is accompanied by thoughts of your inability to cope then a Positive Alternative could be 'I'm strong and capable and can accomplish whatever I attempt'. If it is accompanied by a belief in your stupidity then your Positive Alternative could be 'I'm smart, intelligent and wise'. If you fear that you are hard and unloving and not good enough to have a warm and happy relationship it could be 'I'm a warm and loving person and have wonderfully successful relationships'.

Make the Positive Alternative strong. If you simply change 'I'm unlovable' to 'I am lovable' it will help somewhat but not a great deal. If you change it to 'I am popular, appreciated and much loved' you will get a stronger result.

Keep out all negative words. A Positive Alternative of 'I'm not a failure' still includes the word failure. 'I am a success' is much more positive.

There is a further aspect of affirmations that it is important in helping you to reduce your stress. When you are using them use words, certainly. Hear the positive statement, but use your other senses as well. Visualize the results of what you are saying and feel the effect of your words. If you are affirming that you are in control of your life and all is well, visualize what that will mean in practical terms. See yourself looking relaxed and at ease in situations that currently make you feel tense. Use your feelings as well and develop the feeling of relaxation and inner peace that would accompany that scenario. As you focus on all three aspects, on visualizing, hearing and feeling, you will find your stress levels decreasing.

Using all your facilities is very important. Sports psychologists know that you can improve your performance by watching experts doing what you are training to do. This is not only because you are learning the correct way intellectually. It is also because your body tries to copy what you have seen or have visualized.

There was an American prisoner of war who was in a Japanese camp for three years and in solitary confinement in a restricted space for lengthy periods. He made it a habit to visualize himself playing the 18-hole golf course at his home club every day. He made sure the visualization was accurate in every respect and that the round took as long as it would have done had he played it physically. When he eventually returned home after the war, even though he was weak and unfit, he went out and took three strokes off his pre-war handicap at the first attempt. This active and visual affirmation over the three years of his imprisonment had produced clear and demonstrable results.

Affirmations and visualizations combined can have an amazingly powerful effect. Eliminating your Ultimate Negative Belief and creating the Positive Alternative can do magic in improving the quality of your life and in reducing your stress. The only time these steps won't work is when you think they won't and when you are unwilling to change.

To any objection you make I would simply say 'Only if you think so'. Remember what was suggested in an earlier chapter – be willing to change. This time you are being asked simply to change what you choose to believe about yourself and to change negative, destructive and unproductive statements into repeated positive and constructive ones.

CHAPTER TEN

Face the Worst and
Know You Can Cope

Think of some of the things that worry you. How many of them are worries that relate to something that may possibly happen in the future? Are you afraid you will fail, that someone will criticize you, that someone you love will get hurt, that there is going to be a row or that you will make a fool of yourself? These and many other fears of possible future events can cause you a lot of stress. Yet many times the feared situation does not arrive.

To put the concept into perspective it is again time for you to make a list. List all the worries and fears you have had in the past about things that might have happened to you. Then note beside each one whether or not the feared event did actually happen. Stop reading. Do that now.

You've done it? Isn't it amazing how often you were worried about nothing? Yet the worry and stress were real for all that.

The irony is that, if the dreaded situation does eventuate, all the fear and anxiety that you experienced in anticipation does nothing to reduce the stress of the situation when it occurs. In fact it may have the opposite effect. Because of the stress and anxiety you experienced beforehand you may be less resourceful in handling the situation that does come about.

One way to deal with this situation, with the anticipatory stress prior to whatever it is that worries you, is to be willing to believe in a positive future, to believe that the outcome is going to be good, or, if not, that something even better will come out of it. This concept is explored further in the next chapter devoted entirely to believing in a positive future.

In the meantime we are going to focus on the process of handling those existing fears of future worry, events or possibilities.

Some of these fears may focus on specified situations. Many times, however, they are nebulous fears. You may be afraid that something bad will happen, without ever specifying in your mind exactly what that something bad is. You may worry that 'something will go wrong', that 'people will hurt you or let you down', that 'you will lose all you have' or simply the all-embracing fear that 'something awful will happen'.

It is difficult for someone to help you dispel these fears since you can never grasp them. A helpful friend may try to reassure you by insisting that this won't happen and that won't happen. You may even agree with them, yet the fear of some other situation developing still remains. Since you have riot specified the problem you cannot find a solution.

How do you deal with these two situations? One is the stress of worrying over some known possible adverse outcome or event. The other is the nebulous fear of 'something'.

Obviously all the ideas in the rest of this book apply. However, there is another tool that you can use to break the immobilizing fear that stresses you, pulls you down and stops you being as effective as you would like to be.

Imagine the worst possible scenario

Consider what it is that is stressing you. It may be a divorce with possible battles over children, money and possessions. It may be fear of losing someone you love or of hurt to someone you love. It may be fear of bankruptcy, of failing in an endeavour, of not passing exams. It may be fear of ill-health. It may be fear of a pending row, of someone cheating you or of not being invited or included in activities or gatherings.

Now that you have the particular scenario in mind imagine the worst possible thing that could happen, the worst possible outcome. Do it in full detail.

Let's assume you are afraid that you may not be able to make the mortgage payments on your home and that you could lose it. If this is the case you could be lying in bed at night with this big cloud of misery hanging over you. What will you do, how will you cope, what about the children, what will people say, what about the in-laws, your own parents, where will you put the furniture, will your partner forgive you? On and on it goes as your mind races round in circles or stops dead and ceases to function. During the day it gets worse, your fears intrude into all that you do or, if you choose to bury them, overshadow and spoil things. The next night you fret and can't get to sleep and the following day you are exhausted as the cycle starts over again.

Face up to the situation. Imagine the worst possible outcome. Imagine everything, every little detail, step by step. You know your payments are in arrears, the bank calls you in, you're in the manager's office, your partner is with you, you both recognize that there is nothing you can do. The sale notices go up. You decide you will rent a small flat, the children would have to share a bedroom, you have to choose a less expensive suburb. Plan what possessions you would take with you, what you would sell. Imagine the whole outcome.

Recognize that you would cope

However unwelcome the outcome is, the amazing thing is that you can cope. Whatever the result is there is always some way that you can deal with the situation. You will survive, you will live through it. It may not be what you want but it is not the end of the world. Even if you have spent the last few months saying it will be the end of the world, this is only a figure of speech and it is time your subconscious realized that.

Once you realize that you can cope with the worst possible outcome, you have removed a lot of the nebulous and nameless fears and worries. It is unlikely that the worst possible scenario will develop so whatever happens will be no worse than you have imagined, and possibly better.

You may want to break the problem down into chunks. In our example above you may want to work on the chunk that involves your

immediate family, then the chunk that involves finding new accommo-
dation, then the chunk that deals with your friends and colleagues, then
the one that deals with your personal possessions and the logistics of the
future scenario, and so forth. Just like food, stress is more digestible
when dealt with in bite-sized pieces.

Results

This exercise can have an amazingly empowering effect. You realize you
have unrecognized strengths and resources. The stress of the unknown
has gone.

   While you are doing this keep in mind the ideas in the rest of this
book. Run phrases such as 'The reason this aspect of the situation upsets
me is ...' and 'The thing I fear most is ...' and 'The worst aspect of this is
...'. Find out where the underlying fears are, use the power of your positive mind, believe in a positive future. Do everything else, but also do
this exercise.

Benefits

The next step is to look for the benefits in your worst possible scenario. Your initial reaction to this may be to insist there are none, but
you will doubtless find some. They may not seem to be worth the cost,
but at least by focusing on some positive outcomes you can reduce
your stress.

A legal colleague was very worried about his practice. He went through
a period where he was losing a number of his clients and getting very
few new ones. He said he had reached the stage where he could barely
pay the overheads and have enough left over to support the family. His
worst possible outcome involved abandoning the practice, selling the
large family home and moving to a small home in a small town or
village somewhere. The children would have to pay their own university

costs or leave and he would either find a local job, which would be difficult as he was in his late 50s, or live on his pension.

As he ran the phrase 'A benefit I would get from this outcome is ...', he found a lot, much to his surprise. He and his wife would have more time together. He wouldn't have to spend all his weekends worrying about the upkeep of a large house but could garden and paint instead and the children would learn to be more independent. Best of all he would no longer have the worry that some of his legal clients caused him, the possibility of litigation involving his own actions and work, and he could relax and enjoy life.

In no time at all it was obvious that he was mentally enjoying many aspects of this outcome. If the practice folded he could do this immediately; if not he had, in effect, established what he wanted to do when he retired.

Not surprisingly the removal of the worry that had been preoccupying him for months cleared his mind sufficiently for him to take an active role in rebuilding his practice and he was soon fully busy again. He was then free to make his decision about the future.

Elsewhere you will come across the situation of a man whose business was facing bankruptcy. This did happen and in time he came to realize that it was a blessing in disguise.

Many other examples could be given. Imagining the worst possible scenario and knowing you can cope will not necessarily guarantee that it either does or does not happen. The main point is not to predict the future or to show you how to deal with whatever dreadful or unpleasant outcome you fear. It is to show you that, if the worst happens, you can cope and that, since this is so, you can refocus your energies onto dealing with the problem or doing whatever it takes to avoid the situation that stresses you. In this way you are released from the numbing and counter-productive reaction caused by the stress of believing you couldn't cope.

⌒

Minor worries

So far we have discussed fairly major and specific stresses but the technique applies to all types and sizes of stress. Are you stressed by having to meet a deadline? Perhaps you have to finish the shopping before the shops close, iron some clothes before an event, decide on a purchase. Perhaps your stomach is in a knot and you are wishing life could be relaxed and carefree.

Imagine the worst outcome. What will happen if you don't finish the shopping, will you cope? Of course you will, you can do more shopping tomorrow. If the ironing is not finished can you wear something else? Of course you can. It may not be your first choice of outfit for the occasion but you won't have to go naked. If you make the wrong decision will you manage? Of course you will. Imagine just how you will cope and recognize your ability to deal with the new situation. It may not be your ideal outcome but you could cope and it would not be the end of the world.

Once you remove this fear you can focus on getting on with the matter in hand. You can shop much faster if you're not in a dither and you make much better decisions when you are relaxed than when you are stressed.

Two positive outcomes are accomplished in this way. Firstly you feel less stressed while doing what has to be done. Secondly you are more relaxed, thus better able to deal successfully with the situation at hand and thus lessening the chance of the feared outcome developing.

Reducing stress

Keep in mind our present goal. It is to reduce your stress level. This is not a book about how to solve problems, how to make decisions, how to deal with the practicalities of living. It is a book about removing some or all of the stress from your life by examining the way you view things, by changing the way you think and by examining your attitude and learning from it.

Your mind is wonderfully powerful. Harness this power to reduce your stress, not to increase it.

CHAPTER ELEVEN

Believe in a Positive Future

No-one can know for sure what the future holds. Yet most stress is caused by the fear of some future event. In the last chapter we discussed how you could deal with this by imagining the worst possible outcome and by discovering both that you would cope and how you would cope. We also saw that this supposedly worst possible outcome might even have some advantages. In this chapter we are hoping to take this concept further and assume that whatever is in the future will be for the best, no matter what you think of it at this moment. Here are some common worries and fears:

- You won't get a project done on time.
- Someone will burgle your house, steal your car or attack you.
- You will lose your current lover or not find another lover or partner.
- You may lose people you care about, let them down or they will let you down.
- Your financial future, your health or your job, things that might happen to your children or your parents.
- The decisions your children will make.
- Your exam results.
- Your retirement.
- Flying.
- Making a gaffe at a party.
- Leaving your pets when you go on holiday.
- Breaking a plate when you wash up for someone else.

All these and thousands of other stresses come about because you are afraid of and worrying about some event that may happen in the future. Yet for most people it is true to say that in the majority of cases the thing that worried them either didn't occur or, if it did, turned out to be a good thing after all, a blessing in disguise or at least not as bad as they had expected.

Think back to some of the worries and stresses of your past. Did you worry at school, about your tests, about exam results? In the end you probably passed and found that the worry had been unnecessary. Did you worry about who would be friends with you and to which parties you would receive invitations? Think about your fears during teenage years. Did you worry about getting a job, having friends, getting married? Almost certainly you did. Almost certainly, too, many if not most of these worries turned out to be unnecessary. You may even have thought to yourself, afterwards, how silly you were to feel worried or stressed since, as it turned out, there had been nothing to worry about.

This is not the same as deeming things to have been less important from the vantage point of the present than they were at the time. Any concern, worry or stress can be diminished in this way. It is a recognition that many of the situations, the anticipation of which worried and stressed you, either never came about or turned out to be beneficial.

Perhaps failing an exam at school turned you towards a more satisfying and rewarding career. Perhaps one girl or boy refusing to go out with you left you free to accept another invitation. Perhaps being unable to afford an overseas holiday led to making some good friends close to home.

Stop reading now and make a list. List all the things that worried you in your past. List the big things, list the small things. Put one thing on each line and draw four vertical lines down the page making three columns. Now score them. In the first column mark three points for a major stress, two for a medium one and one for a minor stress. Then go down the list again and mark in the next column the ones that turned out well. In other words the ones about which, had you been able to see into the future and to know the outcome, you would not have worried. In the final column mark the ones for which your worries and feelings of stress actually made the outcome worse.

Perhaps you fretted so much before exams that you were too tense to write your best possible answers when the exams came. Perhaps you worried about not having a boyfriend or girlfriend and not getting married, so you married at your first opportunity and then regretted not having had more single years. Perhaps you worried about money while the children were young and scrimped and saved so they could go to university only to find that either they didn't want to go or they won scholarships. Perhaps you felt stressed before parties yet found you had a good time once you got there. Perhaps you felt stressed at work, afraid of criticism that didn't come.

All these stresses and the others like them came about because you anticipated and feared a negative future. You felt worried, stressed and anxious because of fears as to what would happen if the anticipated negative outcome occurred. Had you chosen to assume that the outcome would have been positive you need not have felt stressed. Consider just how much less stress there would have been in your life had you viewed the future as positive and assumed things would turn out well rather than focused on the negative possibilities and worried about the possible bad things that might happen.

As has so often been said before, today is the first day of the rest of your life. Today is tomorrow's yesterday. If you continue with what you are doing you will be creating more yesterdays of needless stresses. This is the time to consider the possibility of assuming the future will be positive and so cutting down on your experience of stress.

You can take a lot of stress out of your life by choosing to believe in a positive future, by choosing to believe that things will turn out well and by choosing to think that things you cannot change are all for the best. This is true whether, in the end, the future turns out to be positive or negative. At least you have been saved the intervening stress which would have been both useless and destructive.

If the future is good and there was nothing to worry about you have been saved needless stress and worry. If the future does not go the way you would like you have still been spared the interim worry. Note that nowhere am I suggesting that you should lie back and let the future happen. Influence events in the way you want to the best of your ability, then stop worrying and fretting. The following example will further explain what I mean.

Choose the positive perspective

Robyn complained of the stress of trying to get a job. Each time she applied she said she felt tense. She was tense as she waited to see if she would be wanted for an interview. Then she was tense until the interview, fearing she would do badly. She was tense during the interview, still afraid she would do badly. Then she was tense until she got the result, fearing she wouldn't get the job. By the time she saw me she estimated she had tried unsuccessfully for 11 jobs and become thoroughly stressed and anxious in the process.

I suggested that she chose to believe, when she applied for a job interview, that one of two things would happen. Either she would get an interview or that if she didn't, it would be because it was not the job for her and a better one was coming up soon that she would enjoy more. Similarly, before an interview she was told to focus on the belief that either she was going to get the job or, if she didn't, it would be because something better was coming along.

Initially she found this difficult. She said it felt too much as if she was fooling herself. However, with practice, she said she could gradually convince herself. The results, to start with, were simply that she felt less stressed while waiting for the phone to ring. This in itself was a step forward since the main problem she had brought to me was her feeling of suffering from stresses beyond her capacity to bear. In time she got a job. Whether or not she got this as a result of her new, positive and less stressed attitude is debatable. Perhaps she did, but perhaps she didn't. Either way she was a lot less stressed.

You can deal with any stress in this way. Do you get uptight when caught in an unexpected traffic jam? Choose to believe that you are missing something else that is worse. Possibly you would have had an accident had you been able to drive faster. Perhaps you would have caught the boss in a bad mood, perhaps you would have missed out on buying a dress because the shop would not have unpacked it earlier.

Can you know for sure what would have happened? No, of course not. So choose the most useful belief. Why choose to believe a situation or event is bad and make yourself feel stressed? Choose to believe instead that the present situation is better than any other that might have occurred and you will feel less stressed. By what you choose to think you dictate your stress level. So choose to have the belief that the current reality is the best possible reality. If this does bring about any changes they will be changes for the better since you will be in a more relaxed and positive frame of mind for dealing with the situation. Let's look at some more examples.

Mrs B. had been coming to see me for a while and on one visit she told me the following story. She had planned a family gathering and had been very keen for her nephew David to come. Initially he had said he would, then he'd phoned to say something else had come up and that he might not be able to make it, and that if he did get there he would be late.

'It was marvellous,' she said with a rueful grin. 'In the old days I would have got upset and been angry with him. I would have told him he couldn't let something else interfere, he'd already said he would come, I was counting on him, he simply had to come, he owed it to the family and so forth.'

'So what did you say?'

'It was easy. I was focused on what you said and told myself that whatever way it worked out it would be for the best. When he does come he usually argues with uncle Harry so I focused on the fact that if he didn't come there could be one argument less, and that on the other hand if he did come then many of the relatives would be pleased, thus whatever happened it would be for the best.'

'And so what did you say to David when he said he might not be there?'

'I said "That's all right. We would really love to have you but if you can t make it we'll still have a good day. Let me know if you can," and we said goodbye.'

'What happened?'

'He came. You know it was the funniest thing. I really don't think he intended to, so I asked him what had happened. And you know what he said? He said I'd sounded so happy and as if the day was going to be so much fun that he felt he really didn't want to miss it. I think what he really rebels against is the pressure to do what people, and especially the family, want him to do.'

Not only did Mrs B. reduce her tension since she decided not to worry about whether or not David would come but to focus her mind instead on a positive outcome, but, by her change in attitude, she even helped to bring about the situation she desired.

~

Penelope was out shopping and saw the dress of her dreams, just right, she thought, for a dinner party at the weekend. The only problem was that while she was asking an assistant about it someone else arrived and picked up the only one in her size. The other customer, hearing her request to the saleswoman, informed her tartly that she had it in her hand and so she had first choice.

Penelope too had been working with me. She said that in the past she would have argued with the woman, claimed that she had seen it first and, had she lost the argument, would have stormed off in a bad mood muttering to herself things like 'You keep it, you silly old cow, it'll look dreadful on you and I didn't want it anyway.' Since this was blatantly untrue her subconscious would not have been fooled, and she would have been angry and stressed.

Instead, since she couldn't deflect the woman from having first try, she said 'That's all right, go ahead, it may not be suitable for the dinner party I'm going to anyway. I'll look around for something else until you decide.'

There are several possible positive outcomes to this story. She might have looked around and found an even better one, or a less expensive one. She might, by her relaxed attitude, have reduced the other woman's desire for the dress. In fact the other woman did try it on and did buy it but not before Penelope had seen that, on and from a distance, the material looked messy in a way she was sure she would not have noticed had she only looked at herself close-to in the mirror. With a sigh of relief she left and found another, more elegant, dress elsewhere.

~

Mr and Mrs H. were house hunting and found a wonderful cottage that exactly suited their needs. The only problem was the price, slightly above their upper limit. They put in the best bid they could and then settled down to wait. They could have spent the next few days fretting and biting their finger nails. Instead they kept assuring themselves that if they got the cottage it would be marvellous, and if they didn't, perhaps they were going to be saved from unseen wood rot or transport problems. As a result they spent the weekend enjoyably and profitably looking at other properties instead of fretting. They didn't get the cottage but nor would they have done had they fretted through the weekend and at least they were ahead in their search.

Remember, the objective is to reduce the feeling of stress. By all means change the outside situation if this is possible and profitable. If you can't, and even if you can, you can reduce your experience of stress by choosing to believe in a positive future, by choosing to believe that whatever happens will be for the best. In addition, your more relaxed attitude may influence events in your favour. Again it is necessary to stress that for this approach to work lip-service will not do. You must actually convince yourself of the truth of the statements and beliefs, not just mouth the words.

There is one other very important point to stress yet again. It is this. Do not confuse a belief in a positive outcome with a 'couldn't care less' attitude. There is a difference. It may be a fine one, but there is a difference. It would be sad if you took this approach to the extreme and started telling yourself you didn't care about the outcome and that nothing mattered to you any more.

Be warned too of another possible pitfall. Telling yourself you will get what you want anyway and that there is no need to worry may be all very well for your peace of mind, but if it prevents you from working towards your desired goal you may be setting up future stresses when, much to your surprise, you fail. Do whatever it takes at a practical level to achieve your goals but keep a positive attitude in the future at the same time.

Major stresses

So far we have dealt with relatively minor situations, the sort of situations that happen on a fairly regular basis in most people's lives. How, you might reasonably ask, can you use this technique for more serious stresses? You can hardly assume that famine, rape, pillage and murder are for the best. Let's consider this.

Firstly, it is important to keep in mind that you are going to do whatever you can to change the situation for the better, as you perceive it. Note that what you think will be a better outcome may not be what someone else thinks will be the best outcome, but we will not pursue that thought here. We will focus on you.

Perhaps someone you love is dying. Perhaps they are old, maybe it is a parent or someone you have been close to for years and on whom you depend. We will assume you have done all you can and there is nothing more to be done for them. The aim now is not to stifle your grieving but to reduce your feelings of stress and pain.

Believe in a positive outcome. Be willing to give them the freedom to die in their own time. Be willing to believe that it is best for them, that they will be saved further pain and suffering, and that what is happening, since it can't be changed, is for the best. Be willing to believe that you will cope, that you can manage without them. Look also for something positive in the situation, however slight. Perhaps you will have a chance to develop in a way you have not done in the past and be less dependent. Perhaps you will have more time for other members of your family.

Keep in mind that the objective here is to find something in the positive future to which you can work and look forward, rather than focusing on all the painful sides of the situation. You will not care less, you will not necessarily hurt less, but you will feel less stressed.

Perhaps you are facing bankruptcy. You have been running your own business successfully for years, you have borrowed for expansion and growth and now the interest rates are up, cash flow is down and you can't keep your head above water. Do not stop caring and trying. Do all you can to avert the disaster. Then face the future.

You can either focus on the disgrace and the deprivation or you can focus on the best aspects of the situation and believe something good is going to come out of it.

Mr J. did this. When he first arrived in my office he was distraught, worried about his business that was losing money each week, worried about his staff and the firms to which his company owed money, worried about his family and how he would provide for them, worried about what his friends would think, how he would cope, and so forth.

He was also trying to deal with banks and creditors, to run meetings with accountants and lawyers, to plan his course of action over the coming months. During our second session I had him run the phrase 'A benefit I will get from the bankruptcy is...'. Initially he simply gazed at me.

'There can be no possible benefit from going bankrupt,' was his immediate response. However, once we had talked further he was willing to give this approach a try.

The completions he gave surprised him and included '... I won't have to worry about paying the creditors', '... I can have a holiday', '... I won't have to deal with some of the business people I don't like', '... I will have more time with my family'.

By the time we had finished he was looking much less uptight and did say, in mild surprise, that he could indeed see quite a few positive things ahead. Going into bankruptcy might not be the way he would have chosen to achieve these ends but, since he now had no choice, he could reduce his stress level by focusing on the benefits rather than on his loss.

Three years later he wrote to tell me that, in retrospect, losing his business had been a very positive turning point for him. He was back in business again, but this time on a smaller and much more profitable scale with fewer overheads and staff to pay. He was able to earn more than before but work shorter hours and see more of his family. They had moved to a smaller and less expensive town and he spent less time travelling. More importantly, he wrote, as a result of the whole experience he had discovered new capacities and strengths within himself, ones he hadn't known he had, and new friends who had stood by him. He finished the letter by saying that if, during the crisis, he could have seen three years ahead, there would have been negligible stress in the situation.

Consider another major stress. Perhaps someone you love, someone young, has been killed in a car crash. How can you possibly believe that this is for the best and will lead to a positive future? All you can think of right now is your loss and the waste of a life. You cannot change the situation, but you can change the way you feel. You can't change what has happened; the present aim is to reduce your counter-productive feelings of stress. You will not love the dead person any the less for finding ways of reducing the misery you are currently experiencing. Keep this in mind.

The next step is to follow exactly the same procedures we have already discussed. There will be *some* benefit that you can find out of their death, some positive outcome on which you can focus to pull you through your present misery. Certainly you would *not* have wished the person to die to achieve this. Keep this firmly in mind as you read the following paragraphs. And again, keep in mind that you are simply trying to reduce your stress level, a level of stress that is not benefiting you or anyone else and is probably causing further problems.

Mr and Mrs T. lost their elder son in a motor-bike accident and were distraught. Mr T., though upset, was coping with the situation, but his wife was not. He had brought her in to see me fearing that she would have a nervous breakdown. We discussed the above approach and at first she refused to consider it. Mr T., however, could see the benefit of it and encouraged her to try. After running the phrase 'A positive change that will occur as a result of Henry's death is ...' and, very much to her surprise, of course, she found that there were several. They included the fact that with only one boy instead of two to educate they could now afford a university education for the second son.

She kept protesting, and I agreed each time, that none of this was worth Henry's death, and that she felt guilty viewing Henry's death in this way. However, she also came to realize that there were a few positive things she could focus on to help pull her out of her depression. She also recognized that giving in to her grief and possibly having a nervous breakdown would cause untold stress and pain to her husband and remaining son.

If you are thinking that this approach is heartless, stop and think again. Henry had died, that situation could not be changed. The two options for the future were as follows. Firstly, Mrs T. could be over-whelmed by her distress, drown in it, have a nervous breakdown and cause her family further worry. Alternatively she could focus on a positive future, think of her second son and his education and provide a stable basis for the rest of her family.

Six months later she and her husband were indeed able to look back and see this shift in her focus as the one thing that helped to keep the three of them together and save her from a breakdown.

If you believe in reincarnation this will add a further dimension to your ability to feel positive about the future. You can choose to believe that it was best for the person who has left their body to do so at this time. You can choose to believe that they will come back sooner, that you will see them again or that they will be waiting for you when the time comes for you to leave your own body.

I add this only for the benefit of those for whom reincarnation is part of their thinking. It is not necessary to believe in this to achieve help from a belief in a positive future.

Preventing stress

As a practitioner in the field of natural and preventative medicine there is an ever present frustration. In preventative medicine you never know what you have prevented. You may find that, on balance, people remain healthier after they have put the ideas into practice. You may find that, as a group, people who take vitamin and mineral supplements have statistically fewer health problems than people who don't. What you will never know is exactly what health problem you helped to prevent in a specific person. You cannot know for sure how they would have been had they not improved their diet, lifestyle, thinking and so forth.

The same thing applies when working with people suffering from stressful situations. You cannot know what problem has not developed as the consequence of a particular occurrence, even one that you think of as negative and stressful. Keep in mind the process and you can reduce your stress.

In case you are feeling overwhelmed by the attempt to use this method to deal with major catastrophes then let's go back to lesser ones, the types of stress that can happen daily.

You may go shopping and not be able to get the hair dye you wanted. Perhaps you would have reacted allergically to it. You can either choose to feel stressed because you couldn't get exactly what you wanted or you can tell yourself that the original one might well have caused a problem. You still have to use the second choice but at least you can feel less stressed.

You may get to the bus stop just as the bus's tail lights are disappearing out of sight. You can either wait 20 minutes for the next bus in a lather of irritation at the things that delayed you or you can assume you will have a much better ride in the next bus and use the time for some constructive thinking.

Perhaps you were driving and wanted to take one route but missed the turn-off because of heavy traffic in the lane you wanted. Instead of getting angry with the other cars, calling the other drivers names and muttering about getting to your destination late, consider the possibility that something good is going to come out of this situation. Maybe this way you will pass a shop and, if you are thinking clearly instead of crossly, realize that you did want to buy the evening paper and so stop and take advantage of the situation.

Perhaps you are on holiday and get a toothache. Instead of muttering about the time you are wasting getting it fixed, consider the possibility that the new dentist you go to will do a particularly good job. You can't know but at least you can feel less stressed.

You can't know for sure whether or not a situation that has happened is for the best or has indeed been a setback. Since the object of the exercise is for you to feel less stressed it makes sense to assume that the current situation is for the best. Go ahead and practise this, in small and big things in your life that are causing you to feel stressed at the moment.

Intuition

Listening to your intuition can get you out of a lot of strife and reduce your stress. Everyone has intuition. Maybe you listen to yours a lot. Maybe you pay it scant attention. It is an attribute worth cultivating.

Haven't you ever thought of someone and then suddenly bumped into them, or had the feeling you should take an umbrella, decided not to because the sky was clear and then got caught in a shower? Have you ever acted on your intuition and blessed it or failed to act and regretted it?

It is quite possible that what you call your intuition is a much stronger force than you recognize. Practise with it for a while. Be willing to listen to that inner prompting and find out how often it was right. This will mean, for a while, making your intellectual brain chatter and logical tram-line thinking take a back seat.

I do not mean by this that you should do anything foolish. I simply mean that you should not let your conscious mind ride roughshod over the more delicate intuitive messages your subconscious is sending you. If you ignore your intuition it will stop speaking to you. If you pay attention to it you can learn a lot.

Start with small things first. It would not be sensible to decide to invest your life savings in a scheme picked at random from the stock market listing and hope that your choice was promoted by a wise underlying intuition. On the other hand, if you feel a strong urge to invest in a particular company based on intuition, investigate the company or invest a small amount and see what happens. Use your intuition in small ways and then, as you learn to know it better, trust it to a greater and greater extent.

For example, when you are driving home and suddenly, on a whim, decide to go by an alternative route, you cannot know what would have happened had you gone the usual way. Instead of kicking yourself for the greater length of time the trip may now take think of it as a possible example of your intuitive capacity. Perhaps the change was simply a whim, a change from the usual pattern that was of no importance in the general scheme of things; but consider the other possibility. Perhaps it was your intuition or some higher wisdom warning you that on the usual road you were destined to have an accident.

There are many ways in which you can practise working with your intuition and can develop it. Ask yourself something about the coming day and then see if it occurs. You might wonder who you will meet first when you leave the house, who will phone you first, what someone will be wearing, which restaurant your friends will choose in the evening, if you will get a letter, and so forth. Do not make an intellectual decision. Just pose the question or thought and make a note of the first response that occurs to you.

As you work with your intuition you will gradually learn to differentiate between true intuition and your everyday thinking and worrying.

Sue lived and worked in two separate buildings to which she had the sole keys and in each of which she was the sole occupier. Frequently she left either home or work and then fretted that perhaps she had forgotten to lock the door and set the alarm. For months she worried and, when she simply could not remember for sure that she had indeed locked up properly, would go back to check. Every time she went back she found that she had indeed locked up properly. The prompt was not intuition; it was her usual worry pattern. She then learnt to ignore this and trust herself to lock the doors automatically on leaving.

One day she went out to do some quick shopping. As she was leaving a thought flashed through her mind that the door was not properly closed but she decided to ignore it. When she returned it was indeed ajar, though only slightly. Fortunately no-one had entered while she

> was away but she was able to use this experience to differentiate between worry and an intuitive prompt. Practise this yourself.

Now let's relate this back to stress. If you do get a whim to drive home by a prettier route, even if it is a bit longer, do it. The mere fact of doing it will bring some fun into your day so ignore the voice that insists you stick doggedly to what has to be done. Be willing to believe your intuition is not only giving you some fun but is helping you as well.

- It is less stressful to assume that it was your wise intuition that prompted you to forget to buy the meat today, thus leaving the purchase for another day, than to fume at the irritation of having to go shopping again tomorrow. Perhaps today's meat was old; perhaps it was more expensive than usual.
- It is less stressful to assume that the alternative hotel you can stay in will be better than your first choice that is full than to fret about what you might be missing.
- It is less stressful to assume that you were wise to invite those troublesome neighbours for a meal when they virtually invited themselves than to mutter about the bother of it .
- It is less stressful to assume your hunch that you should phone someone, wear a particular outfit, make a particular decision or refuse an invitation is the result of a wise intuition than to fret, unprofitably, about its wisdom after the decision has been acted upon.

Imposed situations versus created situations

During the course of your life you are affected by a number of outside circumstances. You can choose to believe that, in some way, you created them, in some way you are responsible for them, in some way you chose to be present when they occurred. By this means you can stop blaming other people for your problems and can feel that you did have a direct input into them and so you can have a direct input into their positive outcome.

This is a very powerful belief system to have. You can deal with anything in this way from a minor hurt to being present during a devastating earthquake. After all, you made some of the decisions that resulted in you being there and not somewhere else.

Again, if for you reincarnation is a reality, as it is for about 30 per cent of the Western world, then you can choose to believe that you had some choice as to where you were born and the situations which faced you as a result of this choice.

Imposed situations

However, some people, try as they might, are unwilling or unable to take this point of view, even though they lose out in the process. If you feel you must, you can choose to believe that there are some events that are bigger than you and that have come to you from an outside force that you could not in any way control. I repeat, I do not advocate this belief since it offers you the possibility of blame and victim status, but I realize that some people will simply refuse to believe that they could, in some way, have had an input into any situation. For the moment we will take and accept this view of the situation.

These, then, are situations of which you are a part and yet for which you have chosen to feel no responsibility. They exist, they may cause you stress, you will almost certainly want to reduce this stress. This is not going to come about by blaming circumstances or other people.

Created situations

At the same time, throughout your life there will be a wide variety and huge number of situations, relationships, events etc., that you create yourself.

You may like or dislike some of the outside events that occur. You may wish you could disclaim all responsibility for them and for your involvement in them. You may or may not be able to alter them or use them to your advantage. You may like or dislike some of the situations you have created by your words and your deeds and by the decisions you have made.

Your attitude

Both the things that you choose to believe happen to you, the passive recipient, and the things you choose to believe you have created, may be either beneficial or stressful. It is up to you to decide which they will be. It is up to you to decide the way you will handle them.

This handling is the key to your stress levels. The way you deal with the events that occur and the situations you have created determines the flavour of your life and decides the outcome in terms of the amount of stress you will experience.

It is your attitude that is all important in determining how much stress you experience. It is your attitude far more than what occurs, whether you believe you created that occurrence or not, that determines your stress. It is your attitude, after you have said or done something, that determines your stress level, even more than what you said or did.

Keep this firmly in mind for one thing is sure. Your attitude is something over which you have full and total control. No-one else can control your attitude or the view you choose to take of a situation. By using your mind and making the appropriate choices you can choose to have a good attitude to a situation or you can choose to have a bad attitude to a situation. You can choose to feel stressed or you can choose not to feel stressed.

The positive future

In the ways described above and in a million and one other similar ways, you can choose to believe in a positive future, you can choose to have a good attitude, and thus you can reduce greatly your experience of stress.

Keep in mind that if there are specific things you can do, external to yourself, to reduce the stress of a situation, you should do them. Take what you receive or create in life, do the best with it that you can. Make every appropriate effort to generate your desired outcome. Then, when you have done physically all you possibly can, use the power of your mind to control your attitude to minimize any possible stress.

If there is nothing you can do about a situation then move directly to taking a positive view of the future. By taking this positive view of whatever has happened, you can greatly reduce your stress, and that is what this book is all about.

CHAPTER TWELVE

Proaction versus Reaction

How much of your mood is determined by you and how much of it is determined by the people, things and events around you and by what people think of you? If you are to be free from stress you must be able to choose and determine your own mood rather than let it be subjected to and dependent upon other people and the things that are happening 'outside' and over which you have, or may appear to have, limited or no control.

Consider your mood at this moment.

- Are you being bothered by noises going on around you?
- Are there dishes in the sink, papers on your desk or other chores, making you feel guilty for relaxing with a book rather than getting on with the jobs?
- Are you resenting people who are clamouring for your attention?
- If you are travelling, by bus, train or plane, are there external factors that are bothering you?
- Are you fretting about what other people are thinking of you and what you are doing?
- Do you worry frequently about other people's opinions?

Write down your answers to these questions, your comments and your assessments of what this tells you about yourself.

Take this exercise one step further. Is your mind split in two? Are you both considering the answers to the above questions and, at the same time, wondering what point is being made? You may also have part of your mind distracted about things that have been happening in the recent past or things that are about to happen in the future.

It is clear from this that you are not your mind. You are not your feelings. You are something else above these, and you are able to decide upon which of the various things impinging on your consciousness you wish to focus.

The decisions you make in this regard will affect your experience of stress. If you choose to focus on something pleasant that happened recently you will feel relaxed and happy. If you choose to focus your attention on something bad that might be about to happen you could feel stressed. Thus you can choose your stress level. We have considered aspects of this in the previous chapters. However, we can take it further.

The important thing for you to focus on here is not only what you are choosing to think or think about, but also the perspective you are choosing to have, the ultimate source on which you are going to base your thoughts and emotions. If you spend your life responding to the thoughts, ideas, values, criticisms, judgments and comments of other people you are going to experience one level of stress. If you decide what you wish to do, what is right for you and how you want to behave and then act accordingly, you will experience another level of stress. In general, but not always, you will experience much less stress when you freely choose your own emotions than when you jerk around, like a puppet on a string, responding to other people's opinions.

Consider the following circumstance. You are a busy homemaker. You have spent the day working hard at home. You have cooked dinner and set it on the table. After dinner the children are told to wash up and you

plan to spend the evening reading a good book. You know you have
worked hard and you want some time for yourself. You know the children
want to go out and play and resent having to do the washing up. What do
you do?

(a) Feel guilty and tell them you'll wash up so they can play;

(b) Feel guilty so do a chore you will otherwise have to do later, to look
busy, and promise yourself you will read your book, possibly unobserved,
afterwards;

(c) Read your book anyway but get angry with the children, insisting
you have worked hard and they have already been playing while you got
dinner;

(d) Relax, knowing your decisions on the division of labour are fair by
your standards, and enjoy the book.

If you opt for any of the first three outcomes you are being reactive. You
will feel stressed, either because you are not doing what you want to do
or because you are doing what you want but are feeling uncomfortable.
This stress is self-imposed, you are experiencing it because you are
choosing to react to the world around you rather than to make your
own decision and then feel comfortable with it.

Not only are you feeling stressed by being reactive but you are probably also going to stress the other people involved by your guilt,
resentment or other reactive emotion and thus further stress yourself
and, in turn, them. By the end of the evening everyone will feel thoroughly upset. You may well feel angry with the children for interrupting
your reading or resentful of them if you let them stop you and prevent
you following your chosen course of action. One way or other they are
likely to become aware of this; they will feel resentful and you in turn
will feel more guilty or more stressed.

Consider this circumstance. You are the general manager of an office. An important decision has to be made by you on Monday morning and all week long different individuals have been coming to you putting their point of view. Do you spend the weekend fretting about what to do or do you relax? Which of the following best describes your actions?

(a) One colleague phones you up and pushes his or her ideas. You see their point of view and consider perhaps you should do as they think and you let them realize this.

Another colleague phones and you start to worry about what you have just decided and think perhaps you should alter your decision a bit. Then you worry about what the first colleague will think.

You then read the memo from your boss and feel you have to try to do what he would like best, the only trouble is you are not sure what this is.

Then you worry what your customers will think.

All in all you have a pretty stressful weekend worrying about what others are thinking, what you ought to do and what others will think after you have acted. You are too tired, by Monday morning, to have a clear idea of what is best for the company as a whole and your final decision depends on what happens and how you and your staff react at the Monday meeting.

(b) You sit down for a few hours on Saturday morning with all the input you have received and make your own decision as to what you think is best. You thank any colleagues who choose to phone you but let them know you have already gathered all the input you need and tell them you will inform them on Monday. You decide your boss, by appointing you to your job, showed faith in your ability. You have faith in your own ability. You know that when you announce your decision on Monday you will have done what you think is right. You relax and enjoy the rest of the weekend.

In (a) you are being reactive and become highly stressed. In (b) you are being proactive, acting on your own decisions, believing in yourself and able to make a decision without undue stress.

Consider a situation in which you are deciding what to wear to an event. It may be an important social event or it may be something minor. What do you do?

(a) Do you fret about what to wear and spend hours in your bedroom trying on one outfit after another, not knowing whether to dress up or dress down, to wear warm or cool clothes, to wear something new or something old and comfortable?

(b) Do you phone a particular friend and follow their advice?

(c) Do you phone around among your friends, find they have conflicting ideas and wonder which one to copy and if the others will be offended that you haven't taken their advice?

(d) Do you find out from the hostess or organizer what would be the appropriate dress and then make your own choice, wearing something you like and in which you feel good?

If you do any of the first three or any variant on them you are being reactive and will feel stressed. Clearly your feeling of comfort is going to be based on feeling you have pleased the other people who will see you and on getting a satisfactory response from them as to the way you look. When you get to the event you cannot relax as some people will have dressed differently to you and you may wonder if you should have been more like them. Even if what you are wearing is correct you may wonder if the colour or style is right for you and so still depend on getting a complimentary response from other people. Either way you will certainly feel stressed.

If you act as in (d) you are being proactive and you can relax. Even if other people dress differently you will know you look good in what you have on, you will feel comfortable and you will be able to enjoy the occasion. Your peace of mind is not dependent on other people's opinions.

If you are proactive you decide what you will do and how you will feel and then get on with your life. You understand clearly what is right for you and you feel confident in yourself. If you are reactive you will spend most of your time responding to the outside world and wondering what other people are thinking of you. You will look to others for validation of yourself and this never works. It never works because at every point some of these other people will approve of you and some of them will disapprove.

It would be bad enough if the other people referred to were all proactive and secure in their judgments. But remember that they too, by and large, will be reactive and they will be wondering what you are thinking of them, and their thoughts, words and deeds will vary as a result.

Childhood patterns

Most of our reactive patterns go back to childhood. As a child you probably heard phrases such as:

- 'Don't do that, what will other people think'
- 'Don't do so and so, whatever will the neighbours say'
- 'Do or don't behave in a certain way or people will think I've brought you up badly'
- 'You must do well at your studies or people will think you're stupid'
- 'Behave when you are in school uniform or people will think this is a poor school'
- 'Be polite or other mothers will think you have learnt no manners'

These and hundreds of other similar statements are part of most people's childhood. Thus from an early age you have been taught that what other people think of you is of paramount importance. It is other people's thoughts and opinions that, you are led to believe, are all important, not your own.

Your life would have been very different if you had been trained in the following way:

> 'First we will discuss how you think you should behave and what level of achievement you think is appropriate for you. Then you must make your decision and must act as you think best. You will have to recognize that you will have generated whatever benefits or consequences arise from your chosen course of action. Our criteria, yours and mine, in assessing your achievement, will then be based on whether or not you have behaved within your own guidelines. If at any time you wish to change your guidelines as to what you think is the correct behaviour then you are free to do so.'

Obviously the wording will have to change for a very young child but the general concept can still be expressed.

Granted it may be a little difficult to get this concept across to a baby or a toddler but, at least in small ways, it is possible, and people do start learning and developing their attitudes and standards very young. As a child grows older this becomes more and more easy. It is more constructive in the long run to teach a child by direct cause and effect rather than by holding up the spectre of 'what will other people think' as the yardstick by which they will be assessed. When you realize that this latter method can lead to a lifetime of real and imagined stress you can begin to see the value of the former method.

Consider the following examples of some of the things parents commonly say to their children, and remember, the inferences are being drawn by the child, perhaps you in the past, with a child's perspective on the world:

> 'Don't make a mess of your clothes or grandmother will think you're a dirty child and she won't want to pick you up.' Implication: If I don't look good, grandma, and other people, won't love me.

'Be sure to be good and to thank the parents or they won't invite you back again.' Implication: If I don't please the hosts I won't be wanted any more.

'Be quiet and don't make a noise or you'll disturb people.' Implication: I am not important and only get in other people's way.

'Do well at school now, I expect you to come near the top of the class. Your older brother did so I'm sure you can too. Implication: If I don't do well I won't be as good as (as worthwhile a person as) my brother.

'How could you do that? Only nasty people criticize their friends. You want to be popular, don't you?' Implication: If I speak out and express my point of view I won't be liked.

'Behave yourself at table or people will think you don't know how to behave.' Implication: If I behave wrongly in a situation people will think less of me.

'You must wear the right clothes or you'll look silly.' Implication: What I wear or look like is more important than who I am.

Hundreds, probably thousands, more examples could be given. You will doubtless have many you can recall from your childhood. Notice the one thing they all have in common. What other people think is the yardstick by which you are being judged. The clear message to you, from birth onwards, was that to get on in the world, to be a good, acceptable person who is loved and approved of, you must behave in such a way that you obtain other people's approval.

Which group of 'other people' is being referred to is never exactly specified. Mention is rarely if ever made of the fact that these 'other people' will have different opinions and that you cannot please all of them all of the time. There is no discussion as to who gave them the authority to judge you, and certainly you are never told that you are part of 'other people' for everyone else.

Josie was 15 when she first came to see me. Her mother told me that she and Josie were always arguing, that Josie seemed unhappy, that she seemed to resent any authority and all she seemed to want to do was get her own way. Her mother was near the end of her tether saying 'It's as if she resents any input from us, yet we're only trying to do what's best for her.

'One of the worst areas for fights is over the question of what she wears. She always wants to buy the most expensive clothes, she never likes the things I choose and in no time has them looking a mess. So then I have to buy more clothes only they suffer the same fate. I hate to think what other people are saying; they must think we can't afford to dress her properly. And in some ways it is true, she is costing us a fortune in clothes yet she never looks good. I keep telling her she must try to look smarter for everyone's sake.'

Clearly a number of factors are operating here. For a start the mother has been reared on a strict diet of 'What will other people think?' However, my immediate concern was with Josie. After the first session her attitudes were clear.

She had learnt early that she had to be aware of what other people thought of her. She had then developed her own list of people she wanted to please with her appearance, namely her own friends, not her mother's friends. She did also have definite ideas of her own but she was nervous of putting them into practice as her mother had taught her, relentlessly, by example, that what other people thought was important.

As she put it, when paraphrased to its essence, 'I get so confused when I go shopping. Mother wants me to buy one thing, I know something else would fit in with what my friends will be wearing and yet I often like a third thing. We usually get what mother wants. I hate it, my friends laugh at it and so I guess I do treat it badly and it's soon dirty or rumpled. Then there are the times when I do put up a fight and buy the current fad outfit, but though my friends might like it I often feel silly, even though I know they will approve of me. Then because mother dislikes it she tries to stop me wearing it and, because I'm often not mad about it either, I toss it into the back of the cupboard. Occasionally I fight for something but it's usually for the sake of the fight and often means I land up buying something I don't really want. The trouble is I never do seem to have anything to wear and so we have to go shopping and the cycle starts over again. Then mother complains about the price and says I cost her more than my brother and sister put together ... and I know she loves them best anyway. It's not fair, either. I'd cost her less if she let me make my own choices.'

What a lot of trouble is caused by trying to please other people, and what a lot of bother could be saved if each individual was taught from an early age to decide what is right for them and to live by it. In other words, there would be a lot less stress if you were taught from childhood to be proactive rather than reactive.

In Josie's case the solution was surprisingly simple. The family sat down together and the amount spent on the clothes of each child was estimated. Josie discovered that she did indeed get more than her share of the clothing budget. The first agreed step was that Josie would have her own clothing budget. The amount was agreed by them all on the basis of the funds available for the total family and Josie accepted it. She also accepted that nothing extra would be provided when or if this money ran out before the end of the year. It was also decided that she should, for one year, be allowed to choose her own clothes. Further, it was agreed that the people who mattered (both she and her mother were still more reactive than proactive, though they were learning), in this case her friends and her mother's friends, would be told about the arrangement. This meant that her mother could stop taking responsibility for Josie's appearance and that Josie had no-one to blame but herself if she wasn't happy with the way she looked.

The results came in quite rapidly. Josie first sat down and assessed what clothes she thought were important. She budgeted out some of the more outrageous outfits and she declined some of the things she had wanted to buy for effect, either to conform with her peers or to reject her mother's choices. She gradually stopped feeling that she had to please other people and wear the same things as her friends and she stopped thinking that she could blame other people if she looked wrong. This meant she had to make some serious decisions about what really suited her, both her looks and her personality. She then had to buy wisely within her budget.

Very quickly she established her own style. Of course she made mistakes, but soon she found she welcomed some input from her mother, in the form of advice not instructions, and that she and her mother could go shopping together and enjoy it. At the end of the year she even had some of the budget left over. In no time she could feel good in social situations provided she had her own approval and didn't mind what other people thought.

The stress levels for both Josie and her mother fell sharply simply because Josie was allowed to take responsibility for her own looks and was encouraged to dress for herself rather than for 'what other people thought'.

You and what other people think

As we have seen, most people make a lot of their decisions based on what other people think, or, more precisely, on what they think other people think.

It is again time for you to stop reading and do some work. Take a pen and paper and make a list of all the things you do or don't do, because of what other people think. Consider the decisions you make with regard to your family, your social life, your home life, your work, your finances, your hobbies, your appearance, your holidays and travel, your car, your future plans and so forth. Consider how different the decisions might have been if you had not been considering what other people thought but rather had based your decision entirely on what you yourself wanted.

Assuming you have done that, take up your pen again. This time think about the decisions you did make to please yourself but be willing to explore the extent to which this pleasure was affected, at some deeper level, by the way you thought other people would feel about you as a result.

When Graham did this he first said that if he hadn't worried about what his family would think he would have gone to university, studied science and become a researcher and lecturer rather than gone into the family business running a series of retail stores.

When he thought more deeply about this he realized part of the satisfaction would have been the accolade he received from other people on his academic achievement and that what he really wanted to do, deep down and for himself, was to teach science to primary school children.

Instead he was running the family business, not doing it particularly well, resenting the restrictions and the missed opportunity of a teaching career. He felt stressed by the responsibility and resentful of his family. As so often happens in these situations, no-one benefited. The family business would have been more successful had some other arrangement been made and the family would have been happier if Graham had followed his chosen career and resented them less.

Who are these 'other people?'

The next step is for you to start thinking about these other people and what they really do think. Remember that, to everyone else, you are one of these other people.

For most individuals the group labelled 'other people' in this context is a nebulous and unidentified group of people with infinite wisdom. This is the time for you to identify them and recognize each individual, give them a face and thus a character and a set of opinions. Then decide

how much value you really put on each individual person's opinion.
The other people about whom you are concerned probably consist of
your identifiable family members, identifiable friends, identifiable colleagues, identifiable people you meet daily such as shopkeepers, your
banker, your children's friends and their parents and so forth, and even
your identifiable enemies, *plus* an amorphous, non-identified group of
'others'.

As you mentally identify them consider what you know about each
one and about what they think. If you are considering a career move, a
purchase, a decision on a social outing or the behaviour of someone for
whom you feel responsible, even your own behaviour, ask yourself a few
questions. Ask yourself, about each one individually, just exactly what
you think they do think. Consider whether or not you do actually know
what they would think in a certain situation or whether or not you are
simply assuming you know or even guessing. Consider exactly how
much you value each individual's opinion on the particular decision or
matter in question.

Mr D. was thinking of a career move to a job he would like better but
which carried less prestige and a lower salary than his present job. He
was stressed and anxious as he mulled over the pros and cons and unhappy as he decided against it, for the sake of others. He told me how
much he wanted to move but that he knew his wife would hate the reduced income, his children would not like the extra hours it would
entail, his parents would feel they had wasted the money they'd spent
on his education and he worried that his assistant at work would be
left in the lurch. I suggested that he write down what he thought each
person would think, in as much detail as he could, and that he then
approach that person and ask them to be fully honest with him and tell
him what they really thought.

The results surprised him. His wife said the money didn't matter but
that if he would be happier he might be easier to live with and that
would more than make up for it; the present tensions between them

were leading her to wonder how long the marriage could last. His children said they didn't mind if he came home later as they wanted to have more time with their friends, and his parents said he'd more than amply repaid them for their investment already and they only wanted him to be happy. The people who minded his move most were his present employers who hated to lose him. His assistant, John, also said he would hate him to go but later on he found that in fact John was thrilled with the idea as it gave him a chance at promotion.

Often, when you consider the ideas and opinions of others you are merely putting your own ideas out there and mixing them with what you assume other people think and what you think they ought to think. In other words, you can never know what other people really do think. Even when you have told them to be 100 per cent honest with you they may still hide some of their ideas, as John did in the above example.

One thing I have learnt, very thoroughly, after 20 years of advising people on health and related matters, is that you never do know what someone else is thinking and that if you second-guess them you are almost bound to be wrong.

Patients have filled out pages of questionnaires about their symptoms before they have seen me. I have assessed these and come to a conclusion in my own mind as to the problems they will want to discuss with me when they come into my office only to find that, in fact, it is not their digestion, their arthritis or their migraines but rather a problem with breaking nails or their fear of getting cancer. I never try to second-guess my patients. Even during a counselling session, when we are unravelling why they are overweight, why they are unhappy or why they feel stressed, I no longer try to work out what is going on in their mind. You cannot possibly know what other people are thinking. You can only know what you think they are thinking.

Mrs V. had an alcoholic husband who beat her up regularly, a son who was on drugs, a sick mother to look after and no time to do the things she enjoyed. On her first visit she told me she was unhappy and stressed. At one time I would have said 'No wonder, with your husband drinking so much... etc'. Instead I ran the phrase 'The thing that stresses me most is . . .' and waited for her completion. It came as '... I think my husband is seeing another woman'.

Now most wives might well have been thrilled at that. A divorce and a neat division of the ample money they had would, you might imagine, have released her from an unhappy, alcohol-bedevilled marriage and given her the time and freedom to do the things she wanted to do. Yet deep down her real stress was the possible loss of the husband she still loved, in spite of his drinking and his violence.

You cannot know what another person thinks, therefore making decisions about your own life so that you please them or, in your view, will look good in their eyes, is a fruitless exercise. They might say they admire you for your brains, so you study hard and get good grades only to find that they think you are a dry bookworm and no fun to be with. You never can tell.

The situation is worsened by the fact that if you do things to please other people you will not be dealing with just one other person. You will be dealing with tens or hundreds of other people that you can identify and they will invariably have different opinions as to how you should behave. Some will think you should spend more time with your family, others will think you should get out and about more. Some will think you should earn more money, others that you spend too much time thinking about money and not enough time thinking about people. Some will think you should be strong and supportive, others will think you should be more willing to compromise. The list is endless.

Isn't it absurd? You cannot know what other people think, and in any case, different members of this group of other people think totally differently, one from the other. Yet you spend a lot of time being reactive and feeling stressed because of what you think they think about you and what you do and because you might not look, be or do what you think they think you should look, be or do.

The way the world sees you

You can have two views of yourself. One is a view of yourself that you establish on your own. The other is a view of yourself composed of all the feedback you get from the world around you and your assessment and interpretation of this feedback.

> Stop reading this for a minute and do the following exercise. Get a sheet of paper and write down all the comments you can remember other people ever making about you, all the criticisms, all the compliments and all the neutral remarks. Go ahead, do that now.
>
> What have you got?

> One client, Rosalind, came up, in part, with the following list:
>
> - I'm lazy
> - untidy
> - fussy
> - always late
> - always in a rush
> - too clever
> - not smart enough
> - loving and caring
> - hard to get on with
> - too tall
> - too short

- *always putting other people first*
- *selfish*
- *a great reader*
- *not well read*
- *a wonderful homemaker*
- *a stodgy stay-at-home*

Clearly many of these statements are contradictory. Remember that they had been made by a number of different people. Her neighbours were impressed by how well she kept her house but a friend who had built herself an interesting career found her increasingly dull. Her short husband found her too tall but the children complained she wasn't tall enough when they wanted things down off high shelves. Her doctor thought she was overweight, her plump mother nagged at her for always dieting and being too thin.

Rosalind listened to them all and felt like a tennis ball being walloped in ever-changing directions. She worried about each opinion and thus felt stressed a lot of the time. No wonder – she was in the middle of an impossible tug of war. Her stressful reaction to the situation and what was happening to her was why she had come to my office. To help her deal with the stresses that these conflicting criticisms and comments created she was encouraged to make her own assessment of herself. She came up with the following:

- *I am a good wife and mother and I do have a well-run home.*
- *I work hard but I also think it is important to relax and play so I will not feel guilty even if other women are rushing around doing more.*
- *In general I like things to be tidy but when an activity is in progress it is all right if things get a bit messy.*
- *I do read but enjoy lighter books than some of my friends.*
- *I do not want a career and am happy with me as I am.*
- *I am comfortable with my height, and my husband liked it well enough when he married me, but I will lose seven pounds.*
- *I will continue to feel relaxed with my friends and it is all right if I am withdrawn in the company of people I know less well or do not like so much, however I will try to take a greater interest in new people I meet.*

In other words, she did listen to the reflection of herself that came back to her from the people around her but she also made her own decisions as to how she should be. Some aspects of herself she felt satisfied with, others she didn't and so she decided on the appropriate changes to make.

Once she had written her thoughts down she was told to refer back to them any time she felt stressed by the opinion of others and to remember the quiet time during which she had assessed herself. This, she found, had a stabilizing effect on her emotions and cut down on her stress levels considerably.

Keep in mind that the image of yourself reflected back to you by other people is significantly affected by their own view of the world. It is a music-hall joke that the overweight doctor thinks your excess pounds have little to do with your bad health while the slim doctor will tell you to diet. The heavy drinker thinks if you drink half a bottle of wine a night you are only a lightweight whereas the teetotaller will think you are halfway to being an alcoholic. The serious bookworm will tell you that reading fiction is frivolous while the dedicated T.V. watcher will tell you that even reading magazines is heavy going.

Inside your head

Any number of things can happen to you externally but you are always free to choose what you will do with your mind. This takes us back to the ideas expressed at the beginning of this chapter. You are not your mind, you are not your emotions. You are something else above and beyond that. This something else chooses what you will think with your mind and what emotions you will feel.

If you are being reactive you abdicate this control. You forsake the power to make your own decisions as to what you will focus your mind upon and what emotions you will feel. Instead you let the opinions and reactions of other people and outside circumstances dictate your inner experience. In this way you allow yourself to feel enormous amounts of stress.

If you choose to be proactive you will decide what is right for you. You will decide to be your own judge and not allow yourself to be influenced by the judgments of others. You will control your emotions, not by bottling them up but by choosing the way you will feel. In this way you can reduce the level of stress in your life enormously.

Elsewhere I have told the story of an American held in a Japanese prisoner-of-war camp. You will recall that he was often in cramped and solitary confinement and chose to spend the time mentally doing an 18-hole round of golf on his home golf course and making sure it took as long to do it in his mind as it would in real life. By the end of the war he found, when he got home and played his first game, that he had significantly reduced his handicap. Not only is this an example of the power of visualization; it is also an example of the freedom you can have within your own mind even when outside events are not what you would wish. Other men in similar circumstances spent the time being angry and fretful at their confinement, afraid of what would happen to them next and worrying about what their fellow prisoners were thinking of them. One way led to extreme stress, the other to a reduction in stress and a future positive benefit.

Peter came to see me a few months after arriving from overseas. He said he missed his home and family dreadfully, even though he was glad to be studying here, and that he hated being laughed at and teased for his unsophisticated ways. He also said that he knew his mother was hurt that he had left home and that his older sister resented the money being spent on his education. As a result of all this stress and his homesickness his studies were suffering and he was even contemplating giving them up and returning home. He had two tasks to do.

Firstly he had to decide if he felt comfortable with the chance he had been given. Eventually he decided that he was, that he understood how his sister felt but that it was still acceptable in his eyes that he was being given a university education even though she hadn't had one. She might continue to complain but he felt comfortable within himself and thus felt he could stop feeling guilty when he thought of her. He also came to recognize that his mother would feel unhappy whenever he left home but that he obviously had to do it at some stage so doing it now was all right.

Having sorted out these ideas and deciding to be proactive rather than reactive, to be happy with himself rather than react because of his family's attitudes, he was able to feel a lot less stressed. He still had another problem to deal with, his homesickness.

He learnt to do this in two ways. Instead of lying in bed at night, thinking of his family and how far away they were and feeling miserable, he learnt to project himself, in his mind, back into his family life. He learnt, using the method described in the chapter on regression, to visualize himself inside the family home, to turn round mentally and see it from every angle, to walk down a corridor, sit in a room or go out into the garden, then to live through an evening as if he really was at home. From this he derived great comfort which replaced the sorrow he felt when he thought of it as being so far away. He was choosing what he would allow in his mind and using his unique powers as a human being to create an experience that was unrelated to his present circumstances.

Secondly he decided to use another tool discussed in the chapter on a positive future. He chose to take the view that he was in the best possible place both for the present and for his future. He chose to focus his attention entirely on the good features of his present situation and to refuse to dwell on its less satisfactory aspects. He chose to believe that his future was going to be wonderful as he put his training into practice rather than stressful because of alienation from his family. In this way his stress was lessened even further.

Thus by being proactive rather than reacting to his family, by visualizing himself into a nurturing environment rather than dwelling on his loss, by focusing on the good rather than the less good features of the present and by believing in a positive future he was able to reduce his stresses to a negligible level. As a result he did well at his studies, made many friends and derived maximum enjoyment from the experience.

Being proactive

One person I spoke to about being proactive, Mrs G., said she knew all about that. She had already learnt about it and had decided to be proactive but she still had enormous stresses in her life. This gave me pause for thought. After all, if you are truly proactive and are very stressed it can only be because you choose to be stressed, so I asked her what she had done.

'Well,' she said, 'I no longer let other people make decisions for me. I no longer let other people tell me what to do. I make my own decisions now, I do things my way. I have truly taken control of my life. Before I learnt about this concept and about taking charge and being proactive I let everyone else decide what I would do. I was always doing things to please other people. I fitted my life around my children and always made sure I was home from my part-time job by the time they came home from school. I brought work home so as not to let my boss down. I spent the weekend doing whatever my husband and the children wanted to do. I cooked the meals they wanted, helped the children with their homework and dressed the way my husband liked. I tried hard to please people. The only problem was I was tired and grumpy all the time and never felt I did enough for everyone and that they always wanted more. I was enormously stressed.'

'And now?' I queried.

'Oh now it's different,' she said. 'Now I do what I want. I do as much as I can at work and then leave my work behind when I come home. I've told my children they must do their own homework and I cook the sort of meals I like to cook. At the weekends I go shopping and visit my friends. I do what I want instead of running round in small circles helping everyone else.'

'And are you happy?' I asked.

'No,' she said. 'That's the problem. I still feel stressed. There are dreadful tensions in the family, my boss is always criticizing me, there are arguments at mealtimes and my husband and I seem to be drifting apart. They all call me selfish and I feel just as stressed as before I learnt about being proactive.'

Clearly she had missed the point about being proactive. It is not what you do that counts but the way you choose to do it. Being proactive does not simply mean taking the initiative in the things you do. It means being responsible for and comfortable with what you think, how you feel, and how you respond to external stimuli. It means trusting your own judgment about yourself, your life and the way you should be. It means making your own decisions about what is right for you and not being swayed this way and that by the varying opinions and actions of others. It doesn't mean doing things because other people want you to nor refusing to do them as a way of asserting your independence. It means feeling good about yourself and not being dependent on the mirrored view of you that the world returns to you.

Mrs G. had equated proactivity with doing what she wanted, with little thought for others and refusing to do some things simply because other people wanted her to do them. Instead of running round doing what everyone else wanted she was now thumbing her nose at them and saying, in effect, that they could do what they liked; she was going to do her own thing and they could lump it. In a sense she was still being reactive by acting in part out of rebellion.

We discussed the full meaning of proactivity and she returned a month later with a much happier story. She had told her boss that she did enjoy her job but that she also had family commitments and agreed that if it was absolutely essential she could stay back occasionally but that most days she did want to be home in time for the children. She decided that the children should be able to do their own homework but offered to help them, for a limited number of hours a week, if they were really stuck. She explained to her husband that she needed some time to herself at the weekend, which he understood, but that she did also want to spend some time with him.

Best of all she came to understand the real meaning of proactivity and had learnt to decide what was best for herself, within the family context. She had explained this fully to her family while at the same time expressing her love for and her appreciation of them. As a result not only did she have some time for herself but the family understood her needs and their relative roles. The marriage strengthened and everyone felt a lot less stressed.

When you are truly proactive you cannot be stressed by what happens to you as long as you feel you have done what is right and best, as long as you value yourself and as long as you assume that, in your higher wisdom, you have done what is best for a positive future. You cannot be stressed by other people's opinions. You cannot feel diminished if some-one criticizes you. You cannot fall apart if you think you have said or done the wrong thing and someone 'out there' is thinking less of you. If you are proactive you can only feel stressed if you decide to feel stressed, if you decide you have not done the right thing by your own internal code, your own internal standards.

Being proactive does not mean you can avoid pain. If you lose someone you love, if your business fails or you lose your job, if things don't turn out the way you would like – in these and other situations you may feel hurt, you may feel sad, you may experience the loss or the pressure. But the real stress comes about when you choose to feel inadequate to deal with the situations, when you choose to feel diminished by the situations, when you choose to dance to everyone else's tunes, wondering what other people are thinking about you and what you should be doing.

Being reactive is being a slave. Being proactive means you are free. The next chapter on creating your own Life Plan will further help you to define yourself and enable you to be progressively less reactive and more proactive.

CHAPTER THIRTEEN

Your Life Plan

Who are you, what are your values and what is your goal?

In the previous chapter we discussed the concept of reducing your stress level by being proactive rather than reactive. You will recall that this means that you decide who you are and where you are going. You decide what is the right way for you to behave. You do not let one person stress you out by telling you that you have been too lenient with your children and that you will ruin them nor do you let someone else stress you by telling you that you are being too strict and that you will cripple them emotionally. Instead you decide on the way that you want to bring them up and think is right, then stick with that.

Being proactive means that you do not try to do 'the right thing' according to someone else's view and then get tossed from pillar to post as different people give you different feedback. There is no external 'right thing'; there is only your decision as to what is right for you.

This means that to be successfully proactive and so to reduce your stress levels you must have a very clear idea of who you are and who you want to be. You must set your own standards. You must know exactly who you are and what you want to do in your life and what is right for you. Since being proactive means that it is you and no-one else that makes the decisions about yourself and your deeds, you also have to know on what these decisions will be based. You have to have your own Life Plan. Then, provided you live by your Life Plan you do not need to feel stressed when criticized.

If you do not know the sort of person you want to be or the type of life that is right for you then you have no goal or target. If you do not know your destination you cannot possibly know whether or not you are on the right road. You cannot know whether or not you have done the right thing and you will feel stressed anytime you are criticized for not doing the right thing, even if that 'right thing' is measured by someone else's standards and not your own.

If you do not know the type of person you want to be you cannot judge if you have behaved in such a way as to be or become that type of person. You cannot know if you have behaved rightly or wrongly against your own standards since you have no measuring stick of your own. This means that you yourself keep wondering what is the right thing or the wrong thing to do in any situation. The result is stress.

Matters are further complicated by the fact that your short-term goals will vary from day to day and time to time. One day you may want to be relaxed and have fun. You may feel like indulging yourself, to overeat, to be lenient with the children or to agree with a neighbour to avoid an argument. Another day this may seem all wrong and then you feel badly about what you ate, regret the children's lack of discipline or feel like a hypocrite for what you said to the neighbour.

Who are you, what are your beliefs? Do you feel like a leaf tossed in the wind, wondering all the time what you should be feeling and doing and, worst of all, asking the dreaded question 'Did I do the right thing?' as if there is some universal and omnipotent being out there who decrees the absolute rights and wrongs?

> Mrs R. told me that the really stressed time for her was in the afternoon once the children came home from school. She was buffeted on the one hand by her own desire to have the children love her and like her, and on the other by her husband's demands that she should be more strict with them and disciplined so that there was peace and relaxation when he got home from work rather than mayhem.

One neighbour, with an exuberant family of apparently happy but very dirty children who were always in trouble for not doing their homework, told her she was preventing her children from having any fun. The other neighbour, with a spotlessly tidy house and children who didn't say boo to a goose, told her she was teaching her children bad habits and she should train them better.

'One day,' Mrs R. told me, 'I am really strict with them and they are quiet and ready for bed when my husband gets home. The trouble is I feel awful, and I know they won't like me if I go on being so strict with them. Another day I let them play and we have a really lovely time, but I am still putting them to bed when my husband thinks I should be serving him dinner and the rest of the evening is tense. As for my neighbours, I don't know, it seems you can't please everyone.'

That last statement was the truest thing she could have said. If she had had her own Life Plan she could have settled on a course of action that was right for her in the long term, stuck with it and reduced her stress. Since she would have felt confident that she had acted in the way that she thought best, any unwanted consequence would have been acceptable to her as the result of her own reasoned decisions. She would not have had the stress of kicking herself for not having done the right thing and wishing she'd behaved differently.

If you have a long-term Life Plan then you can measure each action against this yardstick. Was one behaviour or deed that was criticized in line with your Life Plan? If so then you can relax and ignore the adverse comments as stemming from the opinions of someone else with whom you do not agree. If it wasn't, then you must recognize it as a temporary lapse, acknowledge the criticism and work on becoming more nearly the person you really want to be. If maintaining your Life Plan is a constant struggle then perhaps it is time to review your Life Plan.

How the plan can work

Here are some examples of how the plan can work. Then we will consider ways in which you can determine your own plan.

> Imagine that your Life Plan involves having a successful career, making a lot of money and being able to provide a luxurious lifestyle for yourself and your family. You want to be a success. You go into a business meeting and negotiate the possibility of taking over a smaller company that will give your own company exactly the resources it needs to double its profits. The price is high but you have a way of negotiating it down. You play your cards perfectly and the company is yours for a price you can afford. At the end of the meeting the people with whom you've been negotiating comment on how determined and strong you are and one of them says 'You're a hard person to do business with'. Because these were necessary attributes for you to be able to reach your goal you take the remarks as compliments. If you had not been clear on your goal, and if part of you had also wanted to be popular, you might have left the meeting feeling stressed and uncomfortable because the other people did not like you or thought you had been too tough.
>
> Back in your office you are praised for being strong and getting the company at the best possible price. Do you feel good? Of course you do, but not because it makes up for the criticisms you received from your opponents after the negotiations, you have no need of that. You feel good because these comments are tacit acknowledgement that you have lived rightly according to your Life Plan.

Here is another situation.

You have joined the parents' committee at the local school and been elected as its chairperson. You've done this and accepted the position because you are on your own now the children are at school and less dependent on you. You like looking after children, you like helping others and doing things with other parents, and you like people to come to you for advice and comfort. You also like to be part of whatever is going on in the social life of your neighbourhood and you want to be thought of as someone anyone can call on when in need.

There is a committee meeting to chastise one of the members for behaving badly and a vote is taken that she should be asked to resign. Not only do you make excuses for her and point out that she had problems at home but, when the vote is tied, you vote in favour of giving her a second chance.

After the meeting some of the parents come over and tell you that you're soft, have no backbone and are weak. Do you feel criticized, wrong and stressed? Of course not. You know you acted correctly by your Life Plan in which you have decided that it is more important for you to help those in need and to be someone people can turn to than to be strong and efficient.

Later, when others on the committee praise you for your compassion, do you feel good? Of course you do, but again, this is not because it makes up for the criticisms; it is because it confirms that you are living according to your own goals, your own Life Plan.

Provided you keep to your own Life Plan it is you who will be the ultimate judge of your behaviour and no-one else. If there are comments that confirm that you have acted according to your own Plan, well and good. If there are comments that suggest you have deviated from this then you may choose to make a mental note to be aware of this and behave differently in future. On the other hand, you may decide that you did the right thing and want to reassess and possibly alter your Life Plan. Keep in mind that this Life Plan is not a fixed and rigid thing. It is yours and you can change it anytime you like. But be sure that you change it after careful consideration and reassessment, not on a daily or even monthly basis in response to the last person who spoke to you.

When you behave in ways that are in line with your Life Plan you will know you have been true to yourself and done what you think is the right thing. You will know you have done the best you can to reach your goals and to enable you to have the type of life you want. If things seem to go wrong, if other people criticize you for what you have done or said, you will be able to thank them for their opinion but rest assured in the knowledge that it is their opinion, they do not know what is right for you, you have already assessed that and done your best.

This is true whatever your Life Plan is. Your Plan may be to put success above people; it may be to be so strong that nothing matters to you and no-one can hurt you, even if this means missing out on family life. It may involve being kind to and agreeing with other people, even if some call you a hypocrite. It may involve being selfish; it may involve being generous. It may involve putting your family through poverty while you pursue spiritual or artistic goals. It may involve putting other people first, it may involve putting yourself first.

It is true whether or not other people approve of your Life Plan. As long as your Life Plan is what you want to do and is important to you then when you live by it you cannot feel stressed by situations that develop as a result of this. They are merely challenges on your way to your goal. It is when you have no Plan or do not live by your Plan that unnecessary stresses develop.

Right thing, wrong thing

Much of your stress is based on the assumption that there is a Right Thing that you should do or should have done at any given time and that there are many different Wrong Things that you should not do or have done. This is nonsense.

The concept comes up in different ways and in different parts of this book but it is appropriate here to outline it starkly. There is no Right Thing that you should do. There is no Right Thing, on which everyone agrees, that you should determine ahead of time and then stick to. There is no Right Thing such that, having done it you will achieve your goals, eliminate all stress and criticism and earn praise all round.

Similarly there are no Wrong Things that you absolutely must not do, that, if done, will cause everyone to criticize you, and you to feel guilty and stressed, and to find that no-one has a good word to say for you.

You may be thinking, at this point, that there are some things that are definitely wrong and that are considered to be illegal or immoral or both. This may be true, up to a point, but it is all too often used as an excuse to remain reactive.

Take a wider view. There may be things that are illegal or immoral in your society but not in another. When making and accepting a statement, namely that there are no Absolute Right or Absolute Wrong things to do, keep this in mind. I am not advocating either anarchy, cruelty or immorality, far from it. I am endeavouring to empower you by making you set your own values. At the same time it is appropriate to keep in mind that if you choose to live comfortably in a certain society it is probably in your best interests to live within the laws and morals of that society, otherwise you have to be prepared to accept the consequences.

Beware, however, that you do not use this suggestion of adapting and fitting in as an excuse to 'bend to ALL the rules', including all the minor, unwritten and unspoken 'rules', just for the sake of it. If you do, you will be back in the position of trying to please everyone and feeling thoroughly stressed. Don't kill, but don't feel you have to live by other people's standards or by what others tell you to do or by what they think you ought to do.

Ultimately, if you do what you feel is right and important you will, by definition, be willing to accept the consequences. You won't turn to blaming other people or feeling like a victim but will know you have acted in the full awareness, from start to finish, of what you were doing, of its importance to you, and you will be willing to accept the likely or possible outcomes.

Whatever you do there will be some people who praise you and others who criticize you.

This may seem obvious when stated so boldly, yet much of the stress in your life is undoubtedly caused by the fear that you have done the Wrong Thing at some time in the past, that you are doing the Wrong Thing right now or that you will do the Wrong Thing at some time in the future.

What really matters is that you decide on what is right and what is wrong for you and then work within that frame.

In the same way there is no Wrong or Right Thing that can occur in your life. It may seem totally wrong that one lover ditches you, yet a few months later a much more compatible lover may turn up. It may seem absolutely right that you got a chance to travel but in some foreign country you may get sick. What is right for you is what fits in with and conforms to your Plan of who you want to be and the way you want your life to turn out.

Blaming others

If you do what you think is right and yet don't like the outcome you have no-one else to blame. This may seem tough as most people are all too quick to blame other people for their misfortunes. They appear to derive comfort from laying the blame on circumstances outside themselves and creating a situation where they were the helpless victim rather than the person in control. This may be an immediate response; it may seem, initially, to reduce the stress and provide some comfort, but it also leaves you in a position of helplessness.

You may choose to resent someone else for giving you bad advice, tell a second person it is all their fault as you did it all for them or a third person that they made you do something and you had really known all along that it wouldn't work. You can do any of these things but it won't help much in reducing your stress level or improving the situation and it may even add to your problem.

You will still feel stressed by whatever went wrong. You will also have added to this the stress caused by blaming the other person and the further stress caused by being angry with them, for which they in turn will blame you, or being resentful of them. In addition you will feel that life is unfair, things are stacked against you and that you haven't got a chance. All of which is conducive to victim status and lots of stress.

Guilt

The next step, very often, is to say that if it is no-one else's fault then it must be yours. If it is your fault and you are to blame then you must be stupid, silly, careless, inefficient, lazy, worthless and so forth. You blame yourself, treat yourself as stupid, silly and so on, and feel guilty. Does this make sense? Will it reduce your stress? Not at all.

Learning experiences

It is perfectly possible to have your Plan, decide what you will do according to it, find that something doesn't work or isn't leading you to your desired goal, and use this as a Learning Experience. By viewing all errors and mistakes as Learning Experiences rather than as stupid acts you can stop blaming yourself and feeling guilty. Instead you can compliment yourself for the learning steps you are experiencing and from which you are choosing to benefit. In this way you can make major strides in reducing the stress in your life. There are other benefits as well.

When you view a mistake you made as something bad and stupid, not only do you berate yourself for it, feel stressed, and then add to the stress by dwelling on the problem, but you lose a chance to benefit. When you view a mistake as a Learning Experience you can pat yourself on the back for doing it in the first place as it has taught you something and you can pat yourself on the back for being willing to put your new-found knowledge to good use and for building it into your strategies for following your Life Plan.

Perhaps you go shopping. You load up the car feeling pleased with yourself, get home and find you have forgotten one key purchase. What do you do? Do you blame yourself, call yourself an idiot? No, probably not. Hopefully you use this as a Learning Experience and decide to make a list next time.

Then what happens? You go shopping and half-way through realize you have left your list at home. Do you call yourself an idiot or do you decide that in future the list will be kept near your car keys? Let's hope you treat this too as a Learning Experience rather than a chance to apply blame.

The next time you take the list with you, use it in the first few shops and then lose it. When you get home you find it in the bottom of your bag along with other bits of paper. By now you may be ready to throw in the towel and really call yourself an idiot. After all these Learning Experiences you are still not achieving your desired goal of efficient and stress-free shopping. Perhaps you really are stupid.

Stop. Remember that the moment you give in and call your action or non-action a mistake, a fault or something for which you are to blame, you will feel stressed. Keep calling them Learning Experiences.

The next step might be to write the list on cardboard, even coloured cardboard. Whatever you do, until you have the system working perfectly, they are Learning Experiences and not mistakes, you are stress-free and, best of all, at the end you will have a marvellous new system that helps you to achieve your long-term goal of doing all the shopping in one successful trip.

This may seem a relatively trivial or simple example but the method applies to all situations.

Perhaps you are looking for promotion at work. To achieve this your division has to improve its output. One of your staff members is not performing and you call them in to tell them so. They resent this and resign. You did not want this to happen; you are now one member short on the team and your boss is upset. Call yourself an idiot if you like and take your stress out on your friends that evening, but you can also call it a Learning Experience. Pat yourself on the back for giving yourself this chance and spend time determining what you could have done differently and how you can apply this knowledge in the future.

By taking this approach you will not get the staff member back, but you will cut down on your stress and you will reap future benefit.

Mr Y. was a sales rep and had been in his present job for nine months. All was going well except with one customer on whom he called who had reduced his order by over 50 per cent in these nine months. Mr Y. felt he was an experienced and good salesman. He had tried all his usual methods to improve sales but to no avail and he had worked himself up to such a pitch that he hated visiting that shop. He blamed the shop for failing to retail properly and so for needing less product and he blamed himself for not getting the order. He was tense beforehand and depressed afterwards. His strategy hadn't changed but his opinion of himself had fallen.

The first point, discussed elsewhere, is to be willing to change what you are doing if what you are doing is not working. Mr Y. felt reluctant to change in view of his many years of experience so the first step was to get him to agree to change his strategy.

At first he was unwilling to do this but in time agreed on the basis that he would go in, not looking for an order but to treat the situation as a pure, and somewhat academic, Learning Experience. He went into the shop with the sole intent of studying the owner and hearing what

> he had to say. When he left he almost forgot to ask for the order.
> Much to his surprise he was called back and given the longest order of
> the year.

Turn stress into a Learning Experience and you can benefit in both the
short and the long term.

The benefits

Even if you do not have any plan in your life there will be times when
things go well. You do the, mythical, Right Thing and everything works
out well. If you do not have a definite Life Plan you may not be aware of
what you have done. In this case you will call it luck, be glad, yet worry
that you may not be able to achieve the same result again. So you still
feel stressed.

> Terry wanted to be popular at his new school. He had no particular Life
> Plan, no particular idea of what sort of person he wanted to be. He
> simply knew that he wanted to be popular and that he was willing to
> do anything to achieve this aim.
>
> One day when he was trying to join in with a group that had stead-
> fastly ignored him he suddenly found himself drawn into the group.
> They all seemed to want to hear what he had to say and he felt a glow
> of belonging. At last he had done the Right Thing and had been
> accepted by his peers. The next day he again tried to join them but they
> did not welcome him.
>
> Terry had no way of knowing what it was that had made him
> acceptable one day and not the other. It could have been that one day
> he had the answers to some homework problem that was troubling the
> group; he could have had some gossip they wanted; they could have
> been impressed with his confidence or his reluctance to tell tales.

> Because he did not have a behaviour pattern that he had deter-
> mined upon he was left with trying to please the others yet not
> knowing how to.

If you suddenly forge ahead at work, get on better with your family, make friends more easily, make a wise investment, strike a closer rapport with your daughter, find you are more relaxed or lose the pain in your chest, and you were behaving at random, you cannot truly claim the benefit as yours and feel confident that you can repeat it. You may even feel a fraud since things are going well without you knowing how or why.

On the other hand, if you have a Life Plan and act within it you will know that all the good things that happen, the things that cause you pleasure and satisfaction, are caused by you, are repeatable and will continue to lead you towards your goals.

Designing your life plan

Now that we have discussed the benefits of having a Life Plan and the problems and stresses that will result inevitably if you do not, it is time for you to create one. You may find this a simple task or you may find it difficult. You may find it an exciting opportunity, a way of spelling out your idea of Utopia and defining exactly all the good things you want. Or you may find it a daunting, difficult and frightening task.

Personally I have thoroughly enjoyed designing my Life Plan and changing it as appropriate and found it a stimulating experience so I was considerably surprised when one workshop participant told me it had been the most traumatic part of the weekend. Since then I have found that many people find it very difficult so do not feel unusual if you come into this category.

If you enjoy the idea then set to and do it. If you find the task too challenging and want to avoid it, all I can tell you is that it is worse if you don't have one. You have already seen how much of the stress in your life comes from having no specific plan. This stress will always be greater than the one of creating the plan, yet it's like having a toothache. Some people will put up with a toothache for days or weeks rather than face the hour of discomfort needed at the dentist's to correct the problem.

Find a quiet time when you can be introspective and have a paper and pen with you. Your aim is to write down your goals in life, the things you want to achieve, the things you find important, the type of person you want to be, the circumstances in which you want to live, the people you would like to have around you, and so forth.

While you are doing this keep in mind that this is a secret plan. Imagine that you will tell no-one what you are doing, no-one will see what you are writing, no-one will know the result. If you write a set of goals that seem to you to be asking too much, wanting to have the impossible or asking for more than you feel you deserve, no-one will know. If you have been pretending that your life is fine and you are happy, when in fact you are in pain with the things that are wrong, don't worry, these inner feelings will not be exposed. If you write the noblest of goals and plan a life of self-sacrifice no-one will read your notes and applaud. This list is for your eyes only. You may burn it at the end or you may keep the latest version and put it in a safe place.

When you have done the very best you can we will consider ways in which you can refine it and possibly even improve on it.

So start now. The steps will, of course, vary depending on your age, sex and current life situation so do whichever of the following applies to you. A final word of advice before you start. Do not let yourself be restricted by the present, by common sense, by convention, by what other people expect, or by your feelings of what you deserve. You have a free hand, use it. This is your chance to create your life and your future exactly the way you want them to be. More importantly, it is your chance to define who you want to be and what is important to you.

Firstly think about the people in your life

1 People generally

How important are people in your life? Do you want to have lots of people around or do you prefer to be on your own much of the time? Do you want to have a large circle of family, friends and acquaintances or just a few?

2 Family

You have existing family and you will acquire new family members as people marry and have children. Plan who you would like to have in the family, how close you would like them to be, how you would like those relationships to be.

Include your parents. Assess your relationship with them now and consider any changes you would like to make or any improvements you would like to achieve. It is common for people to have difficulties and issues with their parents as well as with other family members, no matter how close those people are. The relationships can all be improved.

3 Friends

Do you want lots of friends, a few close friends, different groups of friends for different reasons or do you prefer to be on your own? How much do you value other people in your life? You can learn a lot about yourself from these answers.

4 Marriage/partner

If you are single, do you want to marry? If so, when? If not, what are your reasons and what type of relationship would you like to have, if any, instead? What does this tell you about yourself and what can you learn from it? Go ahead and plan your ideal loving relationship or situation. How close would you want it to be? How much space and freedom would you want within it?

If you are married, is the relationship perfect? How would you like it to change?

5 Children

Do you want children? If so, when do you want to have them and how many? What sex would you like them to be? How would you like your family relationships and activities to be?

What about grandchildren? Answer the same questions in relation to them.

6 Colleagues

What type of people would you like to work with? What sort of relationship would you like to have with those who work for you and with those for whom you work?

Now turn your attention to possessions

1 Money

How much money do you want? Is money important to you and if so why? Is it money itself or the things you can do with it? What does this say about you? What can you learn from this? Consider the financial status that will suit you best and with which you will feel comfortable. Some people feel they would enjoy unlimited wealth, others would feel burdened by it. Some people feel it is worth striving for, others feel it is of secondary importance. Consider how you will feel when you have this amount. Will the effort to obtain it have been worth it or will you feel the struggle has led you to a barren place? Will you enjoy it or will you feel guilty at your affluence?

2 Your home

Is your home important to you or is it of no consequence? If it is, why is this so? What does this say about you? What can you learn from this? Where would you like to live? Which country would you like to live in? Remember there are no restrictions, you can choose to live anywhere in the world.

What type of dwelling would you like – large or small, house, flat, boat, caravan, hotel, or something entirely different? Plan it in detail.

Would you like more than one home? If so, detail them. Now furnish your home or homes.

3 Car

Is a car important to you, and if so, is the type of car you drive of importance? If it is, why is this so? What does this say about you? What can you learn from this? Cars are very important to many people, sometimes for practical reasons, sometimes for image or other reasons. Consider all the types of car that are available and make your choice.

4 Other possessions

What else would you like in your life in the way of material possessions? Are possessions important to you? If so, why? What does that say about you? Make a list of all the things you would like in your life and describe them fully.

5 Assessment

Did this emphasis on material things and possessions excite you or irritate you? How did you feel when focusing on material things? What does this say about you and what can you learn about this?

Remember this is a very private time. There are no brownie points for your answers. You will not score more if you had high aspirations or if you were very non-greedy and non-acquisitive. The important thing is for you to find out as much about yourself and your aims and goals as you can.

Now let's move on to activities

1 Work

How do you view work? Is work important to you as an end in itself, as a means of self-expression, or as a statement of your abilities and interests? Is it a means to an end, a way to acquire the money or the wherewithall to achieve your other goals? What does this say about you and what can you learn from this?

Now consider the nature of your work. What do you want to do and why? What are the important features you would like to have incorporated into your work, the activities, the people, the surroundings, the status? What satisfactions would your chosen work provide?

Do you want to work? Would you rather have limited income and not work at all? Would you rather subsist and have your time free to pursue hobbies? Would you rather make a home and have someone else support you and earn the money?

If you plan to work for a short while, how long would that be? When would you like to stop? If you plan a longer working life, when do you plan to retire? What do you plan to do then? What would you like to be able to do when you do retire?

2 Travel
Would you like to travel? If so, how much, where to and for how long?

3 Hobbies
What are the things you like to do as hobbies, sports or pastimes? How much time do you like to spend doing them? What purpose or function do they achieve in your life? Do you consider them valuable and important or indulgences?

4 Balance
What balance do you wish to have between work and play, between being alone and socializing, between being a family person and being involved in the community at large?

5 Spiritual and religious values and beliefs
What do you believe in? How important is it to you? What time do you want to devote to these values and how much else are you willing to modify for their sake? How do they affect your life? Write down your beliefs and their importance to you.

You

Now we come to the hard part and this concerns you. We started in the above sequence and left you till last because in general this is the part with which people have the most difficulty, though of course for some people this is the easiest part. By now, too, as a result of going through the above you may have learnt more about yourself and have developed a clearer idea than you had before of where you want to go in life.

1 You

What are you like, what is important to you? Do you want to be creative or practical? Do you want to be a success materially or is it more important that you do certain other things that satisfy you? Do you want to have a good time? Do you want to do good for others?

Do not become analytical and worry about whether or not you are being selfish or generous, lazy or successful. Implicit in much that we have discussed elsewhere is the idea that you will have the most to give others when you first fulfil your own needs and are true to them.

What is your purpose in choosing your work activity? Do you want to do what interests you, what helps other people, what is respected by other people or what other people expect you to do? Do you choose to do whatever job comes along, not really caring what it is, or the best-paid job, putting the money first?

Why do you want children – because it is the normal thing to do, because you love them, because you want family for your old age?

Consider your health, how you expect it to be, how you would like it to be and what you can do to create your desired outcome. In early workshops on *Choosing Health Intentionally* participants were given a form to complete in which they were asked what they expected their health to be like in five years' time, in ten years' time, at fifty, at seventy and beyond. Without exception they answered 'Good'. There was no real awareness of the way their body might age unless they took better care of it than they were doing at present. Like the rats we learnt. We soon gave up that questionnaire as being unproductive!

Take a serious look at your own health and the health of your family. Realistically, what can you expect from your present level of healthcare? How would you like to change this to maintain your present good health throughout the coming decades or to improve your health in the future?

What traits do you wish to develop? Do you want to be ruthless and strong, or soft and supportive? Do you want to help others or get the best for yourself? Do you want to create, inter-relate and achieve certain recognitions? Do you want to care for others or be taken care of, study more or have more fun? What, at the end of your life, will have made it all worthwhile?

What are your goals and drives at the personal level? There are so many aspects to this that it is impossible for me to trigger your thinking on all of them. It is time now for you to complete your own personal Life Plan at the emotional, spiritual and attitudinal levels.

2 Your looks

Is the way you look important to you? If it is, why is this so? What does this say about you? What can you learn from this? Plan what you would have in your ideal wardrobe. What figure would you like, are you too slim or too fat? Is your hair the way you want it? Plan the ideal image you would like to present to the world. Obviously there are certain limitations here; you cannot suddenly become three inches taller or shorter, but you might be surprised at the transformations that could be brought about after some radical changes to your diet, hairstyle, make-up, beard and so forth.

Your future

The next part concerns your future. A useful way to assess whether or not you have really chosen the ideal Life Plan for you is to go forward into the future. Having created a very clear picture of the sort of person you want to be and the sort of life you want to lead go forward five years, then ten, then fifty years. If you are older you will adjust your time-spans accordingly.

1 The present

Even the present is really the future, if only moments into the future. How is your present on a day-to-day basis? Is it, following the guidelines that you have created, turning out to be satisfying or are there changes you want to make? There is no point in living every day for some distant future if you are not pleased and satisfied on a day-to-day basis. Sacrificing the present for some distant future is a sure recipe for severe stress. The future may never come, it may not come in the way you anticipate or, when it comes, it may turn out to be other than you expected. Make sure that you enjoy the journey as much as the destination.

2 Five or ten years

Check out how you will feel five or ten years from now as you look back over your past. Has it all been appropriate, has it been worthwhile? Have what you have done, the way you've behaved and the achievements you've had been desirable and satisfying?

3 Distant future

Repeat the above exercise at intervals between your present age and the possible end to your life-span as you approach 100 or more or less. It may surprise you to find that things you think are important now will not seem the same way in the future and in retrospect. Things that stress you now may seem of little consequence five or fifty years into the future.

From the vantage point of these various futures look back on your life as it has been lived according to your Life Plan. Has it been worthwhile? Has it fulfilled your needs? If so, well and good. If not, then reappraise your Life Plan and repeat the exercise.

Corrections and improvements

Even having done this you may not have discovered your real aims and goals. A colleague said that he had chosen his role in the healing professions because he wanted to make people healthier and to serve others. He had designed and described his Life Plan accordingly.

When pushed further he concluded that his real goal was to make the world a better and happier place for people to live. It took a further push for him to discover his real goal, namely that he wanted the world to be a better place so that he would live in a better world which would mean he would be happier.

In other words, deep down his goal was to be happy. In fact his professional life had been frustrating him for some years which caused him considerable stress both in itself and because he kept insisting that this shouldn't be so as he was doing what he really wanted to do.

With this further realization he rethought his life again. He decided to work less hard and to spend more time on the hobbies he had been neglecting. In this way he found a balance that satisfied him, reduced his stress levels and brought joy into his life. He found he could serve others and also be happy himself when he created the appropriate balance of work and play and when he fully understood his goals in life.

A way to delve down to your real goals is to use the 'Running a phrase' technique already described.

Mr V. had determined that making a lot of money was important to him, and that one of his major goals was to be wealthy. He had, in fact, been successful and at 40 he was earning more money than any of his friends and had twice the assets, yet he wasn't happy and he still felt stressed. In fact he felt even more stressed since having made the sort of money he thought was important he still didn't feel relaxed or that he had achieved anything that satisfied him.

He was told to run the phrase 'A reason I want to be wealthy is ...' and came up with conclusions such as '... so I can travel', '... so I can do the things I want to do', '... so I can afford the best hotels and restaurants', '... so that I can have wonderful and glamorous holidays'. When I asked him if he was doing any of these things he admitted that he wasn't, though he could well afford to. He was so programmed into making money that he hadn't thought about spending it or about changing his activity. Not until he realized what his true Life Plan was could he release the frustrations and stresses of his situation and get his life back on track.

~

Mrs A. claimed that her Life Plan was to help other people. She looked after her family, devoted her life to her children and fitted in with her husband's wants and needs, never insisting on doing what she wanted at the weekend but letting him choose what they would do. She helped on a number of committees for her church and her children's school, she would help any neighbour or friend who needed her and she did all she could to support other family members who were in difficulties. She had sufficient income to have a housekeeper and was not run off her feet by all the help she gave yet she wasn't happy and complained of feeling dissatisfied with her life. She even went so far as to say 'If only there was more I could do, then maybe I could feel I'd achieved something'.

It seemed likely that there was some other deeper goal in her life that was not being satisfied so she was told to run the phrase 'A reason I like to help people is ...'. At first she came up with such completions as '... because they need help', '... because it's the right thing to do', '... because I have more than they have' but eventually we got to the heart of the matter. I changed the phrase to 'A benefit I will get from helping people is ...' to which her third and fourth completions were '... they will like me' and '... I will be popular'.

It turned out that her real goal was to be popular and liked. She had been taught in childhood that she should be good and help others, then she would be rewarded, then she would be mother's little darling and mother's little help. As the eldest of three children she had been amply rewarded with acknowledgement and appreciation when she helped out and she had soon learnt that this was the way to be popular.

Having recognized that this was her real aim she was able to act differently and target her energies in such a way that she spent more time on social activities and soon built up a large circle of friends. She still went on helping people – that was deeply embedded in her nature – but she stopped being at everyone's beck and call. She altered the balance in her life between helping others and her socializing in such a way that it was in line with her true Life Plan.

Other people

From the above I hope I have made it clear that it is you and you alone who is designing your Life Plan. Do it for yourself, keep it private and produce a Plan that works *for you*. When you live with this you can reduce your stress and be happy.

I have recently come across several suggestions, in books and in discussion, that you should consider and assess your life, at its end, from the point of view of what other people would say and think of it.

The suggestion has been made that you should visualize your own funeral and imagine what is being said, by your friends and family and all the people who knew you or knew of you and about your life, and that you should value what they think of you. If they do not assess you and your life favourably and in the way you would like them to assess it, so goes the suggestion, then perhaps you should consider changing the way you lead your life.

Alternatively, it is suggested that you should consider what you would say to them at your own funeral, were that possible, as you considered and assessed your life yourself Would you be able to feel confident as you told them what you had done and achieved, or would you feel that they were assessing you and finding your life wanting?

This worries me greatly and, in my view, could set you up for a lot of stress. It takes us right back to trying to please all of the people all of the time, an impossible task.

At the end of my life I want to be able to look back on it, assess it *myself* and find it good. I will then not mind what other people think. In this way there can be no stress inflicted on me by other people. Who are they to judge my life? Only I can do that and only I will live with the consequences. There may be regret, when the time comes, but at least I will know that I did the best I could along the way and by *my* standards. Decide on what *you* want to do and be and what you think is worthwhile, then live accordingly.

The real role of other people

While recognizing that you no longer want to live by what other people think, to live to conform to their standards or to be ruled by their opinion of you, it is still appropriate to consider an outside view of yourself.

How would you like to appear to other people? What would you like other people to say about you? Would you like them to consider you had been a successful leader or a willing helper, a good family person, quietly independent, strong and tough or a gentle and caring provider? Mentally offer up your Life Plan and the results it is likely to achieve to some people you trust and whose opinion you value. Are you happy with their opinion or does it show you things of which you might be ashamed or with which you may feel uncomfortable?

The next step is not, as you might possibly imagine, to change your Life Plan but rather to contemplate quietly why their opinion of the Life Plan you have so diligently fashioned makes you uncomfortable. The reason may give you further information about your early programming. When you have assessed this you can then consider, quietly and in your own time, whether or not you actually do want to change your Plan.

Mrs A. above, felt most uncomfortable when she went through this part of the process. She felt people would criticize her for not continuing to devote all of her time to others and that many of the family

~

might stop showing her the love and affection she valued. As she thought this through she realized that this came from the early patterns her mother had established. She also recalled that several of her family and friends were often telling her to slow down, do less, and have more time for herself. Thus she decided to go ahead with her Plan unchanged.

~

Mr C., on the other hand, had as part of his Plan an aim to be the most successful lawyer in his firm and to pull in the largest fees. He said he was willing to do whatever it took to achieve this so that he and his wife could have a luxurious yacht, invite their friends out sailing at weekends and entertain in lavish style. When he viewed this from the perspective of several other people he found that, although he was comfortable with the opinion of colleagues who might criticize him for being too greedy, he was not comfortable about his friends' view that he was doing it for show, and possibly making them feel uncomfortable since they could not return such lavish hospitality. He then realized that he could have as much fun and find the social acceptance he craved in his new and adopted country by spending more social time chatting with his colleagues at work and meeting up with friends for quiet and casual dinners in the evening. Once he recognized that he didn't need the boat he altered his Plan somewhat. He still chose to strive for excellence but he became more thoughtful and aware of other people and their feelings. In so doing he also developed a confidence that he was liked and wanted for himself and not for the material things he could offer to other people.

Once you have it

This whole process may take time. It could take months or years. Alternatively you may already have a firm idea of who you are and who you want to be. Keep in mind that this is an ongoing and flexible process. At any stage you can change your goals and your aims, but do not, as we have discussed elsewhere, do this on a whim. Any changes to your Plan should only be made after serious thought.

It might help you to create a visual image of the type of person you want to be and the life you would like to have. If you want to be wealthy and travel the world make a collage of pictures from magazines that depict this. Then when people criticize you and say that you work too hard you can smile and picture the far-away places on the collage. If you want to be a homemaker make the appropriate collage with scenes of happy family life, then you can ignore the people who say you are vegetating. If political life is important or a quiet life in the country, then make the appropriate pictures.

Whatever it takes, make a very clear picture for yourself of the type of person you want to be and the things and attributes you value. Then when you are criticized for doing certain things, provided they are in line with your own set of values and your long-term goals, you need not feel stressed. You will only feel stressed when you are untrue to yourself.

To summarize

First make your Plan, then live by it. In this way you can greatly reduce the stress in your life and prevent the endless buffeting as you are tossed from one possible course of action to another. You will not worry and fret about doing, saying or thinking the wrong thing, or that people will criticize you. You will not live in fear that you will have regrets at a later date. You will take charge of your life rather than let life take charge over you.

When you have a Plan that is right for you, you will know where you are going and how to get there in the future. You will also have more knowledge of how you have got to your present position. You will have the peace of knowing that, if you were suddenly to lose everything, you could re-establish your life all over again rapidly and smoothly, knowing exactly where you wanted to go and what you wanted to achieve.

You will no longer be buffeted by the, usually conflicting, views of others. If you want to be wealthy and successful in business and to provide an affluent lifestyle for yourself and your family you will not feel criticized or stressed when someone calls you tough, strong, independent, a go-getter or any such phrase. You have already decided it is all right to be these things; they are part of your nature and you know where they are taking you.

If you want to be a caring family provider, making a comfortable home for your family, being there when you are needed and providing lots of nurture then you need not feel criticized or stressed when your career friends call you dull and uninteresting because you are not up with the latest fashions or stock prices.

If your most important goal is to create great works of art you will not care about people who call you a lazy drifter with no thought for other people.

If you want to lead a life of service and support people in difficulties you need not feel embarrassed by the well-worn furniture when your well-off friends come to visit.

As long as you have a clear idea of what you value, what is important to you and how you want your life to be, and as long as you work towards and conform with these goals, you need not feel stressed by any adverse criticism, and adverse criticism is a major source of stress in most people's lives.

CHAPTER FOURTEEN

You Are Terrific

Self-criticism

Most people hate to be criticized. Some profess not to mind and to use the information thus gleaned for positive goals such as self-improvement. Few, very few, enjoy it. Yet almost everyone criticizes themselves. You probably do.

They criticize themselves to other people, sometimes out of a real belief that they deserve to be criticized; sometimes to get their comments in first before other people criticize them; sometimes in the hope that other people will deny the criticism and thus validate them; and sometimes in the hope of receiving a compliment in reply. They also silently criticize themselves much of the time. You do it, everybody does it, to a greater or lesser degree.

If you doubt this then listen to the conversation the next time you are with a group of friends who feel free to relax and chatter together. Ask people how they feel about themselves. You will almost certainly find they give you more self-criticism than self-compliment. Listen to the chatter going on inside your own head. How much of that is criticism and how much is complimentary?

If you spend time criticizing yourself you cannot be relaxed and happy. If you are constantly criticizing yourself you are going to feel stressed. If, on the other hand, you feel you are terrific, and if you are happy with yourself and with your own judgment, then a stress-free life is going to be much easier to achieve. After all, if you feel good about yourself, like yourself and feel happy with the way you are, then the criticisms of others will merely represent their opinions and will be more a reflection of them than of you, with no power to hurt, wound or stress you.

Just as someone who likes Bach and hates the Beatles is telling you the type of person they are, so someone who likes you and dislikes someone else is also telling you what type of person they are - *not* what type of person Bach and you are on any absolute scale.

Learn to love yourself

It is time to start liking yourself, praising yourself, complimenting yourself for your achievements and for what you are and, above all, it is time for loving yourself. Learn to love yourself not in a narcissistic way, but in the sense of valuing yourself caring for yourself and approving of yourself. Acknowledge yourself for the efforts you have made, be willing to forgive yourself when things have not gone the way you planned. In other words, be willing to be as kind to yourself and do as much for yourself as you would for someone you love.

Now before you jump up and down and say this is conceited, self-centred and egotistical, let's just pursue this further. I am not suggesting that you constantly spend time telling people how wonderful you are and that you are the best possible person and better than them or anyone else. This is not a competition. I am suggesting that you develop a quiet content with the way you are. Equally you do not have to believe you are perfect as you are, and that there is nothing whatsoever that you need to change. That is indeed arrogant and is not what I mean.

It is perfectly possible to like yourself in a quiet, positive but non-aggressive way. It is also possible to like yourself just the way you are, be pleased with what you have achieved and have become and yet still have plans to change, grow, develop and improve further.

Keep in mind also what was said in an earlier chapter about loving a child but not necessarily liking what he or she did on any given occasion. You may think you are wonderful yet still decide that what you did yesterday was not perhaps the best and plan to change the way you behave in the future.

When this happens, still give yourself total love and approval, approval for having done your best at the time, approval for recognizing the need to change it further and approval for being willing to change in the future. You may indeed like yourself thoroughly but want and plan to change some aspect of yourself in the coming months. After all, you no doubt felt thrilled at school when you did well in a particular exam, yet you still planned to study more and learn more in that subject.

Liking and loving yourself in this context means total acceptance of and appreciation for, the way you are right now. It is a quiet, peaceful and positive emotion. It does not need the blessing of other people. They do not have to feel the same way about you that you do about yourself. They do not have to like you for you to have permission to like yourself. It is impossible that everyone will like you. This is an impossible goal and yet this thought can cause you enormous stress if you are not comfortable with yourself.

If you are not comfortable with yourself then you had better do something about this, and you and only you can do it. No-one else can make this change for you. The change comes about in two ways. Firstly stop giving yourself a hard time and decide right now, this minute and with no further change, that you like yourself totally. You may also decide, right now, that there are things you want to change about yourself. That is all right; the two things can happen at once – total acceptance plus a desire to make changes. Liking yourself is an ongoing process, so is life and so is your own development.

Remember that you have been programmed from childhood onwards to put other people ahead of yourself, in what you do and in what you think. You have been programmed to like and value yourself less than you like and value other people. You have almost certainly been programmed *not* to boast about the things you do well, *not* to expect or demand to come first in queues, *not* to expect and demand the best of everything as if by right.

While much of this is good manners and consideration for others the underlying message to your subconscious is that you were *not* good

enough, *not* as good as the others. So it is not surprising if you feel somewhat uncomfortable when you start telling yourself that you are terrific.

To demonstrate what I mean we will start with some of your physical
attributes. Are you overweight? Your answer is probably yes, since most
people seem to consider themselves to be overweight. If you think you are
overweight there is no constructive point in calling yourself a great flat
slob, berating yourself for being a glutton, starting a diet, failing because
you don't really think you deserve or are good enough to be slim and then
berating yourself for this failure.

Instead, tell yourself that you have a great body, that it is temporarily
a little too large and then decide whether or not this is the right time to
do something about it. It is much easier to stick to a diet when you like
yourself than when you consider yourself to be in league with beached
whales.

Your weight is something over which you do have control. Even if you do
have trouble dieting, you can lose weight. Anyone who reduces their daily
intake consistently will see results; you do have the option. (For further help
in this regard see *Choosing Weight Intentionally* by the same author.)

Your height is something about which you can do little so instead of
criticizing the way it is, tell yourself you like it. If you are tall and have
been telling yourself for years that you would rather be small and petite,
stop. You cannot change your height. If you tell yourself you hate being
tall you will be unhappy. If you tell yourself you love being tall you can
relax and like this attribute. Focus on all the advantages of being tall
rather than the perceived disadvantages. You can then walk tall and concentrate on the benefits instead of slouching along trying to look
invisible. Since you cannot change the physical actuality, change your
beliefs and preferences. You may be surprised to find how easy it is to do
this once you have practised a little.

Do you like your hair? If it is the wrong colour you can change it. If it
is straight and you want curls you can create them. If it is light and fine
and you would rather have a thick and heavy curtain of hair there is little

you can do about it other than buy a wig. Do this if it pleases you. At the same time start telling yourself that you love your fine and soft hair and that there are so many things you can do with it that would be impossible with heavy straight hair. Soon you will come to love your hair the way it is. Focus on what works and you have another attribute of yourself with which you are perfectly happy and content.

Start applying the 10 points outlined in the introduction to yourself and to your opinion of yourself. Take control of your thoughts and focus on the ones that serve you best. You may argue that it is hypocritical to say you love being a woman when you would rather be a man, that you love having a large nose when you would rather have a small one, that you love being intelligent when you would rather be attractive. But if these thoughts are making you unhappy then there is little to be gained by hanging on to them.

Work in the same way on your mental and emotional attributes. Consider what they are, consider which ones you want to change and set about changing them if this is possible, but above all come to terms with yourself.

Apply these ideas and exercises to everything about you that does not please you. Accept that you are the way you are for a reason. Accept that, however much you may dislike one of your attributes, there are people who envy you for it and people who benefit from it. If someone calls you uncaring there will be someone else who will value your independence. If you are stupid there is someone who will feel less stupid m your company or who will enjoy the chance to be helpful.

There are many exercises you can do. A common one is to look at your image in the mirror and say 'I love you' and observe the mirror image saying the same thing back to you. Another one is to create the image of someone you love, *feel* the emotions you have for them, and then put your own face into the image while still holding on to the feelings you had. You can do this in your mind or use a photogaph, although doing it mentally is usually much more powerful. Or observe, in your mind's eye, a small child, unknown to you, being badly treated by an adult and experience the warmth, love and compassion you can feel for them, then in your imagination put yourself at the receiving end of those emotions. It may surprise you to realize how much more love you have to give to other people than you can spare for yourself.

Do whatever it takes but learn to love and accept yourself for the beautiful person you are. This one step alone can greatly reduce the stress in your life.

CHAPTER FIFTEEN

Playing God and Being Perfect

There are other situations that can cause you worry and stress that I put in the 'playing God and being perfect' category. For all the best reasons you stress yourself for not having been perfect in the past, for not creating the best possible situation in the present and for not preventing stress in the lives of other people.

Past guilts and letting the past go

Do you feel stressed by things you did in the past? Do you feel guilty over some of the things you have done? Do you have regrets over some of the decisions you have made? Do these past situations and occurrences add to your present stress levels?

You may wish you had chosen a different job or a different partner. You may wish you had said something to a friend in need or not said something during a row. You may have made decisions that caused you to lose money, lose friends or miss opportunities. You may wish you had appreciated people more; perhaps they have died and it is now too late to tell them. You may be able to look back on an event or a time which you now recognize as having been the source of subsequent stresses.

When this happens it is often difficult to let this past situation go. You may keep harking back to it in your mind, blaming and castigating yourself for what you did or didn't do. In this way you are heaping stresses on yourself.

STOP! You cannot change the past. All the worry and fret over it will do nothing to change the future. All you will do is create more problems, for yourself and for other people, as you focus on it rather than on the here and now.

This may be easier said than done, yet dropping the past is one big step in reducing your stress levels. Ask yourself if you meant, at the time, to create problems for yourself. Almost certainly you didn't. Almost certainly you did what you thought was for the best at the time. You acted out of the wisdom you had at that time and the needs you had at that time. It is time now to acknowledge that, not beat yourself up further.

Being perfect

You don't call yourself an idiot for having done some arithmetic incorrectly at seven years old just because you know how to do it now. You did not demand that you were perfect then. You recognize this as a step in your learning curve. Be willing to do this with other things you have done that you are now calling mistakes.

It may even be that you would readily forgive other people if they had done the same thing, yet you are not willing to forgive yourself. It may be that you would have understood the same actions if someone else had made them, yet you are unwilling to give yourself the same understanding.

How arrogant. How come it is all right for other people to have made mistakes, but not you? How come you should be perfect when it is all right if they are not?

Above all, remember your aim here. It is to reduce your present stress levels and to create a less stressed future for yourself. Focusing on errors of the past does not achieve this.

One way to make it easier for you to let the past go is to look for benefits that have come out of it. There may be some major benefits, there may only be minor ones. Whatever they are, look for them, find them, and be willing to focus on them.

One patient came to see me because she was lonely and single. Many years earlier she had been proposed to by someone of whom she was very fond but whom she had not been willing to marry at the time. Now she was regretting it and daily berated herself for a decision that had led her to a lonely life.

She was told to run the phrase 'A benefit I got out of not marrying Jim was ...' and came up with more positive completions than there is space for here. They included a variety of different jobs that she had enjoyed, travel that would not have been possible had she married, a better financial state and many freedoms that would have been denied her had she taken on the responsibilities of marriage and children.

From her vantage point of the present she thought these poor compensation for being married but she did agree that when she focused on them rather than filling her mind with regrets she felt more relaxed and at peace. She was also able to admit that marriage to Jim might not have worked out all that well.

Another patient regretted a career decision he had made to please his parents. By focusing on the benefits he had derived from the choice he had made he came to recognize all the financial rewards and reduce his stress by focusing on those rather than on the frustrations of some aspects of his present job.

Another woman, having been left some money in a settlement, had bought into a business and promptly lost all of it and had to sell her home to cover the debts. When she agreed to focus on the benefits she had derived from the situation rather than the financial loss she was able to recognize she had made some powerful contacts. Out of these she started a new business venture which, happily, involved no risk capital and turned out to be very lucrative, such that within two years she was again able to buy her own home and have income to spare.

Had she continued to focus on the wrong decision of the past she might never have accomplished this.

Some

A man had recently retired and, getting bored, decided to buy into his own business. This too lost money. When challenged to find a benefit that came out of the situation he did admit that his marriage had looked very rocky when he was at home all day. With this new challenge his wife had joined forces with him and they were working together as a team in a way they both appreciated.

Some

Another man was full of regret about his relationship with his parents. He felt he had not appreciated them in the past. He had left home at the earliest possible opportunity, feeling he had outgrown them, and led his own life, sharing little with them. Now, with children of his own, he recognized many of the positive things his parents had done for him and appreciated some of the difficulties they had experienced as his education and activities took him in directions in which they couldn't follow. Since they were both dead he couldn't communicate with them and his guilt caused him a lot of stress.

Focusing on the benefits to come out of this situation brought little comfort to him until it was suggested that he use these insights to help him in his communication with his own children as they grew up and thus to acknowledge the benefit deriving from the otherwise stressful memories of the past.

Accept yourself

Be content to be less than perfect. Above all, keep in mind that you cannot change the past. You are not omnipotent. You cannot change what you have done. If there is something you can do to right the wrong then do it. But if there is not then focus on the benefits that have come from it. Wonderful children from a bad marriage, helpful learning experiences from past mistakes, wonderful friends from a poor choice of job, new friends when you hurt old ones, learning to think before you speak after you realize how easily your sharp tongue can hurt someone. Benefit from the past where possible then forgive yourself and let it go. Do not continue to berate yourself for your mistakes and for being less than perfect.

For some people there is a sin in this freedom and redemption. It's as if, by continuing to feel guilty, unhappy and stressed about the past situation, as they burden themselves with regret they in some way expiate the sin. Not so. You will not help the other people involved in the past situation by continuing to feel stressed yourself in the present. You will not be less caring, less loving or less regretful when you forgive yourself for what you are perceiving as past errors, but you will feel less stressed in the present.

You are blaming yourself for not being perfect in the past. Would you blame other people for not being perfect or do you understand that they are fallible, they are doing the best they can and that we all make mistakes? If you can be understanding about them but not about yourself it is time you considered this. Why should you be better than them? You are human and fallible too.

Mrs K. was telling me all about the mistake she had made when she persuaded her husband to buy their present home. He had wanted to buy another newer one that she thought had no character; she had opted for an older and larger cottage with wonderful old beams and rooms that showed off their antiques to advantage. Their current stress was due to the many costly repairs the house had needed in spite of the good builder's report they had had prior to purchase.

'I should have known,' she said, 'I should have let my husband choose, I should have realised the building assessor was being too optimistic. I shouldn't have insisted on the extra space.'

She went on in this vein for some time, insisting it was all her fault that they had bought the old house and were in their current financial difficulties.

Try as I might I couldn't stop the flow of words as she pointed out the many reasons why it was all her fault. Finally I took a stand and, looking as severe as I could, I said:

'Stop being so arrogant.'

That did the trick. She paused in mid-sentence and was about to tell me how rude I was when I continued.

'You are assuming you should have known more than a specialist in the field. You are assuming you have total capacity to dictate to your husband and that he had no say in the matter whatsoever. You are assuming that he and everyone else in the family had to do, and did, exactly what you said. Do you think so little of your husband that you deny him his input into the decision?'

'Well,' she sat back and started to think things over in the light of these statements, 'I suppose you're right. When you put it like that I suppose he could have refused to buy it. I suppose he did agree to go along with my choice rather than insist on his. I suppose too that it was more up to him than to me to investigate the credentials of the building assessor. After all, he did appoint him, not me.'

We continued the talk in this vein. When she realized that he had indeed had some input too she was gradually able to absolve herself of some of the guilt, but what really did the trick was my use of the word arrogant and her recognition of the implications behind this point of view. When she considered this she was able to forgive herself and give up the self-criticism and the stress this was causing her now.

~

Mr T. was a somewhat similar case. He blamed himself for errors he had made in business as a result of which it was not as successful as he felt it should have been. This meant that the family had less money than he would have liked. They were less well off than their relations. His wife's sister had married well and her brother had been very successful in his career. As a result, at family gatherings he was conscious that his children were less well-dressed than the others and that their car was the shabbiest in the drive. He felt dreadful when his wife complained in a similar vein. She also entertained less and less and was lonely. He insisted on taking an extra job in an effort to supplement their income but then had little time for his family. Marital relations were clearly deteriorating.

He insisted it was all his fault they had so little money, his fault the business was not doing well, his fault that they had three children when they only wanted two, his fault his wife had so few friends, his fault that the marriage was looking increasingly shaky, his fault for being stressed and so not having the patience to deal with the situation at home.

Again it took a strong statement to stop his flow of self-blame. This time it was:

'Stop being so selfish.'

'What? That's one thing I am not. I may have been stupid in the past but I am not selfish. I am trying to do all I can for my family and for my wife.'

'I know,' I explained, 'but you are not willing to share responsibility with her. You are not willing to recognize that she had input into the situation too. She chose to marry you, with all your strengths and all your weaknesses. She contributed to having three children. She chooses to place more importance on the way she and the children dress than on the family relationships. She, as well as you, has had input into the situation you are both now in. By claiming total responsibility what are you doing to her? You are not allowing her to share in the problem, you are not acknowledging her as an adult, you are not willing to let her go out and earn some extra money, now the children are at school. That's what I mean by you being selfish. Above all, by demanding for yourself all the blame you are more stressed than you need be and are thus contributing to problems within the family and you are denying her the right to contribute to a positive solution.'

Again it was this new way of looking at the situation that changed the way he was willing to view the past. He was then able to discuss things much more fully with his wife, as a result of which they were able to make important changes in their lives. By being willing to stop blaming himself and not insisting that he should have been perfect he was able to be less stressed and this was of benefit to other people as well as to himself.

Being omnipotent

Stress may also come when you worry about other people. You want your partner to do well. You want your children to be happy, to have the right job, to marry well, to be successful and safe. You want your friends to be happy. You feel stressed when you think of things happening to them that will distress them.

If they are not happy and safe you may even feel that it is your fault, that you have in some way let them down. You were not the correct partner, you did not bring your children up as well as you could, you should have known better, you should have advised your friends differently.

These and related stories and fears can cause you a lot of stress.

It is natural for you to want the best for those you like and love. It is natural for you to want the best for other people. But you can take this too far.

Mrs F. was a nervous wreck when she came to see me. Her husband had recently been promoted and then developed stomach ulcers and she blamed herself for not looking after him better. She worried about her eldest daughter's marriage and blamed herself for not pointing out to her daughter sufficiently strongly the type of man her husband was before they got married. She was afraid her son would lose his job because he was being slapdash in his work and fretted that she couldn't make him work harder.

In the end I had to tell her to stop being so possessive. This was the word that finally got through to her.

'Possessive, never,' she said. 'That's the last thing I am. I just want what's best for them.'

'I know, but you're not willing to let them take responsibility for their own decisions. You're not willing to recognize that they and only they know what is best for them. You don't; only they can know that.'

'But I do, or I should. I'm their mother.'

'Did your mother know what was best for you?'

'Well no, I guess not. She wanted me to get a job first but I just wanted to marry Denis.'

'Did you feel she had the right to stop you doing what you wanted?'

'No, of course not.'

'Even if she was sure she knew best?'

'No. Oh, I see what you mean.'

'Furthermore,' I said, wanting to push my point home, 'you're not willing to trust them and their ability to lead their own lives. Isn't this belittling them? Isn't this being possessive and refusing to give them their freedom? Isn't this refusing to acknowledge them for being competent human beings with a right to choose their own destiny?'

That settled it for her. Suddenly it was as if she had permission to let them go, permission to stop worrying about them, permission to hand over responsibility to them, and permission to stop feeling so stressed.

Consider these things in your own life. How much unnecessary and unwarranted stress are you taking on simply because you choose to believe you should have been perfect in the past, because you choose to believe you and possibly you alone are responsible for whatever stressful situation occurs to people around you and because you choose to believe that it is your responsibility to ensure that other people's lives work out for the best?

The sad irony is, that while you are doing what you think is best and being as caring and responsible for others as you feel you should be, there are negative consequences as well. The extra stress you are thus putting on yourself will almost certainly cause ripples through their lives as well. Your stress will cause tension in them. It may stress communications between you. They may feel stressed by the stress they feel they are causing you. They may want to rebel against your assumption of responsibility and thus increase a gap between you. The possibilities are endless.

What is the answer? Give other people their freedom. You are not responsible for them. Care about them, do what is appropriate but do not take on their stress. If something unfortunate or bad happens to them, so be it. They have to do what they have to do. They have the right to make their own choices. You will not help them by choosing to feel stressed beforehand as you consider all the things that could go wrong in their lives.

Do your best but be content to be less than perfect and less than God.

CHAPTER SIXTEEN

Summary

Now it is time to go back to the Introduction, particularly to the notes that you made about the points itemized in it and to your list of stressors. I hope you did do this for now is the time to reap your reward. When you compare the way you thought then with the way you think now you will realize just how much you have learnt and how much your thoughts and attitudes to stress have changed during the course of reading this book. For they have, haven't they? This in turn will help to clarify for you the new directions in which you can head in the days, months and years ahead as you move towards a progressively stress-free future.

It is not uncommon for patients to come back on their second visit to the clinic, having listed a number of physical health problems on their first one, saying they have not improved. They may have come in originally with 10 symptoms including headaches, and the conversation on their second visit may go something like this.

'How have you been since your last visit here?'

'Not too bad, but nothing much has changed. I'm still getting headaches.'

'What about your indigestion?'

'Oh that's gone, I can eat anything now, but I'm still getting lots of headaches.'

'What about your skin, have you had any more pimples?'

'Oh no, that's been clear, it's the headaches that still bother me.'

'Is your nose still blocked or can you breathe properly now?'

'No, my nose is clear,' said with a puzzled frown.

'What about your insomnia and the need to get up in the night?'

'Well, no, but there's still the headaches.'

'You mean you no longer get indigestion after meals, rumblings in your stomach, diarrhoea or wind. Your skin has cleared up, you have no boils or pimples, and your sinuses are no longer blocked or hurting you. You're sleeping well, probably because you can breathe properly and don't have those digestive pains. All that is left for us to deal with now is the headaches?'

'Well yes, I guess so. If you put it like that.'

It is all too easy to forget the strides, large and small, that you have made. This is true in relation to stress as well as to physical health problems. You may have put many of the ideas you have learnt from this book into practice already and forgotten about the stresses you have thus eliminated. You may have made great strides in the way you handle stress and in your self-knowledge and wisdom. You may fail to recognize this unless you consciously sit down and think back to your ideas and attitudes before you started to read this book and assess any changes you would now make to the list of things that stressed you then.

If you have read this book over a period of days or weeks you have, hopefully, been putting some of the ideas into practice, bit by bit, as they applied to you. As such you will have learnt how to dispense with certain of the stresses in your life as you recognized and dealt with the reasons for them. Just like the patient whose conversation was quoted above, you may have forgotten the resolved problems and now only be aware of the ones that remain.

Going back to the comments you made when you were first faced with some of the concepts discussed in this book is a helpful way of recognizing your present achievements and the new ways in which you are willing to view your reactions to situations and to stress.

This is one of the reasons I suggested at the time that you write down your reactions to the statements when you first read them in the Introduction. Another is so that you can recognize the learning experiences you have had about your past. Your list will also help you now as you make conscious decisions about the way you will lead your life in the future.

Now it is time to review what we have covered as well as the changes you have made.

A first and preliminary instruction, when handling the things you find stressful in your life, was to do all you could to change the external factors that stress you, as far as that is appropriate. If you hate your job and are sure it is just this job and not your attitude to work in general, then look for a new one. If you are lonely then go out and take active steps to meet new people. If the lack of money worries you then explore, and be willing to explore, all possible means of increasing your income. If the children's behaviour is giving you headaches and heartaches explore new and alternative ways of discussing and possibly changing this. When all these avenues have been explored, and even while you are still exploring them, do all you can to learn more about why certain things make you feel stressed and how you, by your change in attitude and self-knowledge, can reduce the stress.

Point 1

'Stress is your own experience. It is personal to you and generated by you. It is not directly to do with things outside yourself; they are only the triggers to a response from within you, a response that is individual to you.'

We started with the concept that there is no such thing as an objective stress, external to yourself. There is no such thing as a universal stress, one that causes everyone to feel stressed to an equal degree and in a similar way. This being so it means that the real stress comes about by the way you, as an individual, react to specific external situations, events or possibilities.

As you have read this book it is probable that you have come to rec-ognize, more clearly than in the past, that it is your hidden fears, worries, uncertainties and needs that cause you all the stress that you have so far attributed to outside events and to understand what some of these fears, worries, uncertainties and needs are.

It may be your fear of failure and the fear that you are not good enough that causes all those exam nerves, or the terror of public speaking, or that anxiety that makes a challenge a stress rather than an excitement. It may be your inner fear that if people knew what you were really like they would not want to be your friend that stops you trusting your friends and revelling in their warmth and company and leaves you unhappy anytime you are not included in an invitation. It may be your insecurity about your value, in your own eyes and hence to other people, that makes you aggressive when not given the attention you think you deserve. It may be your conviction that everything is your fault that has you sabotaging any pleasant event by your nerves and uncertainties as you spend the time anticipating what will happen when things go wrong.

You may hate to be alone, fearing it means no-one loves you. You may fill your life with endless activity, afraid of what you would find during a spell of quiet contemplation. You may long to drop out, not from a desire for quiet country life but to avoid demands being made on you. It may be your fear that you are not loved for yourself but for what you do for others that has you rushing around doing things for every-one and becoming tired and stressed in the process.

In all these and many, many other ways, we have discussed and illus-trated the idea that your stress comes from within you, not from outside. It is what you choose to think and how you choose to assess outside events that causes you to generate your own internal stress.

The real cause of stress is rarely the obvious reason but usually the more deeply buried one. By discovering this you have made a first and major step in stress reduction.

Questions

    (i) In the light of what you have read in this book, how do you now view this concept?

   (ii) What thoughts are you now having about the stresses in your life?

  (iii) How do they relate to the thoughts you had at the beginning and when you wrote your original comments to the Introduction?

  (iv) Write a list of all the things that stress you now.

   (v) How does this list vary from your original list?

Point 2

'Feeling stressed is your choice and you can choose to continue or to stop. There is no such thing as a universal stress.'

The exciting consequence of this is that if you choose to view outside events differently you need not feel stressed. If you choose to view a criticism as helpful input and genuine concern for your growth and development by the person involved it cannot be stressful. If you choose to view your omission from a particular party list as a recognition that your interests are different from those of the other people invited you can enjoy the extra time it gives you to pursue your own chosen activity. If you choose to view a tirade from someone else as a reflection of their own insecurities you can make use of the opportunity to help them. If you choose to believe that a setback is opening the way for a better opportunity it can be exciting rather than stressful.

Stress is very much a matter of the thoughts you choose to have and the interpretations you choose to put on events and situations. Since feeling stressed is your choice you can choose to continue or you can choose to stop. Since there is no such thing as a universal stress you have the exciting concept that you can choose to eliminate stress any time you wish.

As we explored the power of your thoughts and of your thinking and the way you choose to think it is likely that several things became obvious to you. You can choose to think things are going well or you can choose to think they are going badly. You can choose to believe that the future will turn out the way you want or to believe that it is bound to be difficult and contrary and cause you stress and grief. You can filter, in many different ways and against a variety of different criteria, the input you choose to receive and acknowledge and the inputs you choose to ignore.

By the way you view your world you can also affect your world. By choosing to act positively you will get different results, in big and small ways, to the ones you will create if you choose to act negatively.

In these and in other ways, by the power of your thoughts and the ways you choose to use them, you can have a powerful effect on the level of stress in your life.

Questions

(i) What thoughts are you choosing to have that are stressful to you?

(ii) What things are you choosing to change in your life as a result of reading this book?

(iii) In what way could your life improve if you change your thoughts on a particular aspect of it?

Point 3

'You can use the awareness of what stresses you to learn more about yourself and then use this knowledge for change (of yourself)'.

From the above two points we developed the concept that an important step in your stress reduction programme is to learn more about yourself and your past programming and thus to understand better the underlying reasons why specific situations are perceived, by you, to be stressful. You can use the knowledge of what stresses you to learn more about yourself. You can, in turn, use this knowledge to enable you to feel less stressed.

Learn as much as you can about yourself and your past. Use the technique of running a phrase to find out more. Go back into the past in your own mind, either on your own or with the help of someone else to guide you. The greater your self-knowledge, self-awareness and self-confidence, the less stress you will experience.

This process is never complete. There is always more you can learn. It is like peeling off layers of an onion. When each new layer is exposed it is an exciting discovery. The new knowledge is fresh and piquant. You work with it, use it and feel that now, at last, you understand why you get stressed.

Then this new layer dries, it becomes part of the landscape, it loses its piquancy, the first excitement of discovery is past. Certainly you feel better, but you also do find you are still getting stressed. It is time to delve deeper. Peel off the next layer, learn even more about yourself, use this knowledge for growth and development and repeat the cycle. The layers may seem endless but you will find each time you remove one that life takes a step forward, it gets better, more peaceful, more exciting and much much richer.

Questions
  (i) What have you learnt about your past that affects your present stress levels?
 (ii) What self-recognitions have you had of things that were not so deeply buried, were even half-guessed at though not fully acknowledged consciously?
(iii) What have you learnt about your past that caused you surprise?

Point 4

'Be willing to change what you are doing – if what you have been doing has not been working, be willing to do something different.'

Many times you become stressed in certain, often repeated, situations. There are probably a number of things you do that result in a response or outcome that stresses you. It is also probable that you do little to change your tactic for dealing with these situations. It is surprising how often this happens in people's lives. For some reason inertia takes over and you make no effort to change either the situation, your way of deal-

ing with it or your attitude to it. Commonly this results from the fact
that you are getting some other benefit from this situation such as
recognition, sympathy, or the infliction of guilt or discomfort on the
other person or people involved.

Questions
   (i) What have you learnt about yourself in this regard?
  (ii) What benefits are you deriving from not contributing to the
       reduction of stress in each specific situation in your life?
 (iii) How does your attitude to this concept vary from the attitude
       you had when you started this book and wrote your original
       comments?
  (iv) What can you do to change your current behaviour in such a way
       that you will avoid certain specific stressful situations in the
       future?

Point 5

*'You are responsible for, and have had some input into, all that happens, and
has happened, in your life. Be willing to assume that you are in total control.
Be willing to give up victim status.'*

A major step in managing and reducing your stress levels comes about
when you make the decision to accept responsibility for all that has
happened in your life and all that will happen, and to accept that you
had at least some degree of input, no matter how small, into every situation. There are few if any circumstances in your life when you did not
have some degree of control. Even in a car crash deemed to be the other
person's fault you did decide to be on that road at that time.

Once you accept this degree of responsibility you can then stop blaming others and railing against fate. This is useful in several ways:

1 Blaming fate and other people leaves you in a thoroughly bad
  frame of mind, thus causing you more stress.

2 Blaming other people can worsen your relationship, with them and other people, in the future which could in turn cause you further stress and unhappiness.

3 By taking responsibility you become free from that person. As you no longer acknowledge them as the cause of your problem you also acknowledge that they no longer have power over you.

4 You come to recognize that, just as you had some measure of input into the past you can have input into your future, and this being the case, you can have some control over it. This, properly recognized, can give you the feeling of power and control over your future and hence over whether or not you will choose to be or feel stressed.

It is important, when recognizing your input into and responsibility over, the past, that you do not go into self-blame and thus generate more stress. It may be tempting to say 'Oh well, if I'm responsible for my life and it's bad then I'm to blame, it's all my fault, I'm stupid and so now I (choose to) feel even more stressed'.

Keep in mind that there is no intention of applying blame. After all, only you can know what is right and wrong for you and who else is to say otherwise if you decide on a certain course of action. It may seem wrong or stupid to them yet lead to results that you consider right and appropriate for you. Do not judge other people and do not accept their right to judge you. Only you can decide on what is right for you. Of course you, in turn, have to accept the consequences, good or bad, of your choices; you cannot blame anyone else. This in itself is stressful for some people who love to ask advice and then have someone to blame if things go wrong, yet ultimately this course of action can never lead to a happy and stress-free life. One of the riskiest things to do in life is to lean on and depend on other people for your support or to expect them to know what is best for you. Remember, they have enough problems orchestrating their own life to their own satisfaction. How should they be able to manage yours better?

Questions

(i) In what ways do you currently depend on other people?

(ii) To what extent does this empower you?

(iii) To what extent does this weaken you?

(iv) In what ways could you take over control of your life?

(v) How do your present views in this regard differ from those at the start?

Point 6

'Get clear on your outcome – what are you really trying to achieve? Are you trying to prove someone else wrong, to force someone else to be different, to have something to complain about, to get sympathy or attention? Do you really want to reduce your stress?'

It is important, in situations you find stressful, to be very clear on your desired outcome. Are you really trying to reduce the stress in your life or are you getting some unseen benefit from the way things are?

As we saw in earlier chapters there are many times when the stressful situation is being used for some subtly perceived yet unacknowledged benefit. You may, for instance, be proving the other person wrong or using the situation to get sympathy, recognition or acknowledgement. You may be endeavouring to force the other person or people involved to change as a way of increasing your own sense of power or importance. You may be choosing to make them feel guilty or uncomfortable as revenge or justification.

Questions

(i) In any stressful situation in your life are you trying to prove someone else wrong?

(ii) Are you trying to force someone else to change to the way you want them to be?

(iii) Do you benefit from having something to complain about?

(iv) Do you use stress as a way of getting sympathy or attention?

(v) What else have you learnt about yourself in this regard?

〜

Point 7

'Know you can cope. Avoid the stress caused by fear of the unknown. Imagine the worst possible scenario. Find out how you would deal with it. Then get on with handling the present.'

So much of the experience of stress is due to fear – fear of what other people think, fear of the consequences of past actions and, above all, fear of the future. Fear of some dreadful thing that is about to happen, that could happen in the distant future or that might possibly happen at some time unspecified.

More often than not these fears do not materialize. Think back to the times that you worried about an event that didn't happen or worried that something important might fail to occur yet it did. Did you fret that you might not be invited out, might not be given the job, might not cope with a dinner party, might not be strong enough to deal with a situation? Did you worry that someone you loved might be hurt, that something dreadful would happen to a friend? Did you worry that you had given an inappropriate present, that your clothes would be wrong, that the job you had done would not be good enough? In all or any of these situations you may have worried needlessly, causing yourself a great deal of unnecessary stress in the process.

If you are afraid of something happening in the future then anticipate it mentally and find out how you will cope. Commonly you will find that if the worst did happen you would survive. You would have found ways of handling the situation and you may well even find some benefits in the situation. They may not, from your vantage point of the present, seem sufficient to be worth the losses along the way. However, they will be there as beacons should the worst happen.

Once you find you can cope with the worst possible outcome you can then free up your worry time and your energies and apply them to dealing positively with the situation and thus give yourself the best possible chance of a positive outcome while feeling less stressed in the meantime.

The point here is to reduce your feeling of stress. This can best be done by defusing the situation and this you can do in the way suggested.

Questions

Think of the worst possible scenario for something that stresses you at the moment.

- (i)   What is the probable outcome if the worst possible scenario occurs?
- (ii) How would you cope if that occurred?
- (iii) What possible benefits can you see in this situation? List at least three.
- (iv) Having done this, how has your present stress level changed?

Point 8

'Believe in a positive future, that whatever happens is, and will be, for the best, but do this without ceasing to care and without developing a laissez-faire attitude.'

The next step in reducing your feeling of stress is to believe in a positive future. If you do not get an outcome you want, and there is nothing you can do to change it, then it is less stressful to believe that there is something better coming along than that you will never have another opportunity. If something bad happens and there is nothing you can do to rectify it then it is less stressful to believe that something good will come out of it and to focus on this than to focus on the distressing event.

Again I repeat, there is a fine line between this and choosing to build a wall round your emotions and not care. That is not at all the same thing. When you lose someone you love you will not love them less if you choose to focus on some positive benefit, however small, rather than to focus on your loss and misery. Keep in mind that the purpose is to reduce your feeling of stress and to help you to deal in a more positive and constructive way with a situation that stresses you.

When someone says something hurtful you might decide to put up your brick wall and hide behind it, claiming you no longer like them, want to be their friend, or care what they think. In this way you lose out on many of the wonderful exchanges of emotions and ideas between people. Instead focus on the possible benefits that could come out of this criticism, the things you can learn about them and yourself and the ways in which you can contribute to and enrich this relationship in the future.

Questions

(i) Think of something that has gone wrong in your life recently. What possible benefit could come from it?

(ii) How could a recent, apparent disappointment lead to something better?

(iii) When you do this what happens to your stress level?

Point 9

'Much stress is caused by your fear of other people's opinions of you and your deeds. Decide who you are and who you want to be. Get a clear statement of purpose, develop your own Life Plan. Keep the plan clearly in your mind, live by it and many of your stresses will dissipate.'

It is for you to decide the person you want to be. By determining your own Life Plan, by deciding exactly who you want to be in life and the course you want your life to take, you can avoid a lot of stress. Determine what is right for you, the right way for you to behave. Decide on the things you consider to be important, the values and goals you wish to have. Once you have done this then live by these guidelines. When you do that you need no longer be tossed around on the whim of other people's criticisms, other people's comments about you or other people's opinions of you. You know what is right for you so get on with it.

If you act outside your own guidelines, if you do something that you personally do think was wrong, then treat it as a learning experience. Acknowledge the deed, learn what you can from it and focus on ways to avoid it in the future. Do not apply blame, unless of course you did it deliberately, wittingly and intentionally, any more than you blame a toddler learning to walk each time he or she falls over.

Questions

(i) Have you written out your own Life Plan?

(ii) Are you happy with it?

(iii) What have you learnt in the process of doing this?

(iv) How do you think this will help you feel less stressed?

Point 10

'You are terrific. Most stress comes from your feelings of inadequacy. Develop full confidence in yourself, be willing to like, love and approve of yourself. If you don't, who will?'

Much stress comes about as a result of underlying doubts about yourself. You may believe you are not good enough, not likable, not lovable, not clever, not wanted. All these and many more are belief systems built in during your early years. They are all belief systems that have demonstrable flaws. Most importantly, they are belief systems that can be changed.

However badly you feel you have behaved, you can think of times when you behaved well. For all the things you think you can't do, you can think of other things you can do. For all the people that don't like you, you can think of others that do.

As said elsewhere, one of the hardest things for most people to do is to like and love themselves fully, deep down where it counts. This is not the same as being boastful or selfish. It means having a quiet inner core of strength and certainty in yourself. Developing this inner security can, in turn, give you the peace that frees you from many of the stresses you used to experience.

Several other strategies have been discussed as tools and aids along the way to developing yourself and your emotional balance to the point where the challenges and trials of life can be dealt with without causing you undue and unnecessary stress and pain. These included not demanding perfection of yourself but only that you tried, and not trying to play God and take over responsibility for other people's lives and stresses.

Above all, when you are attempting to reduce the stress in your life, be aware that you have the choice. You can choose whether to feel stressed or not. It may take a large effort of will and a strong focus but you can make this choice. The way in which you view your past is your choice. What you are thinking at this moment is your choice. The expectations you have of the future are your choice. The interpretation you put on an event, on something someone says, on the way a person looks, is your choice.

When you have these choices you can choose to feel stressed or you can choose not to feel stressed. Use whatever it takes to aid your personal growth and development to help you make the choices that best serve you.

Do this, have fun doing it, take control, choose wisely and enjoy your stress-free life.

CHAPTER SEVENTEEN

Conclusions to Part I

From all that we have said there are clearly some specific steps to take to reduce the experience of stress in your life.

- Start with two practical things. Do all you possibly can, practically, to improve the situation. Then face the worst that could possibly happen and work out how you would cope with it. Above all, realize that you could cope with it.
- Then start working on yourself at the mental and emotional level. Realize that you do choose what you think, you own your thoughts, they do not own you. By delving into your past you can find the basis of most of your attitudes and assumptions. When these are seen in the clear light of day you will probably want to change many of them, as a result of which many things that now stress you will no longer do so.
- Having recognized that you can control your thoughts it is now time to decide what sort of thoughts you want to have. Decide what sort of beliefs are causing you stress and so should be dispensed with and what sort of beliefs and thoughts would lead to a more stress-free life.
- Be willing to change, since what you were doing in the past left you stressed. Be willing to accept responsibility for all that happens in your life and to stop blaming other people and outside events for your stresses. In this way you can stop being a victim and take control of your life.

❧ Check out your addictions and preferences. Develop your self-confidence to such an extent that you know there is nothing you absolutely have to have if you are not to fall apart. Learn and feel comfortable with the idea that your own inner core is inviolate and that you can, at some level, deal with whatever happens and turn it to some advantage. Be willing to look for the benefits, however small, in any stressful situation and to believe that all will be for the best and thus decrease your stress.

❧ Work on deciding upon the type of person you want to be and the type of person you will be happy being. Learn to love, value and appreciate yourself. Once you have yourself and your Life Plan worked out all you need to do is live in alignment with that. Then whenever people criticize you or you feel threatened you can check yourself against your own chosen blueprint and, provided you have lived and acted within that framework, you need not feel stressed by their comments.

❧ Above all, recognize the choice is yours, take control, believe in yourself and in a positive future.

PART II

THE
Physical
Aspects of Stress

CHAPTER EIGHTEEN

Your Mind and Your Body

Stress and its effect on your body

Any experience of stress has a seemingly automatic effect on your overall body, although here, in fact, you do actually have some control. When you feel stressed it is likely that your facial muscles change, you frown rather than smile, your forehead is creased, your eyebrows come together, the corners of your mouth turn down and so forth. Most, although not all, people look stressed when they feel stressed. You may tense the rest of the muscles of your body. Your shoulders may tense and hunch, you may bend over in a protective gesture rather than stand straight and tall. You may cross your arms and legs too, in an effort to achieve protection and to ward off the threats. These are things you can change voluntarily and relatively easily. If you are tense before a meeting it is not too hard to school yourself to relax your muscles, stand up straight with shoulders back and put a smile on your face.

The unconscious physical movements are harder to control. These include all the nervous mannerisms you have ever observed both in yourself and in other people when they are under stress. Some people play with a pen, twist a handkerchief, fiddle with objects near them or stroke their ears or some other part of their body. Your eyes may dart around, you may have trouble making eye contact. All these and many more physical movements are part of the physical expression of stress.

Adrenalin

There are other ways in which stress affects your body. Most people are familiar with the effects of the rush of adrenaline that occurs when you just miss the car in front of you, just stop a valuable object from crashing to the floor, are subjected to a sudden horror or startled by a loud noise. In the face of any such sudden event or stress adrenaline is pumped from the adrenal glands. These glands are situated over your kidneys, and the adrenaline flows in the bloodstream throughout your body. It affects all the cells as it passes by. Your heart will pump faster, your skin will sweat or go cold and clammy, your muscles will tense ready for action, your hands may shake, and so forth. All these are signs of the sudden stress you have experienced and are the body's preparations for whatever flight or fight activity may be demanded.

The nervous system

There are other changes that take place in your body, and to understand them fully we need to learn a bit more about the way the body functions.

Firstly, consider the nervous system. There are many ways of subdividing it. One is to consider the two parts that are known respectively as the sympathetic nervous system and the parasympathetic nervous system. Never mind how those seemingly odd names came about, let's consider what each system does.

The sympathetic nervous system

The sympathetic nervous system is the part that deals with the outside world. It includes what is commonly referred to as your fight or flight system. The one objective of the sympathetic nervous system is to enable you to run or fight when you have to. In other words it is helping you to cope with stress by being physically more active. This means that it ensures your resources are all focused on this end.

As a result of increased activity of the sympathetic nervous system the blood flow to the muscles of your legs and arms increases so that they have a greater supply of oxygen to enable them to do the increased work that could be demanded of them as you fight or run. Conversely, the blood flow to the outer skin is restricted and 'goose pimples' form. The blood circulation to the structure of your lungs and the flow through your lungs is increased so you can achieve maximum oxygen uptake for the exertions that may be required. Your pupils dilate so you can see better and improve long-distance as opposed to short-distance vision. Other changes occur to your heart, your ears and many other parts of your body. A number of hormonal and chemical changes occur that result in increased blood-sugar levels, increased energy output and increased tendency of the blood to clot.

You cannot suddenly increase the potential output of parts of your body like this without having to pay the price. The extra blood supply to the lungs and legs, for instance, has to come from somewhere. Consider what aspects of your anatomy and bodily processes you can put on hold while running and fighting. It is not difficult to see that you do not need to be digesting food at this time. In fact not only is it unnecessary to digest food at this time, it is inadvisable. The last thing you want when fleeing from a tiger is to have to go to the toilet; there is no 'time out' in the game of nature. You can attend to this later, if you are still alive. These are aspects of your bodily functions that the sympathetic nervous system can safely ignore while the crisis is on.

The parasympathetic nervous system

The parasympathetic nervous system directs the function of your bodily processes that deal with internal housekeeping. These do include the process of digestion, kidney function and so forth. It is your parasympathetic nervous system that directs the flow of digestive juices, the saliva to your mouth, the hydrochloric acid to your stomach, and the alkalis from your pancreas. It directs the production and secretion of digestive enzymes into your mouth, stomach and intestines. It dictates the peristaltic action that propels the partially digested food along your digestive tract. It triggers the sensations that send you to the toilet to get rid of waste matter. Similarly the parasympathetic nervous system works on your kidneys, directing their level of activity and triggers the messages you get to tell you your bladder is full. It causes your eye lenses to bulge so you can focus close up rather than long distance.

This is all very well, but the two systems would seem to be in competition with one another, and indeed, in a sense, they are. They cannot both function at once. So who is the boss? Which is the dominant system that gets first choice as to whether or not to be active?

Not surprisingly it is the sympathetic system that is the boss. When you give it some thought you will realize that this makes sense if you want to survive. You can afford to delay the digestion of food if necessary, but if you delay in your attempt to run from an oncoming car you may not be around to digest the food.

The moment there is any sort of stress or alarm your sympathetic nervous system is switched on and the parasympathetic one is switched off. Think about the times you have had a fright. Has your mouth gone dry? Have you lost your inclination to eat or drink or known that you 'couldn't eat a thing', even if you tried? Have you been unaware of the need to go to the toilet or unaware of pain?

In some parts of your body there are nerves from both the parasympathetic and the sympathetic system, acting in opposition, either one or the other being turned on according to what is happening around you. In other parts of your body, however, there is no parasympathetic system, it being sufficient to leave the sympathetic in total control. In your leg muscles, for instance, there are no parasympathetic fibres. Once the sympathetic system is turned off, your blood flow then returns to the relaxed condition.

This distribution of labour was all very well in caveman times or in a more physically violent age when stress meant you had to be ready for physical action. Today it has its problems. It means that if you are stressed but need emotional rather than physical resources to deal with it, your body will still respond as if it might have to be physically active. If you are stressed and try to eat a meal you are likely to get indigestion. If you insist on eating while you are stressed this may go from feeling uncomfortable to getting heartburn and even ulcers. At the very least it is unlikely that you will either digest (break down) the food you eat or absorb much of the nutrients it contains.

The only way you can turn on the parasympathetic nervous system is by turning off the sympathetic system. This means that you simply do have to slow down and relax so you can get on with the business of processing food and nutrients and doing all the other things that we have labelled internal housekeeping. If you don't do this the stresses you feel will translate into serious health problems caused by lack of parasympathetic activity.

This is the background reason why mental stress can lead to physical health problems. It comes about, at least in part, because you are trying to do the internal housekeeping activities while actively feeling stressed.

Stress can also cause health problems due to an excessive amount of sympathetic activity, even when you don't try to do the things that need parasympathetic activity. If you choose to have adrenalin pumping through your body for long periods of time the target organs will become exhausted. Your heart cannot go on pumping harder and faster than usual for ever. If you try this you could well be headed for a heart attack. The increased tendency for your blood to clot was all very well when there was the increased possibility of a physical accident but when prolonged, this extra 'stickiness' of your blood gives your heart more work to do and could increase your blood pressure. The extra adrenaline and other stress-related hormones flowing around your system are damaging to a wide variety of cells and organs if their action is prolonged and can eventually lead to total exhaustion.

Notice how many of the prolonged actions of the sympathetic nervous system lead to the symptoms we think of as the consequence of stress. They include headaches, heart problems, high blood pressure, digestive upsets and ulcers.

You may think that, when under stress, you can grit your teeth, plaster a grim smile on your face and cope. You may fool some of the people all of the time and all of the people some of the time but you are unlikely ever to fool your own body. It will still experience the stress and it will still react and suffer accordingly.

The solution is to change your experience, to change the way you respond to situations. Do this and your body will thank you for it. After all, your body is your home for this lifetime; treat it well and you will have a good home for as long as you want it. Treat it badly and it is likely to let you down when you most need it. Then where will you live?

Mental control of your body

We have seen what happens, automatically, when you experience stress. Now let's consider ways in which you can change this experience by the power of your mind.

If you generate peaceful and relaxing thoughts this will help to relax the sympathetic nervous system and make it less active. Your body will then reflect this; it too will relax and experience less stress. In this way you can, by the nature of the thoughts you choose to think, actually change what is going on in your body. This is the basis of using relaxation techniques, deep breathing, meditation and so forth to deal with stress. Keep in mind, however, that it does not eliminate stress or its basic cause.

It is worth taking this concept of relaxation further. It has been shown by many yogis and people with similar skills that it is possible, simply using the power of your mind, to control the rate at which your heart beats, slowing it down or speeding it up at will. It is also possible to increase or lower the temperature of your skin.

In one example a Swami, by the power of his mind, was able to make one side of his hand become hot and red and the other cold and pale in colour with a temperature difference of 10 degrees Fahrenheit. Other people with similar skills have been able to change their pulse rate from 70 beats a minute to 300, or to slow their breathing to such an extent that they could be enclosed in airtight spaces for considerable lengths of time.

In other words, you can be less stressed by learning the passive techniques of relaxation or by using active techniques of mind control. With this mind control you can choose to control what you think and feel and you can choose the way you allow your body to respond to situations. Even before you learn the techniques the Swami used you can consciously stop your shoulders tensing, stop your stomach muscles clenching and so forth.

All these techniques will lower your experience of stress and reduce the damage that stress can do to your body. Clearly there is an intimate interaction between your mind and your emotions on the one side and your physical body on the other, at all levels.

While you are working with the ideas discussed in the main part of this book you can also work on your physical body. In time, as you eliminate stress, you won't even need to.

CHAPTER NINETEEN

Stress and Overload

It is now time to make a distinction between two types of stress. In Part I, I referred to the confusion caused by giving the word 'stress' several meanings. It is used to designate what is applied to you, and it is also used to describe the way you feel. We will now call them 'overload' and 'stress' respectively.

Stress

Stress is, therefore, what we have been dealing with in Part I. Stress is your emotional and mental response to a situation, any situation, be it physical or emotional. It is, as we have seen, your own response, which could be very different to anyone else's. It is based on what you think about any given situation and what you then think and feel as a result of those thoughts. It is a state of mind you impose upon yourself by your thoughts. By changing your thoughts and responses to a situation you can change your experience from being stressful into being something else entirely; you can reduce your level of stress. Your response could become neutral, interested or positively pleased, and as a result of making these mental changes you can feel a lot more relaxed and life can be much more fun. You are fully in control. By changing your thoughts you can reduce your experience of stress.

For most people, achieving this state is a gradual process. It is made up of many learning steps, mostly upwards but sometimes downwards. At some point you may find yourself on a plateau – you've solved some problems but you can't seem to get any further. Or maybe you're in a cul-de-sac, having tried some of the approaches already discussed but seemingly stuck in a new, and still stressful, behaviour pattern, still trying to figure out how to resolve it. While all this is going on it is likely that you will continue to feel stressed. You may feel less stressed than before because you have resolved some of the situations. Or you may even feel more stressed because indeed you have resolved some of the situations but your expectations are higher and so the (stress-free) end is still not in sight. Or you may be berating yourself for not being instantly successful in applying what you have learnt here.

With time and perseverance, with a willingness to look inside, to listen to the hidden and buried patterns and work on them, you can certainly reduce the stress in your life to either manageable or negligible proportions.

Overload

Overload is primarily a physical problem. It occurs when more demands are being made on you than you can cope with, when there is more on your plate than you feel you can handle. Overload is when you have to work excessively long hours, when you try to juggle home, family, career and other obligations, when the physical and practical demands on your time and energies seem to be more than you can manage. It occurs when there is so much to do that you burn the candle at both ends, have no time for a holiday or a day off at the weekend, go short of sleep and still cannot get everything done, or when several different people are all demanding you do different things, now, instantly.

If possible you should reduce your overload. If the demands on your energy and your time are more than you can handle, the sooner you recognize this and do something about it the better. If you don't, the level of overload will increase, your health will deteriorate and you will then experience the stress of worrying about how you can cope and what will happen if you don't.

Perhaps you do decide to reduce this overload. You may resolve to change jobs, insist the children do more to help around the house, resign from a committee, make fewer commitments to help in various situations. You may decide that it is more important to relax than to have your house, garden or clothes in an immaculate state.

Alternatively, there may be reasons why you decide not to reduce the overload. You may be worried about money and afraid of what will happen to you or your family if you give up your second job or the overtime and there isn't enough income to meet the demands (stress). To deal with this situation you may work on the stress, the underlying fears. Perhaps they stem from a feeling of inadequacy or insecurity. What will others think of you if you cannot provide? You have many tools now to help you reduce the stress. However, if you still want to help your children through college you may decide you simply do have to hold down two jobs (overload) to earn sufficient to pay the bills.

If you decide you absolutely have to remain in overload (not a course to be recommended, but one that can be understood) then it is of paramount importance that you look after your health, and that is the focus of Part II of this book.

Stress and overload

Although the above brief outline discusses stress (mental and emotional) and overload (physical and temporal) separately, they are in fact closely linked and inter-related. Overload can lead to more stress as it generates fears and concerns – fear that your health will suffer from the extra work, fear that you might not be able to keep going, fear of what will happen if people find you are not living up to their expectations. There are clearly many other reasons why overload can lead to stress and you will doubtless have your own examples.

If the physical demands on your time and energies are such that they lead to overload this will in turn lead to failures in your physical body and the way it performs. These health worries will cause you anxiety and worry, increasing your stress at the mental and emotional levels. Even the fear that the overload can be such that physically you won't be able to cope can lead to stress. So overload can lead to stress as your body fails to cope.

Overload is generally composed of things you have to do rather than things you want to do. If you are hectically busy but love what you are doing you are more likely to think of each new task or activity as an exciting challenge and rise to it with enthusiasm than to feel stressed. We might cause this a 'high load' rather than an overload. High loads are very much less likely to lead to stress, though if prolonged excessively they may still cause damage to you at the physical level.

Stress can lead to overload for many reasons. Perhaps you feel compelled to do more to deal with the situations. If you think someone disapproves of you, you may feel you have to strive harder to please them. If you interpret your boss's frowns as being directed at you (instead of his own problems), you may be in fear of losing your job and so spend longer hours at work.

Stress can also lead to overload because of the harm it does to you physically. Ultimately, most experiences of stress result from what your mind and emotions generate within you. This stress sets in motion many changes to your body at the physical level. Since, if prolonged, these changes are usually detrimental to your body, a time comes when your physical body cannot cope with what your mind is dishing out. As a result it experiences overload even when the external demands on your time and energy have not increased. In other words, stress can lead to relative overload even without increased external pressures.

What does all this mean?

To deal with stress you must work with Part I of this book, whether the stress be mental and emotional ('stress') or physical ('overload') and the consequent 'stress'. To become stress-free you must also deal with overload, either by reducing it or dealing with the physical causes or consequences of it, or both.

How you reduce lifestyle overload practically and physically is up to you. It is your decision as to whether you do less, get more help or make changes to your routine. This book is not the place to discuss that topic. Here I am going to assume that you have reduced the physical overload as much as you can or as much as you are willing to. I am now assuming that what you need is the best possible physical body to cope with your (residual) over-load and (as yet unresolved) stress. This is the task of the rest of Part II.

Your physical body

When your physical body is run down, undernourished and not operat-ing at its best, you will feel tired and sluggish; you will be more tense, irritable and moody than usual. As a result your response to both stress and overload will be less resourceful, more acute. You will fly off the handle or flare up more quickly than you do when you are healthy and well-nourished. All of which means that both stress and overload will occur sooner than they need in relation to the strides you are making mentally, emotionally and practically to deal with stress in your life.

So although this is primarily a book about your mental and emo-tional responses to stress, it is now time to consider how your body responds to any type of stressor. It is time to learn what you can do to support your body physically, in its overall health and in its ability to handle both stress and overload.

Happily improving your physical state will accomplish many things. Not only will it increase your ability to handle stress and overload, it will also enable you to be more relaxed and happy and, inevitably, improve your total overall health in many ways, increase your energy and general wellbeing and in turn raise your threshold to overload. This will mean that you can actually do more yet feel more relaxed.

Taking care of yourself physically is important. Yet it is all too easy to ignore this aspect of stress-management, at least initially. You tell yourself you are too busy to think about food or nutritional supplements, that you don't have time to relax, get enough sleep, exercise or do whatever it takes to recharge your batteries. So you push to one side the thought that you are doing physical damage to yourself as you put up with stress and overload. This is made easier by the fact that the very early damage will lead to no obvious external symptoms. Things can be going wrong internally for some time before they become so bad that you are consciously aware of problems. The ulcer can be starting, the allergies can be developing or your ability to maintain a stable blood sugar level can be failing for some time before obvious overt symptoms develop. When they do you may even be surprised, wondering what has gone wrong and why you can no longer cope the way you once did. It's a bit like living on capital and then wondering why a cheque for five pounds is suddenly bounced.

It is all too easy to assume you can cope. Think of the times you have been in a stressful situation, perhaps a job you didn't like, a relationship that wasn't working out ('stress'), or perhaps you just had too much to cope with ('overload'). Perhaps you found that you could grit your teeth and keep going. It may even have surprised you to discover how much overload you could take without cracking up. As a result you may then have assumed that this situation could continue without causing you harm. Not so. Dealing with prolonged stress, even if you seem to be coping, is still doing you harm physically. Remember Selye's three-step stress response? If you have reached this Adaptation Phase and done nothing about it you are harming your body, you are still living on this (health) capital. The next phase, the Exhaustion Phase, is approaching.

It may even be that you have become aware of minor problems de-veloping, yet have chosen to ignore them. I am dismayed when I hear patients saying 'there is pain, but nothing I can't handle', as if this was some heroic act of bravery or show of strength. In fact it is more nearly an act of stupidity not to listen to these early warning signs and do something about them. Sadly, it is often not until a major health prob-lem occurs as a result of stress, including unresolved 'stress' and 'overload', that many people's attitudes change. Under severe stress and/or overload you may have developed an ulcer, developed high blood pressure or diabetes, had a heart attack or stroke, suffered from a variety of infections or developed muscular and skeletal problems. You may then wish you had

a) resolved the stresses sooner,
b) reduced the overload and
c) taken better care of your physical health in the meantime.

My suggestion is that you pay attention to your health right now. Follow the steps outlined below and reduce the risk of future harm.

Every tension you feel at the mental and emotional level, from major stresses down to the slightest disturbing thought, has some effect on you at the physical level. Even thinking about standing on a 10th-storey window ledge will change the level of adrenaline, one of the stress hor-mones, circulating in your bloodstream. Getting tense leads to a tightening of the muscles round your arteries and changes in your blood pressure. Think back to the negative thoughts and then the positive thoughts you were fed in Chapter 3. Even they, just simple thoughts, had an immediate effect on your body. You were aware of this exter-nally. You may even have been aware of some of the changes that occurred internally. You can be sure that hundreds of other changes also occurred at the cellular and molecular levels. All of these changes and reactions have long-term effects on your physical health and wellbeing and this, in turn, feeds back to your level of stress. Who can feel relaxed when they are in pain or in fear of another heart attack?

〜

Even pleasure leads to cellular and chemical changes and makes demands on your nutrient intake. In the pages ahead we will be taking a closer look at the mind-body connection and consider in more detail the effects that stress and overload have on your body at the unconscious and automatic level, at the level at which you exert no conscious control.

CHAPTER TWENTY

The Mental-Physical Connection

Stress and its effect on your body

Stress changes many parameters within your body at the molecular, cellular, tissue and organ levels. The results impact on

- your adrenal glands
- your arteries and your blood pressure
- your heart and its function
- the blood flow to your brain, hence your moods and thoughts
- your blood sugar level, hence mental alertness and stability as well as your energy level.

We could continue this list, but it is enough to say that the following discussions and suggestions are based on a recognition of the changes that can occur within your body when you are in overload or stress.

The symptoms of stress

Early physical symptoms of stress are many and varied. They are often experienced indirectly – you may think you are becoming physically ill as well as being stressed, not realizing that stress is the cause of the physical problems. Let's take a look at some of the more common symptoms of stress and overload in greater detail.

Fatigue

One of the first impacts that stress has on your body is on your energy level. Stressful experiences put a large energy demand on your body physically. The extra thoughts as you worry and fret take energy. The extra tension in your body takes energy – you use more muscles to frown than to smile. The extra activity and workload use up energy. Much of this activity, as you frown, grit your teeth, clamp your stomach muscles, clench your fists, drum your fingers, stamp your feet or pace round the room, is wasted energy but it still uses up your reserves. Then there is all the necessary activity as you deal with the stressful situation; you work harder, travel further, do whatever it takes to try to deal with the situation.

Food as fuel

You do not have an unlimited amount of energy. The energy you experience is a direct result of the conversion of the macro components (fats, carbohydrates and, to a lesser extent, proteins) of the foods you eat into energy.

Dietary Fats
The main fat-rich foods are
- the visible fats on meat
- butter
- margarine
- the oils used in cooking and salad dressings
- cream.

Other fat-rich foods include
- cheese
- nuts and seeds
- olives
- avocado pears.

Many man-made foods are very rich in fats, often hidden; these include

- sausages
- fried foods and batter
- creamed soups
- sauces
- pastries
- cakes and biscuits
- ice cream and a range of desserts.

Many other foods contain a surprising amount of hidden, and often un-suspected, fats. Even lean meat, poultry and fish contain significant amounts of fat. Beans such as soy beans and chickpeas contain fat, eggs contain fat and even grains contain a significant amount (think of corn oil and wheat germ oil). All these fats are broken down by the digestive system into glycerol and free fatty acids. These fatty acids are taken up by individual cells within your body and converted into carbon dioxide and water, and the very large amounts of energy they contain are then released for use by your cells.

Carbohydrates

Carbohydrates come from nearly all the plant foods you eat. The grains, including wheat, rye, barley, oats, corn and rice, contain significant amounts and are the foods people most readily identify as carbohydrates. However, all vegetables contain carbohydrates, from the starchiest ones such as potatoes and carrots to the less starchy onions, tomatoes and green leaves. A further source of carbohydrates in the diet is sugar. This includes the natural sugars found in fruits and some vegetables and con-centrated sugars such as table sugar and honey. Sugar is added to so many processed foods that it is often difficult to find ones that are sugar-free. You would expect to find sugar in desserts, cakes, cookies and sweets of various sorts but you may be more surprised to know it is added to many soups, stews and a wide range of savoury sauces and salad dressings.

The carbohydrates from all these foods are broken down in the diges-tive system and are ultimately converted into glucose. This glucose constitutes the sugar that travels through your bloodstream and is referred to when your 'blood sugar level' is measured. Glucose then travels throughout your body and is available for any cell that needs it for instant energy.

Vitamins

For the proper use of these fat and carbohydrate fuels and their ultimate conversion into usable energy (as opposed to their conversion into unwanted fat that is then stored in your body), a number of complicated steps have to occur. Many of these are catalysed by members of the B-group of vitamins, particularly vitamins B_1, B_2, B_3, B_5 and biotin. So if you are short of any of these B-vitamins you may be short of energy, no matter how much you eat.

Protein

Even protein can be a source of energy. You need some protein in your diet every day to replace the amount that is lost from your muscles and other tissues. Any excess that you eat over and above that requirement is converted into energy in a process that requires ample amounts of vitamin B_6 in addition to the other energy-producing B-vitamins.

Energy-production

All this may sound relatively simple and straightforward. It may even sound as if all that you need to do to have sufficient energy to cope with stress and overload is to eat more. In this vein you might even consider stress to be a helpful way to lose weight, as you use up all those extra calories. But no, as every person, steadily gaining weight and feeling tired at the same time, knows, this is not the case. In fact, many hundreds of steps are required for the production of energy and they rely, absolutely, on an adequate supply of all the micro-nutrients as well.

For fats to enter your cells and become available for energy you need an amino acid called carnitine. Carnitine is obtained from animal (flesh) protein foods. It is also made from two other amino acids, methionine and lysine, both of which are found in rich amounts in animal proteins, including eggs. Lesser amounts are found in vegetable proteins. These three amino acids have to be eaten in the diet; you cannot make them in the body. Thus a low-protein diet or in inadequate vegetarian diet may be part of your fatigue problem. Since you also need extra amounts of vitamin B6 for the conversion of the latter two into carnitine, your diet must also contain a sufficient amount of this vitamin.

For glucose to enter your cells you need a correct output of the hormone insulin. For the production of insulin you need zinc and for insulin to function properly you need a substance called glucose tolerance factor (or GTF) which contains another mineral, chromium, plus vitamin B_3. For the release of stored glucose (as glycogen) from your liver, other nutrients are needed.

This is a very brief and simplified overview of your body's energy production; the whole story is a lot more complex. Clearly, however, the quality of your diet, which often suffers when you are stressed, is crucially important to the amount of energy you produce.

If you are stressed and eat badly, as so often happens, your nutrient intake actually decreases at the time when you need it to increase. You probably rely on refined carbohydrates such as white bread and pasta or on sugar-rich foods and snacks that are low in vitamins, instead of on good quality proteins and a generous supply of vitamin-rich vegetables, and so will be short of the nutrients needed for energy-production. Furthermore, when you are stressed your body actually uses up larger amounts of these essential trace nutrients, particularly some of the minerals and B-vitamins, in producing the stress response and the various hormones that act to help you cope with situations as they arise. This may deplete, for instance, your level of some of the B-vitamins to a point where there is insufficient left for the efficient production of the energy you need.

What does this mean in practice? It means that when stressed you need more than your usual intake of micro-nutrients and you probably consume less. It means that one of the early symptoms of stress and one of the earliest consequences of stress is fatigue, both physical and mental. This will be worse if the quality of your diet deteriorates as your

⤳

stress level escalates but can be prevented or reduced if you pay attention to the 10 Steps in Chapter 22.

Adrenal exhaustion

Your adrenal glands, situated on either side of your lower spine, on top of your kidneys, play a critical role in your stress response. Adrenaline and noradrenaline, produced by the adrenal medulla (centre), are possibly the ones that come to mind first when stress is being considered. However, cortisone and many of the other steroid hormones produced by the adrenal cortex (skin) are also involved in the stress response. In addition they are involved in many other aspects of your metabolism, including the function of your immune system, sexual function and fluid and mineral balance.

What does all this mean? Initially, when you are stressed, your adrenal glands cope, provided of course that your diet is providing sufficient amounts of all the essential nutrients they need. If this is not the case then you will have limited capacity to cope with stress. Eventually, as your stress continues, your adrenal glands become exhausted. The more stress you experience, the sooner this will occur. The result is not only fatigue and reduced ability to handle stress and overload but includes a range of consequences to your immune system, your sex life and other aspects of your health, as we shall soon see.

Once you have reached the stage of adrenal exhaustion, stresses and activities that, in the past, you could cope with relatively easily, will now become major mountains to climb. I hear so many patients saying 'I always used to be able to cope in these situations. Now it seems I can't. I don't know what's changed. Perhaps it's my age.' Age it may be, though usually that is an inadequate explanation. More often than not they have passed from the Alarm Phase, through the Adaptation Phase and have now reached the (adrenal) Exhaustion Phase. It is time for serious therapy.

Headaches

Tension headaches

When you are stressed there is a sudden uptake of glucose by the cells of your body as they endeavour to deal with the situation. As a result, and particularly if your adrenal glands are exhausted, your blood sugar level can fall. This then means that insufficient glucose gets to your brain. All the other tissues in your body can use glucose, fats or even amino acids for energy, but your brain insists on a pure and steady supply of glucose. This lack of glucose to your brain can lead to headaches and mental fatigue.

A normal blood sugar level and a steady supply of this glucose to the brain is essential for normal brain health and function. But before you rush for the sugar caddy, stop. Ironically, eating sugar is not the answer to this problem, as we will discover in more detail when we discuss hypoglycaemia. What is needed is the nutrients indicated above that you need for the proper management of your blood sugar level and for the conversion of glucose into energy.

Headaches can also be caused by other factors, many of them stress-related. They include maldigestion, constipation and the creation of toxins within the digestive system.

Migraines

In some people stress can lead to migraine headaches. These may be caused by spasms of the blood vessels supplying the brain which in turn lead to a reduced supply of blood to the brain. They may actually start after the spasm, when the muscles relax and there is a surge of blood to the brain.

The migraines may occur as you hunch up your shoulders, strain your neck and put some of the vertebrae out of alignment. Such situations can often be helped by osteopathic treatment.

Many people suffer from allergies, particularly masked food allergies (*see below*), without knowing it. When these are recognized (a simple blood test will do it) and avoided the sufferer can avoid the migraine headaches. In the meantime any stress may be the last straw. A food that you can eat when you are relaxed becomes, when you are stressed, too much for your system to cope with, and a migraine results.

Indigestion

There are many ways in which stress affects your digestive system. In Chapter 18 we discussed the sympathetic nervous system and the parasympathetic nervous system. You will recall that your sympathetic nervous system deals with stress, with your fight and flight mechanism, and that your parasympathetic nervous system deals with your internal house-keeping. You will also recall that you can turn your sympathetic nervous system on or off but that you cannot directly control your parasympathetic nervous system. Only when you relax can the latter come into play.

This means that when you are stressed your parasympathetic system switches off automatically. As a result your digestive system closes down. Saliva does not flow, digestive enzymes are not produced, stomach acid and pancreatic alkaline juices do not flow, the peristaltic action that moves food along the system stops. You may articulate this by saying 'My stomach is in a knot'. This is the reason you are told to relax when you eat, and this is necessary and important even if the rest of your life is stressful.

Nausea

Because of the way your digestive system has closed down you may feel nauseous and unlike eating. Don't eat. When you are acutely stressed there is little point in eating. There is little point in ramming food down a system of tubes that has stopped functioning. When you are angry, when you are on a high state of alert, food is the last thing your body needs.

Clearly if the stress is prolonged you must start to eat again. However, it is important, no matter what the stress you are experiencing, to make a particular effort to relax and slow down while you are eating. Otherwise not only will you get little nourishment from the food but you can also start to create other digestive problems, as we shall see below.

Heartburn

Heartburn actually has nothing to do with your heart. It is a burning sensation caused by acid from your stomach venturing up the tube, your oesophagus, that leads back to your mouth. This tube is normally protected, like the rest of your digestive system, including your mouth, by a mucous lining. This is meant to protect the walls from abrasions that could be caused by the food you have eaten or by damage from the various digestive juices and enzymes. You only have to think of the difficulty you have swallowing when your mouth is dry to realize what this mucus does. It also protects you from the possible damage that could be caused by the millions of micro-organisms which inhabit your digestive tract.

When you are stressed, two factors come into play here. Firstly, the protective lining becomes compromised and less of the protective mucus is produced yet, in all probability, you have continued to eat, to push food down the tubes. This leads to damage and abrasions which become painful. Secondly, for a variety of reasons the muscles at the top of your stomach can become weakened or part of your stomach can protrude up through your diaphragm. Either of these situations allows acid from your stomach back up into the oesophagus. This can cause pain and damage itself because your oesophagus is not expected to have to deal with the strong acid from your stomach. If it is occurring in addition to local oesophageal abrasion, the pain can be even more intense and you could develop a hiatus hernia.

Ulcers

The acid produced by your stomach is extremely strong. It is much stronger, for instance, than the citric acid found in lemon juice, the acetic acid found in vinegar or even the ascorbic acid of vitamin C. It is even stronger than the battery acids found in car batteries. It is concentrated hydrochloric acid, so strong that if you left your finger sitting in it the skin would start to peel off. So why does it not harm your stomach? Your stomach is lined with a particularly strong and acid-resistant mucus and so it is safe.

What happens when you are stressed? Yes, you've guessed it. Because the stress mechanism is reducing local parasympathetic activity the lining weakens, becomes damaged, is not repaired and the acid penetrates it. The acid then reaches the underlying muscular lining of your stomach and the resulting pain is intense. This is the start of an ulcer. If the situation is allowed to continue the ulcer will grow and the stomach wall can be perforated. The contents of your stomach can then enter your abdominal cavity and the consequences can be life-threatening as the various chemicals and organisms do their damage to the rest of your body.

If the ulcerated area occurs in the stomach itself it is a stomach ulcer. If it occurs in the duodenum it is a duodenal ulcer. The duodenum is the tube leading from your stomach down to the small intestine proper. It is a U-shaped tube lying on its side and the stomach contents, as they leave the stomach, have a direct impact on the internal bend of the U which is often the site of the ulcer. Again this can be caused by stress. As before, it is likely to occur because the normal function of the digestive system has slowed down and the usual protections are not in place.

There are other reasons for digestive ulcers that could be stress-related. It is now thought that they can be caused by a variety of organisms, particularly heliobacter pylori. As we shall soon see, stress can affect your immune system and this can in turn leave you more vulnerable to invasion by a variety of harmful bacteria and other organisms including the ones that can damage your digestive tract.

Ulcers, be they stomach or duodenal, can lead to headaches (another cause of stress-related headaches) and back pain as well as local pain.

Flatulence

Under this heading we will include the gases that you belch up, the wind that you may pass out downwards and the associated bloating due to the presence of these gases within your digestive system.

Imagine a meat and vegetable stew with a thick rich gravy. Put it, mentally, into a casserole dish with a lid on and leave this sitting in a dark cupboard at 37°C (blood temperature) for several days. What happens? It starts to ferment. Not only will it go green and grey as various moulds form but gases will be formed and start to bubble up. If you had sealed the whole thing in a large plastic bag, the gases produced would have caused this bag to balloon up to its full size and, if the pressure was sufficiently strong, to explode.

If you have food in your digestive system and become stressed then digestive function decreases, the processing of food slows down and its passage along the intestinal tract may almost cease. Instead of normal and healthy digestion taking place, putrefaction occurs and a variety of unwanted gases can be produced, hence the flatulence.

Because there is reduced output of stomach acid and other digestive juices when you are stressed, the chemical nature of your intestinal tract changes and can become more acceptable to a variety of unwanted bacteria. *Candida albicans* (the cause of thrush or candidiasis) can flourish as can many other moulds. Pathogenic bacteria can flourish. Many of these produce gases and cause bloating.

Intestinal problems

There are many inflammatory intestinal problems that are either caused by or aggravated by stress. It's the same story as before. Because your response to stress has turned on your sympathetic nervous system and turned off your parasympathetic nervous system, this lower part of your digestive system is also affected. The walls become vulnerable to damage, they become inflamed and can be ulcerated too. Crohn's disease is an inflammatory condition of the lower part of the small intestine that can be inherited but can also be caused by and is certainly aggravated by stress. It can become so bad that permanent and serious damage can be done to the intestinal lining. Ulcerative colitis is a combination of ulceration and inflammation of the colon. It too can be caused, or aggravated, by stress and for similar reasons.

Diverticulitis

The lower part of the intestinal tract, the colon, is a relatively wide tube with muscular bands round the walls that propel the material along. During stress, inflammation, periods of flatulence and other digestive problems, part of the colon lining can bulge between the muscle fibres creating pockets (diverticulae). Faecal matter accumulates in these pockets; it then ferments and leads to more gases plus local inflammation and damage (diverticulitis). The result is a painful condition that flares up each time you feel stressed.

IBS

Irritable Bowel Syndrome is yet another stress-related intestinal problem. Again the lack of normal digestive function can lead to the bowels becoming inflamed. This in turn can lead to pain and cramps. IBS may also be caused or aggravated by allergies and we will see later that these too can be stress-related.

Leaky gut

It should come as little surprise to learn that all the various types of damage mentioned above can so harm the lining of your digestive tract that it can become 'leaky'. This means that a variety of toxins and partially-digested foods can enter your bloodstream. This can lead to a variety of problems ranging from headaches and mental symptoms to a range of allergic reactions as your body challenges the various undigested foods.

Ironically, this situation can also lead to a loss of nutrients. Many minerals, for instance, need a particular carrier molecule to get them across the gut wall and without it, even when the wall is damaged, they may pass straight through you and out in the stool.

Constipation and diarrhoea

The lack of normal of digestive activity can lead to the system closing down, to a lack of peristalsis and so to the lack of bowel movements. This means that waste material remains static within the colon instead of being expelled. This in turn leads to putrefaction, the production of gases and toxins, and to inflammation and related damage. These toxins can enter the bloodstream and travel throughout your body causing a wide range of problems including headaches, nausea, malaise, fatigue and a variety of other symptoms.

On the other hand, the various inflammatory conditions that we have discussed, such as Crohn's disease and IBS, can lead to diarrhoea. This commonly leads to dehydration and to the loss of a wide range of nutrients. It can also lead to the loss of those very important vitamins and minerals that you need in additional amounts at this time to enable you to deal with the overload in your life.

Infections

Weakened immune system
Stress leads to a number of changes in your immune system. There is clear evidence that stress and distress lead to a reduced number of white blood cells. It is these white blood cells that fight, engulf and destroy the many hundreds of different pathogenic or harmful organisms that are constantly battling at your system. When you are healthy these white cells have no difficulty in destroying these organisms. When you are stressed the organisms can get the upper hand.

Stress also depletes your level of the beneficial nutrients that your cells need to help protect you from viruses. Vitamin C is an obvious example here but in fact a wide range of vitamins and minerals is necessary for proper immune function. Many other changes, too many to discuss here in detail, can come about as a result of stress and weaken your immune function. So this is yet another reason to boost your nutrition at this time.

Common Infections
When your immune system is weakened you are more likely to suffer from colds, flu and many other infections. The exact nature of these infections will depend on your own particular weaknesses. If, for

instance, you are prone to bronchitis and other lung infections then you are more likely to come down with bronchitis when you are stressed. If your bladder is vulnerable and you have a history of cystitis then stress is likely to lead to another attack of cystitis.

It is a common experience to find that people who have recently been bereaved become ill. Elderly people who lose their partner often develop pneumonia or some other dangerous infectious disease. They may even die from it. Think how often you've heard the comment 'They just couldn't live without him [or her], they simply pined away'. This may be true, at least in part, but there is another explanation. The stress of the loss led to a weakened immune system which in turn led to the easy invasion of infectious bacteria and to the illness. Because of the stress and its effect on their resources they did not have the strength to overcome the illness.

Antioxidants

Another important function of your immune system is to protect you from oxidizing agents. Oxygen is an important substance and we soon die if we are deprived of it. However, it can also be dangerous. Oxygen is needed to 'burn up' the food you eat, to turn it into carbon dioxide and water. In a similar manner your own body (like that of the cow, pig or sheep you eat) can be 'burnt' in oxygen and converted into carbon dioxide and water. To prevent this happening you need and produce a range of antioxidants, substances that protect your own body from this oxidizing action.

Some of these antioxidants are enzymes, catalytic proteins produced by the various cells within your body. Others are coenzymes, small molecules that you get from food which help these enzymes to do their job. These coenzymes are commonly vitamins such as vitamins A, C or E and minerals such as selenium, zinc, copper, manganese and others.

Oxygen is not the only substance that can do oxidative damage. Chlorine and other oxidizing agents and compounds called free radicals can do similar harm. Chlorine occurs in drinking water. Free radicals occur in many processed foods, in pollution and in other environmental hazards.

You produce some in your body during metabolic processes, particularly if your diet includes lots of toxic chemicals. When you are under stress the various reactions that occur within your body lead to an increased production of these free radicals and an increased need for these antioxidant nutrients. However, because of the stress reactions, these same (nutrient) coenzymes may be being used up elsewhere in your system at just the time you need them to assist your antioxidant enzymes.

When you are not protected with an adequate amount of antioxidant activity you are much more likely to develop a number of health problems. These could include artery damage and heart problems, headaches and mental and emotional disturbances and even cancer.

Cancer

It should now be clear that many of these stress-induced health problems can lead to cancer. This can come about in the digestive tract because of the various digestive problems that develop and the build-up of local toxins that are carcinogenic. These may affect the colon or they may be absorbed and affect other parts of your body.

Cancer can come about because of the oxidative damage that we have already described and a probable lack of sufficient antioxidant nutrients. It can come about for a number of other reasons related to a weakened immune system.

When you sit an exam there is a pass mark. You are allowed to make a number of mistakes but still survive and pass the exam. This is a luxury not allowed to your immune system. The only acceptable pass mark for your immune system is 100 per cent. Every single time a carcinogen enters your body your immune system has to detect it and either destroy it or eliminate it. If it fails to do this you can develop cancer. It is estimated that we are all exposed to thousands of carcinogens daily and that many pre-cancerous cells form but that as long as your immune system is healthy and vigilant it can deal with them. When you are stressed there is the very real chance that this may not happen successfully.

Heart problems

The effect of stress on your heart is part of history. Most people can recall some elderly person in the family clutching their chest and saying 'No, oh no, my heart, you know how such things distress me' whenever there is a scene or an unexpected trauma. It may not always be true; in previous generations it was sometimes considered lady-like to be frail and to invoke a weak heart when stress occurred. However, stress can have a very real and adverse effect on both your heart and your circulatory system.

High blood pressure

The causes of most cases of hypertension or high blood pressure are unknown. In some (a very few) people, high blood pressure can be caused by an excessive intake of salt. More commonly it can be caused by a deficiency of calcium or magnesium. In most people with a tendency to high blood pressure it will rise during times of stress. High blood pressure in turn has an adverse effect on the walls of your arteries and veins and on your heart.

Raised cholesterol levels

The medical profession is at last coming to realize that cholesterol is not all bad, nor is it a true predictor of heart disease. There are other more important markers for heart disease, such as the level of homocysteine in your blood. However, it still seems true that it is better to have a level of cholesterol that is within the normal range than one that is significantly higher. In part this is because when your total cholesterol level is high, necessarily your level of substances called LDLs (Low Density Lipoproteins) is high as this is the type of lipoprotein that carries the most cholesterol. These LDLs also carry much of the fat-soluble toxins in the bloodstream. So for as long as your LDL level is raised you have an increased level of circulating toxins and are at increased risk of the dangers that these toxins can cause. Whereas when the LDLs are broken down, generally by your liver, the toxins they carry can be dealt with and eliminated.

It is timely to throw in a few words in defence of cholesterol – you need it for many reasons. You need it for the production of vitamin D and hence the absorption of calcium; for the production of sex hormones and the production of bile so you can digest fats. It is so important to your brain that there is twice as much cholesterol in that organ as there is in the same weight of eggs. It is also needed by your total nervous system and it is an important component of the walls of every cell in your body.

From our point of view here you also need cholesterol for the production of those important stress hormones, the corticosteroids such as cortisone, hydroxy cortisone, corticosterone and others. This means that when you are under stress there is an increased flood of cholesterol-related compounds into your bloodstream.

Many years ago the drivers in the Le Mans motor race were cholesterol-tested at each available opportunity. When they were relaxed their cholesterol levels were low. As the tension mounted, towards and during the race, their cholesterol levels rose alarmingly. The level continued to rise for some time after the race and took many hours to finally return to normal. I do not recall that LDL levels were measured specifically, probably not since it was some time ago, but it is almost certain that they rose too.

Heart attacks

Stress can indeed bring about heart attacks. This may in part be to do with the way cholesterol is metabolized. However, it may also occur for other reasons. Stress can, for instance, cause a constriction of blood vessels. If this leads to a reduced supply of blood to the walls of the heart muscle itself then the heart can fail to operate properly. In mild cases this can cause angina. In severe cases it can cause an actual heart attack. Stress can also lead to damage to the artery walls and hence to atheromas and atherosclerosis.

Impotence

Male or female, you make a variety of sex hormones. These include the group of oestrogens, progesterone, testosterone and several others. Women make the female sex hormones in their ovaries. Men make their male sex hormones in the testes. However, men also make female sex hormones and women make the male hormones. Since women don't have testes and men don't have ovaries they have to be made somewhere else and the chosen place is the adrenal glands.

When your adrenal glands are exhausted not only does the output of stress-management hormones become exhausted and fall, the output of sex hormones can also drop. In addition, stress can have other effects on sexual function and these can come about in a variety of ways. Sex is less appealing when you are tired. Impotence is more common in men when they are stressed.

Mental symptoms

Stress can change the physics and chemistry of your brain and these changes, in turn, can affect the way your brain behaves. It is these physical and chemical changes that we will be considering here. Your brain needs nutrients; it needs additional amounts during stress and if these are not available, with the best will in the world, your attempt at positive thoughts and personal growth and development will be restricted.

Insomnia

Stress may well keep you awake at night as your mind works over and over the problems that are concerning you. However, for good sleep you need a number of essential nutrients. The amino acid tryptophan is important for the production of serotonin and this must be obtained from your diet; it cannot be made in the body. Thus a poor diet, particularly the sort of nutrient-poor 'comfort' diet that many people resort to under stress with lots of sugar and fat-rich snacks, may, of itself, create insomnia.

An increased intake of alcohol, often used as a remedy for insomnia as well as for stress, leads to several problems that actually have the opposite effect. These include the damaging chemical effect of the alcohol, the reduced intake of nutrients that results as alcohol calories replace food calories and the loss of nutrients as a result of the effect of alcohol on the body and its diuretic action.

Tryptophan is an unusually large amino acid and may lose out as it competes with other amino acids for passageways into the brain. Its success in this is improved if your blood sugar level is adequate but is hindered when your blood sugar level drops. Tryptophan is found in particularly high concentrations in milk and dairy products and animal flesh proteins, thus giving the theoretical explanation of grandmother's insomnia cure, hot milk and honey. Several B-vitamins are needed for sleep and if these are used up because of the changes occurring in your body as a result of stress then their deficiency may contribute to your insomnia.

Irritability and anger

We have already seen that when you are stressed and need more energy your blood sugar level can fall. When that happens there may be insufficient glucose for your brain and you are likely to feel tired. This has further consequences. You will also be more cross and irritable. This means that in addition to your mental response to the stress which may include anger and irritation there will be extra anger and irritation as a result of the chemical changes that are occurring in your brain.

Confusion and fuzzy thinking

There are a number of amino acids, derived from the protein foods that you eat, that make up necessary messenger molecules, called neurotransmitters, within your brain. Many of the amino acids must come from your diet, others you can make provided you eat sufficient protein. The metabolism of the amino acids and the synthesis of the neurotransmitters involves reactions catalysed by vitamin B_6 and some of the other B-vitamins. You need greater amounts of these neurotransmitters, and hence of these nutrients, when you are stressed and your brain is working overtime. Without adequate amounts of them you are likely to feel the stress at the mental level, again experiencing irritability, confusion, muddled thinking and lack of motivation.

Poor concentration and memory

Memory and concentration can be affected by many of the changes we have already mentioned including nutrient deficiencies, a low blood sugar level and inadequate neurotransmitters. They can also be affected by other factors.

If, for instance, you suffer from candidiasis this problem can be worsened when you are stressed for a number of reasons, including the stress-related changes that can occur in your digestive symptom. When *Candida albicans*, the organism most commonly involved, becomes dominant within your digestive tract it converts large amounts of glucose into alcohol. The amount thus produced can be sufficient to give the feeling of being slightly drunk. This alcohol is then converted into acetaldehyde and you may experience many of the symptoms of a hangover and these can include changes in the way you think and concentrate. Allergies and masked food sensitivities, likely to be more troublesome, as we shall see, when you are stressed, can also lead to poor concentration, reduced mental clarity and memory and poor decision-making.

Finally

This is only a very small and somewhat superficial sample of some of the physical and chemical changes that can and do occur when you are stressed. It should be sufficient however, to make several points clear:

- Stress and overload make a huge impact on your body and your health.
- Even when you feel you are coping with the stresses you experience, they are taking their physical toll on your body.

𝕊 When you are stressed you need even better nutrition than when you are relaxed yet it is all too likely that your nutrition is allowed to deteriorate at this time.

𝕊 There is virtually no health problem or situation that could not be caused or aggravated by stress.

𝕊 Even if stress is not the initial cause of a health problem, the experience of stress can almost always aggravate the problem.

In the interests of your health you should not continue to put up with stress; you should aim to resolve and eliminate it.

CHAPTER TWENTY ONE

What Your Body Needs

It's time now to take a look at what your body needs to function with optimum efficiency, even, and perhaps particularly, when under stress. It needs something approaching 50 essential nutrients. It also benefits from a diet rich in many other compounds such as additional anti-oxidants, plant sterols, hundreds of bioflavonoids and related compounds called OPCs and many other phytonutrients.

Few people get sufficient quantities of these nutrients from their diet to create exuberant and vibrant optimal health. Sadly, as a result, many people operate at a sub-optimal level of health, often without being aware of it. Many patients have said to me, after appropriate dietary and nutrient intake changes, that they hadn't realized how good they could feel, how much better they could feel than the level of health they had assumed to be normal.

When you are stressed you are more likely to reduce the quality of your food and nutrient intake, rather than increase it. When people are stressed they tend to turn to alcohol for relaxation, to drink more coffee, tea or other caffeine-loaded drinks, to consume sugar-laden sweets for energy or to eat comforting creamy and sugary cakes and desserts.

Thus just at the time when you need extra nutrients you are probably consuming fewer. Let's see what you should be doing.

What your body does not need

There are thousands of toxins in the world around you. They come in the form of physical pollution, chemical toxins and biological organisms. Some of them you cannot avoid.

If you live in a city and travel to work there is only a limited amount you can do to avoid the pollution in the streets and on public transport. You can reduce your exposure to mobile phone energy frequencies by using yours (if you have one) with discretion, but you cannot avoid living in a world where the atmosphere is interpenetrated with radio waves of thousands of different frequencies.

You can buy organic food and drink purified water at home but if you eat in restaurants you cannot help being exposed to whatever chemical additives are in the food, the aluminium from the cooking utensils in which the food is cooked and the chlorine from the cooking water.

There are thousands of pathogenic organisms around us at all times. You can take steps to boost your immune system and you can avoid the use of antibiotics so that you remain protected from most of them, but they will still be there.

When you are under pressure you are more than usually vulnerable to these various toxins and so it becomes particularly important at this time to reduce your exposure to toxins where you can and to take extra protective measures to help you where you can't.

Additional Help

In addition to avoiding your toxic load you should do all you can to ensure a super-abundant intake of all the essential nutrients. There are also other steps you can take to help yourself at this time. These include the use of relaxing herbs, appropriate exercise, muscle-relaxing massages. Have stimulating foot treatments where the reflexology points that relate to all parts of your body are worked on. Take morale-boosting steps such as having a facial, a new hair style or buying new make-up or clothes and more.

All the above considerations are part of your 10-step plan to better relaxation, less stress and more fun. These steps are outlined in Chapter 22. All these steps will help you to improve your handling of the stresses with which you have not yet dealt and the overload you are under. However, on their own they are not the answer; they are not the solution to your problem. The answer to how to handle stress is to apply both Parts I and II of this book.

After over 25 years in clinical practice I have seen many people resolve their stressful situation by the methods outlined in Part I. Although it is much easier to do this if you also follow the steps given here, I have seen it done even without some of the considerations outlined in the following chapter. On the other hand, I have never seen anyone solve their problems when they totally ignored all the steps in Part I, no matter how well they ate and how well they nourished and cared for their body.

You can spend countless thousands on upgrading to the most magnificent computer equipment but if the program is not right the results will be unsatisfactory.

CHAPTER TWENTY TWO

Your 10-step Health Check and Stress-reducing Regime

There are many, many things you could do both to reduce the chemical and physical stressors on your body and to reduce the effects on your body of the mental and emotional stresses that are in your life. Many of them are included among the steps indicated below.

There are several ways you can use this list of steps, depending on your level of commitment and the extent of your desire to make positive changes. Clearly you could read the whole list and do all the steps at once. If you feel like doing that, that's fine. I have had many patients over the years who are enthused by the ideas of positive change and like to make a clean sweep all in one go. If this is how you feel I can only encourage you to go for it. On the other hand, this might seem like a stress in itself. If that is the way you feel then do the steps in sequence. Take one step at a time, each day adding the next step to your regime. Alternatively, you could tackle one step a week, again adding each new step to the growing regime. In that way, at the end of 10 days or 10 weeks, you will have done a significant amount to reduce the physical stressors in your diet and to improve your ability to deal with the mental and emotional ones.

If at the end of the Basic 10-step Programme you recognize that there are still problems in your life, that you are not as healthy, relaxed and full of energy as you would like to be, then take on the Advanced 10-step Programme. You can do these steps in the order indicated or you can pick the advanced steps that seem particularly appropriate to you. If you think you need it, do get professional advice. Just so much can be achieved by a book. When trying to improve your health and well being through making positive changes in your life there is indeed much you can do yourself; but there are also many times when professional help is useful or even necessary. A naturopath or nutritionist should be able to help you. In the nature of the problem, such practitioners are almost certainly better placed to help you than doctors, who tend to deal with named and recognized diseases rather than many of the more nebulous symptoms related to stress. Furthermore, the solutions are more likely to come from nutritional sources than from medical drugs.

If, when you have read the following, you decide that it is all too much, that there are too many changes you would have to make and that you simply don't have the time or the inclination to make the effort, then there is a Mini 10-step Programme you can follow. It will certainly lead to some improvement but, as with so much in life, you cannot expect too much if you do not make too much effort. I seriously encourage you to follow at least the Basic 10-step Programme so I have put the Mini 10-step Programme at the very end of this section.

The basic 10-step stress-management programme

Step 1 – Timing Your Meals

Eat three meals a day and make breakfast your most important meal.
The first thing to think about is the timing of your meals. Your body is programmed to:

a) turn the food you eat in the morning and at midday into energy and

b) turn the food you eat in the late afternoon and evening into body fat stores.

This made terrific sense in ancient times when we lived in caves and the search for adequate food was a daily concern, usually carried out in daylight hours. Then there was great survival advantage in using this food and energy efficiently and there was little to do after the sun went down. Now, it's true, this hormonal and metabolic pattern is a bit of a bore. However, your body has not yet caught up with the changes in civilization so we have to live with it.

This means that it is very important, if you are to have the energy and resourcefulness you will need throughout the day to cope with your problems, that you start the day with a good breakfast, have an energy-sustaining lunch and that you eat lightly in the evening. Boring, isn't it? How many times have you heard that before? Yet it remains a truth, even if you have little time for breakfast, less time for a quick lunch at your desk and endless time to entertain and eat a large meal late at night. As a graduate student I timed my meals all wrong, swearing I simply couldn't eat breakfast, wasn't hungry and didn't need it. Now I wouldn't give you the time of day without a good breakfast but I can happily skip dinner if necessary.

You may be screaming that you do not have time for breakfast. There are the children to see to and breakfasts to prepare for other people, that you'd rather sleep in that extra 10 minutes. Believe me, you don't have time or the energy *not* to have a good breakfast. It need not be an elaborate meal, but it should be a good-quality meal. Below is a recipe for Fresh Fruit Muesli. Other breakfast suggestions include scrambled egg or an omelette into which you incorporate as much vegetable as possible – try sautéed onions or sweet pepper, chopped tomato and herbs, and serve it with mashed potato instead of the ubiquitous bread. Poached eggs are also delicious on mashed potato.

Be adventurous. Have some of the leftovers from the night before. You might even cook extra for this purpose. In many countries the same foods are eaten for breakfast as for dinner; it is only the English that insist there are certain foods that are breakfast foods and that vegetables are, by and large, not included.

Fresh Fruit Muesli

This is the real thing, muesli as it was meant to be, as it was designed in the Swiss sanatoriums, before it became distorted by the commercial food companies to a form where it could be stored on shop shelves for months. It is essentially a fruit dish, a fruit salad or a bowl of just one or two fruits, chopped, with the sustaining addition of a small amount of a soaked raw grain and decorated with a few chopped nuts:

Ingredients (per person):
- 1 tablespoon raw porridge oats or other grains
- milk, fruit juice or water
- 2 or more pieces of fresh fruit, such as an apple and a pear. Use fruits in season and thus vary the dish.
- 2–3 tablespoons plain yoghurt, or dairy substitute such as soy, rice or oat milk, or fruit juice
- 1 dessertspoon sunflower seeds or chopped almonds, brazils or other nuts or seeds

Method
   a) Put the oats in a bowl, add the milk, fruit juice or water, just sufficient to moisten the oats.
   b) Chop the fruit and put on top of the oats.
   c) Add the yoghurt or other liquid.
   d) Sprinkle the seeds or chopped nuts on top.

This is a quick and easy dish to prepare. It is also an excellent meal. The fruit supplies short-term energy and the grains and nuts or seeds will provide energy all the way through to lunch time. You will get protein from the oats, yoghurt and seeds, carotenes from the fruits, B-vitamins from the grains and seeds, vitamin C from the fruit and vitamin E from the seeds. The oats, milk and yoghurt provide calcium and the oats and seeds are rich in a variety of other minerals and in fibre. The seeds or nuts provide essential fatty acids.

Now that you have got the day off to a good start don't spoil it by snacking through the morning or skipping lunch. You need a snack mid-morning? Then increase the size of your breakfast or provide yourself with some fruit or nuts to nibble on. You don't have time for lunch? Not true. Again, it is a case of you don't have time *not* to have lunch. The boost you will get from a proper meal in the middle of the day and of allowing yourself 20 minutes during which to relax and eat it will enable you to get so much more done for the rest of the day that you will more than make up for the amount of time involved.

If you are at home there is no need to have a sandwich for lunch. Sandwiches are only for those who simply must eat food that they can hold in their hand. Otherwise the best lunch you can make is a large bowl of fresh vegetables, chopped, tossed in a light dressing and accompanied by a moderate amount of protein food such as fish, an egg or some cheese, preferably low-fat. I hesitate to call this a salad as for most people a salad means a few leaves, possibly with the addition of some cucumber, tomato and tinned beetroot. Instead, try grating carrots, parsnips or beetroot, chop up broccoli and cauliflower, use spinach and beet leaves, and of course add the more normal salad ingredients such as celery, tomato, sweet peppers and so forth. If you like you can also add some fresh fruit, a grated apple or a chopped banana. You can also incorporate cooked vegetable leftovers.

When it's time for your evening meal, keep it light. This does not mean that you cannot have a good time socially. You can still go out to a restaurant or dine with friends. Simply eat less, and avoid all the rich and high-calorie foods. These foods might tempt you but you also know they will leave you over-full, sluggish the next morning and definitely lacking in the energy and wellbeing you need to tackle the day ahead. You can even have three courses in a restaurant, if you want. Start with a green salad or a single cooked vegetable, pick a simple fish or meat dish for the main course with a vegetable and follow with fruit for dessert. Better still, you might like to choose two light starters and then go straight to the fruit.

If possible, have your evening meal several hours before you go to bed. This will give your body time to digest and assimilate it for a few hours before your system slows down. I know this is not always easy in today's busy world, but this just highlights yet another benefit of having a large breakfast and a small dinner.

If you want to snack, do so. There is even some evidence that it is healthier to eat little and often rather than one or possibly two large meals in the day. The real problems with snacking are two-fold. Firstly, snacks tend to be eaten on the run, causing all sorts of digestive problems as we have already discussed. Secondly, most snacks are high in calories and low in nutrients. Choose your snacks wisely. Do not snack on chocolate bars and crisps. Snack on fresh fruit, vegetable crudités, perhaps with a lemon or French dressing dip, on a few raw nuts, or on a piece of cold meat or chicken. Wrap something savoury in a couple of large lettuce leaves. If you put your mind to it you will be able to think of all sorts of nourishing snacks. If you do snack, make sure your meals are correspondingly smaller or you will add the stress of being overweight to the other stresses in your life. And, of course, relax while you snack and for a while afterwards.

Step 2 – Your stress-reducing diet

Learn all you need to know about diet and make determined efforts to improve yours.
Start in the bookshops or your local library, visit your local health-food shop and then move to your kitchen. This is the time to learn all you need to know to create the perfect diet. There are countless books available on diet – you may even have some already – if not, buy or borrow some. At least at the start you will need to have them on hand as reference to keep you on the straight and narrow and stop you slipping back into your old ways. There is not the space here to include all you need to know about nutrition and good diets but do make yourself a promise that you will follow all the guidelines that have been given in this book.

At this time it is particularly important that you eat well. So it is essential the moment you feel stressed to consider making, at the very least, some basic changes to your diet in a positive direction and to stop yourself sliding into a non-nutritious diet of overly-processed, comforting junk foods.

You probably already have a fair idea of some of your bad habits in the diet department. Go through your kitchen cupboards and put to one side all the foods you know you should not be eating. Throw them out or give them away. If you honestly can't afford that, then put them to the back of a cupboard and use them when you are entertaining friends who have made no such commitment to a healthy diet.

Get rid of all those sugar-laden products – the cakes, biscuits, sweet deserts, chocolates and sweets. Get rid of all the sauces and flavourings that are labelled with E numbers. Replace white flour and pasta with wholemeal varieties, white rice with brown, white bread or 'wholemeal' bread that is so light it probably contains either white flour or chemical additives with true wholemeal bread that is heavier than white and a lot more satisfying. Rearrange your shelves and refrigerator so there is much more room for fresh fruits and vegetables. Get rid of soft drinks and cordials; replace them with mineral water and pure fruit juices. Then get to the shops and fill your trolley with (preferably organic) fresh fruit and vegetables.

Step 3 – Adequate Protein, of Good Quality

Include good-quality, low-fat protein in your diet every day.
Choose from fish, poultry and lean cuts of red meat. If you prefer non-flesh sources, include eggs, cottage cheese and soya proteins such as tofu.

It is important to have a good protein intake. There is obligatory nitrogen loss from your body daily which means that some protein breakdown is occurring every day. All your muscles are made of protein. This includes the muscles that you control, that you use to move and to exert force. It also includes your involuntary muscles, the internal ones that keep your system working without conscious control from you, such as those that pump the blood around your body or those that move food along your digestive tract. Your internal organs are made of muscle. You probably already know that foods such as liver are high in protein and low in fat.

Every day some of this protein is being broken down. Every day new protein is needed to replace the old tissue with new tissue. In other words, some of your body protein is lost daily and must be replaced. When you are stressed this amount increases as extra demands are made on your body. More muscles are used, more hormones and neurotransmitters are needed, your immune system's protein requirement goes up, and so forth. This protein is needed both to help you cope with stress and to prevent health problems that might otherwise develop.

Unfortunately, when you are stressed you often feel you can't be bothered to cook a proper meal. Instead you rely on snacks or fast foods. These are likely to be high in saturated fats and refined carbohydrates and low in good-quality protein. These are not the foods you want.

Your protein intake can be of either animal or vegetable origin. Meat, fish and chicken are fine. Eggs are good, in fact they are an excellent and compact source of high-quality nutrients, supplying all the developing embryo needs for its developing life, no space is wasted on unnecessary padding. Cheese is good protein but most cheeses are too high in fat to be your main protein source. Cottage cheese is a healthy option, unless you are allergic to dairy products. If you prefer to be a vegetarian or to eat very little in the way of flesh foods then make sure you include tofu and other soya products, beans, lentils and other legumes.

This is not the place for a discussion about vegetarianism, and I personally prefer to eat very little of the flesh foods of commerce, but it is worth thinking about your diet in an evolutionary sense. For millions of years our diet was based essentially on fruits, vegetables, nuts, seeds, fish and meat. We certainly weren't vegetarian. Nor did we eat grains or dairy products. If you are in any doubt about foods that are good for you, or if you think you might have allergies but choose, for whatever reason, not to have them tested, then this Cave Age Diet has about the best chance of being your healthy option.

Back to the proteins. Remember we have said that a vegetarian diet could leave you short of carnitine, methionine and lysine so include eggs and, if you can, fish at least. There are certain amino acids you need in times of stress and to maximize your energy production. In general these come in far greater amounts from animal proteins than from plant proteins. You might think that you just need to eat more of the plant proteins. However, that gives you more of the amino acids but does not change the proportions. You would still be relatively short of the ones mentioned. To a certain extent they compete with each other for absorption and so you will do best to try to consume them in the right proportions. In this regard the protein from eggs is used the most efficiently, followed by that obtained from fish, milk products and then meats.

Specific amino acids and their tasks

We have seen that the relative proportions of amino acids in different protein foods, and specifically certain individual amino acids, are important, as well as the actual amounts.

You will recall that **tryptophan** is one of these important amino acids. It is needed by your brain to help you relax, unwind and sleep as we mentioned when considering insomnia, yet it has to compete with the others for uptake by the brain. It is found in relatively high concentrations in dairy products and flesh foods.

Phenylalanine and **tyrosine** are two amino acids needed for the synthesis of adrenaline and noradrenaline and so are needed for the activity of your adrenal glands and the production of adrenaline and noradrenaline. These same amino acids are also necessary for the formation of thyroid hormones, the ones that dictate how much metabolic activity you are capable of and hence how much energy you derive from the foods you eat.

The branched-chain amino acids – **leucine**, **iso-leucine** and **valine** – are needed for muscle protein, so if your stress involves you in a lot of physical activity that demands muscular strength, these are three amino acids that will be important to you.

Carnitine is important for energy production so choose foods rich in it plus those rich in methionine and lysine. Such foods include, you've guessed it, eggs and flesh foods.

All the other amino acids are important, but these ones are particularly so. Make sure that your diet contains at least as much protein when you are stressed as normal, possibly more. Ideally it should be low-fat protein so choose lean cuts rather than high-fat sources. For this reason fish, other seafood and chicken are better than pork and ham. Avoid highly-processed sausages as the chemical load they provide will simply give your liver more work to do.

Step 4 – Getting all the vitamins you need

Include vitamin-rich foods in your diet and buy a top-quality multivitamin supplement.

We have already mentioned a number of vitamins that are important when you are stressed. I don't propose here to go through all their functions, deficiency signs and therapeutic uses. There isn't space and these are covered in hundreds of different books that concentrate on these features. However, it is worth mentioning briefly how vitamins, or a lack of them, could impact on your ability to handle stress. Once we have done this you will, hopefully, be more than ever committed to making the positive changes to your diet that will be needed at this time if you want to get the best results.

The **B-group vitamins**, particularly vitamins B_1, B_2, B_3 and B_5, are needed for the production of energy by every single cell in your body from brain cells to those in your feet. You cannot have sufficient energy to handle stress if you are deficient in these nutrients. Vitamin B_5 is needed in additional amounts for the production of several of your stress hormones from the adrenal glands and you will almost certainly benefit from additional amounts of vitamin B_3 if the stress starts you thinking you are about to 'crack-up' mentally (whatever that phrase means to you). Vitamin B_6 is essential for the amino acid and protein metabolism already discussed. Folic acid and vitamin B_{12} are essential for the proper use of iron by your red blood cells; a lack of these nutrients can lead to anaemia and fatigue and so to reduced ability to handle stress.

Three other nutrients loosely associated with the B-group are **biotin**, **choline** and **inositol**. Biotin is needed for energy production, for the metabolism of fats and to help if your hair starts to fall out. Choline and inositol are needed for the proper functioning of your liver, for its role in fat and cholesterol metabolism, hence protecting your heart, and in handling all the toxins to which you are exposed and those that you generate when stressed.

Specific B-group vitamins

Here is an extra guide as to which particular B-vitamin you might need in extra amounts when stressed. If your stress is leading to increased nervous tension, the jitters, the shakes and cravings for either sugar or alcohol, you could benefit from an extra supplement of vitamin B_1 and glutamine, an amino acid. If your stress and overload are leading you to feel that you cannot cope, that you are going quietly mad and may even crack up mentally under the pressure, then take an extra supplement of vitamin B_3. If you are suffering from overload and think that your adrenal glands are exhausted, take some extra vitamin B_5 and C.

Vitamin C is essential for many aspects of stress-management. It is essential for the production of adrenaline and noradrenaline by your adrenal glands. It is also essential for the preservation of these hormones. Without an adequate amount of vitamin C, adrenaline and noradrenaline are converted into highly toxic compounds called adrenochrome and noradrenochrome respectively. Vitamin C is essential for your immune system and so will help you not to succumb to infections, a common consequence of high stress levels. It also protects your arteries from a build-up of atheromas and cholesterol deposits, thus again being important for your heart and for reducing the effects of stress on that organ.

Vitamins A, C and **E** are antioxidants. One of the by-products of stress is the increased production of toxic oxidizing agents including free radicals, a topic we have already discussed.

So what to do? It is important to make sure that your diet contains increased (not decreased) amounts of vitamin-rich foods at this time.

These include all the vegetables, fresh fruits and whole grain products such as brown rice, wholemeal pasta and true wholemeal bread made with only wholemeal flour – no added refined flour. You would also be well-advised to take a multivitamin supplement. You may even find one that specifically focuses on the nutrients needed for stress (e.g. 'Adreno-Max' available from the author).

Most vitamins are water-soluble; the others can, in moderate amounts, be readily handled by your body and an excess can be eliminated in the urine. Taking a multivitamin supplement is rather like offering your body a smorgasbord of nutrients and allowing it to select the ones it needs in the amounts it requires. At reasonable concentrations, as found in most multivitamin supplements, there is negligible danger of taking too much.

Step 5 – Checking out your minerals

Eat a mineral-rich diet and take a supplement if necessary.
As a minimum you should include mineral-rich foods in your diet and take a multimineral supplement. It would be even better if you determined which specific minerals you need and supplemented appropriately.

A lot of minerals and vitamins work together. We have discussed vitamins. Minerals are the other half of the partnership.

Calcium and **magnesium** are needed for proper relaxation. This includes muscle relaxation and your ability to relax mentally and to sleep. Most people recognize that during times of stress there is a danger of your blood pressure rising. This is less likely to happen if you include adequate amounts of these two minerals in your diet. It is also a good idea to cut out high-salt foods such as chips and crisps, and to reduce the amount of salt you add to your foods.

Zinc and **chromium** are important for the proper management of your blood sugar level. We will be discussing this topic later in more detail (*see Advanced Steps*). Here, suffice it to say that you need zinc for the proper activity of insulin, the hormone that prevents your blood sugar level from rising too high, and chromium is needed so that the circulating blood sugar can enter your cells and be used for the production of energy.

Selenium, zinc, copper and **manganese** are important antioxidant nutrients.

Iodine is important for your thyroid gland and **iron** for your red blood cells so both these nutrients are needed for the production of the extra energy you will want, and be expending, at this time.

Mineral-rich foods are the vegetables. In general they even contain as much or more calcium (on a per calorie basis) than milk and other dairy products. They are certainly the best source of many of the trace minerals.

Unlike vitamins, if you are going to take a mineral supplement it is not enough just to present the body with a spread of minerals and ask it to help itself, although this is a good start. For the best results, it is important to find out just what you need as the minerals can compete with each other for absorption and transport. There are several ways of determining your needs. A relatively simple way is to get a chemical analysis done of a sample of hair. There are many laboratories that will analyse this for you and many practitioners who can help you interpret the results. For other testing methods you may need professional help and it would be wise to consult a naturopath at this time.

Step 6 – Eliminate toxins

Recognize the dangers and clean up your world.
You live in a toxic world; it is important to recognize this. It is important for your general health since toxins can cause damage to all the systems of your body. In addition, many of them affect your central nervous system and so can reduce your mental and emotional stability and your ability to handle the stresses in your life or make the appropriate changes.

Toxins include toxic chemicals, biological pathogens and harmful physical factors. The range of chemical toxins is vast. It includes emissions from petrol and other fuels, other environmental pollutants, industrial hazards in the atmosphere, medical drugs (all of which do have toxic side-effects) and many more. Even your own home is not safe. There is the vast range of agricultural and food additives that you consume on a daily basis; there are the toxins in the water supply and the various chemicals and sprays used in the bathroom (including toiletries and make-up), the kitchen (including the detergent on the plates and utensils on or in which you cook or serve your food), the home in general and the garden.

Biological pathogens include such simple organisms as *Candida albicans (see pages 296 and 305)* and those that cause common infections as well as the more serious pathogens. Physical hazards include the well-publicized effect of mobile phones, the emanations from televisions and the electromagnetic fields that surround all electrical objects. There are the hazards of the myriad radio and television waves that permeate the atmosphere, such problems as toxic building effect – the effect of air-conditioning, fluorescent lights and other similar hazards – x-rays and radioactivity.

Many of these toxins, and others, are outside your immediate control. You cannot suddenly create a pure world, nor can you opt for life on a (relatively) unpolluted mountain top. However, you can reduce the load considerably. Your strategies should start in the home. Go through your kitchen cupboards, get rid of those aerosol sprays and use more environmentally-friendly alternatives. Replace your aluminium kitchen ware with stainless steel or Pyrex. Replace your chemical detergents with some of the less toxic ones that are around, available in most health-food shops. Buy organic foods whenever possible and make a point of looking for foods that are marked 'GM-free' (not genetically-modified).

Look round your bathroom. How many toxic chemicals are in the substances you are using in the hope of improving your appearance? If clothes have been dry-cleaned, hang them out to air before putting them away. Become aware of smells; many of them (and you will surely be able to tell the difference) are not pleasant and natural perfumes but come from a variety of man-made chemicals, many of which can be harmful. Find the sources and, where possible, eliminate them.

Consider your medical cabinet. Do you really need those headache pills? Could you not have your allergies tested, correct your blood sugar level and/or take herbal tranquillizers? Do you really need to take antibiotics or could you replace them with large doses of vitamin C and lots of fresh fruit? You almost certainly don't need those antacids – almost no-one has too much stomach acid; many people have a deficiency. Correct the problem with stomach-healing agents such as aloe vera and vitamin E.

Even the sitting room merits attention. Do you sit directly in front of the television? Move it. You can see very nearly as well from a sideways view and you are less vulnerable to disturbing rays. Consider the back of your television too and remember that electromagnetic rays can pass through walls. I once had an eight-year-old patient, a boy who had recently become hyperactive. His problem was traced to the day his parents rearranged the sitting room so that the television in it backed directly onto the head of his bed in the adjacent bedroom. When his bed was moved out of this direct line his behaviour settled back to normal.

If you go out to work then check out your work place. If possible, open the windows. Unless you are in an area of high pollution this is probably a healthier option than the recycled air in the building system. Move your desk so that you do not sit directly under a fluorescent light. Become aware of smells. It is not appropriate to say 'what a bad smell, but I can get used to it'. A bad smell should alert you to the fact that molecules of some foreign substance are entering your system. They are certainly passing the smell detectors at the back of your nose and are probably entering your lungs.

Choose the non-smoking areas in public places. Hold your breath or breathe out rather than in when large lorries belching fumes drive past you. As you consider your daily life you will doubtless find many such small steps that could reduce your intake of toxins. Each may seem, on its own, to be a very small step, yet collectively they can make a significant difference to your intake of toxins.

We cannot discuss here all the possible toxins to which you could be exposed but there is one that is worth focusing on. Most people have silver or mercury amalgams in their teeth. Mercury is a toxic metal. Each time you chew or swallow saliva you could be swallowing a small trace of this toxic substance. Mercury can lead to any of the following symptoms:

⌒

Psychological
anxiety
apathy
appetite loss
depression
dizziness
drowsiness
hallucinations
insomnia
irritability, angry outbursts
manic depression
poor memory, poor
    concentration, brain fog
nervousness, shyness
low self-confidence
poor self-control
tremors

Mouth
bad breath
bleeding gums
bone loss
increased salivation
inflamed gums
inflamed mouth
metallic taste
loose teeth
pigmentation
ulcerations
white patches

Digestive tract
abdominal cramps
colitis

constipation
diarrhoea

Cardiovascular system
changes in blood pressure
chest pains
fast heart beat
slow heart beat
weak pulse

Immunological
allergies
asthma
rhinitis
sinusitis

Nervous system
dizziness
frequent headaches
noises in the ears
tremors – eyelid, lip, tongue,
    hand or feet

Respiratory system
breathing difficulties – shallow
    breathing, irregular breathing
emphysema
persistent cough

Others
anaemia
blurred vision
cold skin
clammy skin

fatigue	muscle weakness
fluid retention	poor co-ordination
increased sweating	reduced vision
joint pains	speech difficulties
loss of appetite	weight loss
low temperature	

You will easily see that these symptoms could be contributing to your feeling of being stressed. To follow this up further you should seek advice from a dentist who is aware of the toxic effects of mercury and experienced in removing the amalgams and replacing them with a safer material. (The British Society for Mercury-Free Dentistry can be contacted on 020-7370-0055 or at 225 Old Brompton Road, London SW5 0EA and will, on request, send you their regional directory appropriate to where you live.)

Consider going on a detox programme. You could plan one for yourself, based on a week (preferably more) of eating organically-grown, simple foods. Go on a fast – there are many books available with instructions as to how to do that. Or follow my own Liver Detox Plan.

Step 7 – Reduce your use of social drugs

Cut out coffee, tea and chocolate, reduce your intake of alcohol and, if you're a smoker, try to give up cigarettes.

Coffee

You may feel your day simply won't start if you don't have a cup of coffee, possibly two. This simply shows that your adrenal glands are becoming exhausted and have to be whipped into action to get them going. It also means that there are some fundamental changes that simply must be made if you don't want to break down. Remember what we said about Hans Selye and the three stages of stress *(see page 291)*? You have gone through the Alarm Phase. You have proceeded a fair way along the Adaptation Phase and your adrenal glands are pretty tired. If you need coffee to keep you going you are running out of adaptive resources and heading for the Exhaustion Phase. Once this occurs there will be serious health problems for you to deal with.

Coffee, by the usual definitions, is a drug. It is an addictive behaviour-modifying substance. If it was to be newly introduced into society today, perhaps by a natural therapist, it would almost certainly be banned.

Coffee provides no real benefit, nor, if you give it up, are you socially deprived. There are also many alternatives – instead you can drink herbal teas or dandelion coffee (excellent for your liver and to help you detoxify).

Some people can cut down on coffee gradually; others will give up cold turkey. If going without leads to a headache then it is already having a serious effect on you. The usual headache painkillers are not the answer and will probably have no effect. The only thing that will stop the headache is ... of course, a cup of coffee. Put up with the headache and in a day or two you will be through the crisis. After that, you can leave the coffee alone.

Tea

Tea is, in many ways, a milder version of coffee. It contains, per cup, about a third of the amount of caffeine as is found in coffee. A 'social cuppa' can readily be replaced by a cup of herbal tea for the same social effect. If you must drink tea then change to green tea. New evidence does suggest that it has some health benefits due to the presence of a number of antioxidant compounds.

Chocolate

Chocolate is a highly addictive compound. It can also have a number of undesirable effects on the body, including premenstrual syndrome and pimples. Very often people who say they crave chocolate turn out to be allergic to it. The problem may be the chocolate itself; it may also, in part, be due to the sugar and milk (other common allergens). Using chocolate to solve your stress problems may provide a temporary indulgence but it crowds more nutritious foods out of your diet and thus leads to a lack of the essential trace nutrients, a lack of real energy properly produced and an increase, ultimately, in nervous tension.

Alcohol

Many people use alcohol as a prop when they are under pressure. They turn to alcohol to help them relax or in an, often vain, attempt to sleep better. Unlike coffee, tea and chocolate, the suggestion here is not to give up alcohol totally, but to make sure you keep it down to a couple of drinks a day at the most. Enjoy it but do not use it as a crutch or to excess.

The amount of alcohol in two drinks a day (possibly half a drink less for a woman, half a drink more for a man) can be dealt with by the liver. With a couple of drinks you can relax and unwind after work, you can share a glass of wine over dinner. Wine even gives you some benefits. It helps to improve your digestion, stimulates your digestive juices and may even provide some beneficial compounds that can protect your heart.

Going without alcohol altogether, in our society as it is today, may mean you miss out on or are excluded from some social situations. It may mean you don't relax and share a quiet time with your partner. It may mean you rush dinner. It may even mean you are not invited to some parties or situations. Losing these benefits could be more detrimental than the effects of the alcohol itself.

However, drinking more than two glasses a day is definitely a problem. Using a heavy intake of alcohol to drown your troubles will not solve them and is of only temporary and superficial benefit. The additional amount of alcohol damages your liver, reduces its function and decreases its ability to detoxify your system and do the many thousands of beneficial things it does for you (see my book, *Liver Detox Plan*). Increasing your alcohol intake also crowds out nutritious foods and so decreases your intake of essential nutrients, thus reducing your ability to handle stresses.

If you have trouble reducing your intake in social settings, use the following trick. Put sparkling mineral water into a wine glass. At a restaurant you can have both this glass and one with your wine side by side on the table. You will be surprised to find how much of your pleasure comes simply from sipping from an elegant wine glass and that this strategy can lead to a greatly reduced consumption of wine.

Step 8 – Herbs that pacify

Use herbs to help you remain calm.
If you have been using tranquillizers, get rid of them and use herbs instead to help you relax. Even if you are not using drugs, there are several herbs that can help you relax and can be of positive benefit when you are stressed. By taking them you can become calmer and better able to handle and deal with whatever is stressing you. When you are calm you can think better and respond more productively to situations that arise. In this way you can handle stress better; you may even be able to reduce some one-time stresses to events you can handle without discomfort.

Herbs that come into this category include passion flower (passiflora), skullcap, valerian and chamomile. These and other herbs are calming; they also help to prevent insomnia, a frequent companion to and aggravation of stress. They can be drunk as herbal teas or taken as tinctures or tablets. They can be taken individually or found in combinations in different anti-stress preparations.

Passion flower (passiflora)
Passion flower helps you to relax both physically and mentally. It acts on the nerves to reduce pain and is an antispasmodic, relaxing tense muscles. This also means that it is helpful in the treatment of asthma and you will know, if you suffer from that problem, that the symptoms are often worse when you are stressed, so for you this is a particularly useful herb.

Skullcap
Skullcap is particularly useful for nervous tension. If you get the fidgets, can't keep still or find yourself uselessly twitching, scratching

or performing other involuntary actions under the effect of stress, this could be the herb for you.

Valerian

Valerian is one of the most effective relaxing herbs. Use it when you are particularly tense and uptight. Like passion flower it is an antispasmodic; it is especially useful if you find that tension hits you in the stomach as it helps to soothe stomach cramps and digestive colic. Many people find that stress gets their 'guts in a knot' or gives them indigestion; if you are one of them, this could be the herb for you. It helps to relieve pain and is particularly useful if you are prone to tension headaches.

Chamomile

Chamomile is probably the most comprehensive of this group of herbs, having a number of different uses. In addition to its ability to relieve anxiety and tension, it helps to relieve indigestion and flatulence, and reduces pain and inflammation. If your eyes are tense or inflamed you can use the warm tea bags as soothing eye pads. Gargle with it if you have a sore throat or laryngitis and use it as a mouth wash if you have mouth ulcers or sores. This is the most readily available of the herbs in this group; it can be bought in most health-food shops and even in most supermarkets as a herbal tea. It is strong and effective yet gentle enough that it can be given to small children and even to babies to help relieve colic.

Lime Blossom

This is another relaxing herb which is particularly helpful when nervous stress and tension are associated with migraine headaches or raised blood pressure.

Wild Lettuce (*Lactuca virosa*)

I have added the Latin name for this herb as there are many different types of lettuce and they should not be confused. Wild lettuce is excellent in cases of restlessness, anxiety and insomnia. It helps create the relaxation needed to overcome insomnia and is useful when stress affects your digestive system and contributes to colicky pains. Like chamomile, it is particularly useful for children. It helps when their stress or tension lead to restlessness and over- or hyperactivity.

Step 9 – Have fun and sleep soundly

Make sure you get sufficient sleep and that you have time for some fun every day.
You are probably already telling yourself that you should get more sleep. However, this is often more difficult to achieve than it sounds. Many people, when they are stressed, find that adequate and relaxing sleep is hard to come by. Perhaps you are so busy trying to deal with your stress load that you are burning the candle at both ends as you try to find the time to solve the problems. Do you work late into the night trying to deal with all that has to be done and then rise early, after a disturbed night's sleep, trying to get an early start and keep up with what has to be done? Or perhaps you are going to bed in good time but, night after night, find yourself lying awake with your mind racing and eyes wide open as sleep eludes you?

Sleeping Tablets
Taking sleeping tablets is not the answer to your insomnia. They may knock you unconscious for a few hours but they do not give you a relaxing night's sleep. Nor do you wake up refreshed afterwards. The normal brainwave patterns of natural sleep as measured by EEGs are well known and the brainwave patterns of your brain in chemically-induced sleep are quite different to those of natural sleep. In normal sleep there is a rhythmical and developing pattern of deep sleep (non-REM or NREM sleep), alternating with periods of rapid eye movement (REM) sleep. It seems that REM sleep is the time when you may be dreaming. As you get closer and closer to waking up, the periods of REM sleep increase and it appears that these periods are important. If volunteers are deprived of REM sleep by waking them up every time they

enter this phase they become tense, anxious and irritable. When subsequently they are allowed to sleep normally they spend a lot more time than usual in REM sleep, as if to catch up. Many sleeping tablets both interfere with the normal sleep patterns and reduce the amount of REM sleep that occurs. This is one of the reasons why you wake up more tense and feel less refreshed after a night of chemically-induced sleep than after a night of natural sleep.

Remedies for Insomnia

So how can you overcome insomnia without taking sleeping pills? You have probably already thought of part of the answer. Use the herbs discussed in Step 8. Passion flower, skullcap, valerian and chamomile can all be taken before bedtime to help you relax. Hops can also be added to the mixture.

Two tissue salts, called Kali Phos and Mag Phos, are readily available from most health-food shops that specialize in supplements and remedies. They can help you to relax and sleep. Mag Phos helps your muscles to relax and Kali Phos helps the brain and nervous system to relax.

Grandmother's classic remedy, hot milk and honey at bedtime, is valuable for reasons that are now better understood. Remember milk protein is particularly rich in the amino acid tryptophan. This is needed for the production of serotonin which in turn is needed for the production of slow wave (NREM) sleep. However, as tryptophan is a particularly large amino acid, it has to compete with the other amino acids for entry into the brain. This entry is facilitated by the honey sugars in the bloodstream.

Enjoy Yourself!

In addition to getting sufficient sleep it is important that you have some fun. No matter how much is going on in your life you will achieve better results and do so more efficiently if you set some time aside each day to do the things you really enjoy. Plan to spend some time doing something you look forward to, something that gives your heart a lift and a glow. It's not for me to tell you what it should be as that is a highly personal decision. It might be doing something active or it might be simply giving yourself time out to do absolutely nothing. It might be something other people think of as a chore, such as gardening or tidying out old boxes in the attic. It might be self-pampering, such as having a massage or a facial. It may involve people or being alone. Whatever it is, if you have it planned, if you have it to look forward to, then some of the things you have to do in your crowded schedule will seem more tolerable. Don't argue that you haven't got sufficient time. Like so many of these steps, you don't have time *not* to do this one. The time you spend having fun will be provided by the increased efficiency and energy you have when faced with the next crisis.

Step 10 – Exercise

Use your body. Exercise regularly each day as a matter of routine.
Exercise is essential for more reasons than we have room to discuss here. Of course there are all the obvious reasons – it tones your muscles, benefits your heart and keeps you slim – but there are more benefits than that. By increasing your circulation it increases the flow of blood and the nutrients it carries to all the cells throughout your body, thus improving your skin (an obvious and visible result) and the function of all your tissues and organs. It also stimulates your lymphatic system and helps your body to get rid of toxins. Being physically active and putting weight-bearing pressure on your bones helps to prevent osteoporosis. By increasing your exercise and keeping fit you are less likely to suffer from a wide range of diseases; you will also feel more alert, more refreshed and better able to deal with stress.

This does not mean that you have to find time to go to the gym each day. There is a vast difference between working out at the gym daily and being a couch potato. Whatever you are doing now, you can do a bit more. If you travel to work by public transport, commit to walking part of the way. If you go up and down in lifts, stop, learn to walk up the stairs. Don't stand on escalators – you haven't suddenly lost the use of your legs – walk. Housework and gardening are terrific, but they don't increase your heart rate or oxygen consumption. So run up and down stairs, run from one point in the garden to the next. There are many ways you can build small and frequent amounts of physical activity into your life.

Go to the gym if it suits you. Swim – it doesn't strain your joints. Find a sport or activity you enjoy. I wouldn't move a muscle if asked to go for a run but offer me a game of tennis before work and I'm up and at it. If your sport has social benefits as well it will be even more enjoyable and you will do it more consistently. If exercise is anathema, try going dancing (the more energetic kind).

Advanced 10-step Programme

If you are working on your mental and emotional issues and have put the Basic 10-step Programme into practice yet still do not feel well or relaxed, then consider the following Advanced 10-step Programme. You can follow each of the steps in sequence or you can pick the one or ones you feel might be specifically appropriate for you. Whatever happens, consider all of them, one after the other, until you start to feel better.

I apologize in advance for the fact that in the following steps there are frequent recommendations to read other books or get professional help. There simply isn't room here to cover all the options. However, knowing the direction in which you should or could go will get you off to a good start. You may well find that you need professional help as we are getting into more complex areas here but there are also several things you can do on your own.

Step 11 – Improve your digestion

There are two aspects to stress and your digestive system. Firstly, as we have seen, stress can cause enormous damage to your digestive system, ranging all the way from mild indigestion to full-scale ulcers or such serious illnesses as Crohn's disease or IBS.

To reduce the damage stress can do to your digestive system:

a) make a serious attempt to relax before and immediately after eating

b) eat slowly and chew your food thoroughly

c) drink aloe vera juice once or twice a day (it helps the healing process)

d) take tablets of pure slippery elm or a teaspoon of pure slippery elm powder before lunch and dinner (this is the equivalent of putting an internal plaster over damaged areas until they heal).

Secondly, an upset digestive system can interfere with your normal absorption of nutrients and so reduce their availability for the cells throughout your body. Your digestive system is the route via which all nutrients enter your body, are digested and absorbed into your system. You will by now have realized that nutrition is important to you at many different levels. Remember there are around 50 or more substances your body absolutely needs to get from foods. There are many other nutrients from which it can benefit. Swallowing (ingesting) them is one thing; this is a matter of conscious decision on your part. Releasing (digesting) them from food and absorbing them into your system is another and your capacity to do this is both unconsciously and adversely affected when you are stressed.

Do you have any of the following symptoms?

- bad breath
- coated tongue
- mouth ulcers
- bleeding gums
- burping
- heartburn
- stomach or duodenal ulcers
- pain at the bottom of your right rib cage
- abdominal bloating
- abdominal cramping or pain
- alternating constipation or diarrhoea

💰 constipation (fewer than three bowel motions a day)
💰 haemorrhoids or itching round the anus

Any of these symptoms could mean you should improve your digestive function. Either find out more for yourself or get professional advice.
Use the following simple self-treatment programme:

a) 1 teaspoon of pure slippery elm powder (if there is acid or burning pain)
b) aloe vera juice (it comes in different strengths so consult the label)
c) acidophilus or other probiotics (especially if you are bloated or have any of the symptoms of candidiasis)
d) hydrochloric acid with digestive enzymes (to aid digestion)
e) a soluble fibre such as psyllium hulls or linseeds (if constipated).

If these don't solve the problem you could have food allergies and may need professional advice. Keep in mind that antacids are only palliative and, in the long run, do more harm than good. You need the acid for proper digestion. The pain occurs if there is damage to your digestive tract lining, not because you have excess acid, and it is this that should be repaired.

Step 12 – Make sure you're not hypoglycaemic

Read the following and, if you suspect you are hypoglycaemic, follow the suggestions given. If you are not sure, or if the application of these suggestions does not change your symptoms, then consult a professional. You cannot deal successfully with stress when your blood sugar level is unstable.

A normal blood sugar level is essential for both proper energy production and proper relaxation, both of which are needed in normal circumstances and even more so when you are under stress. As we have seen, your brain is particularly dependent on blood sugar rather than fat. A low blood sugar level leads to irritability, tension, jitters and many other signs of stress. When your blood sugar level is low you will fly off the handle very much more easily than at other times.

Your body needs energy for every single thing it does. This is true of you as a whole; it is true of all your tissues and each of your organs and it is true of each of the individual cells that make up those tissues and organs. Within those cells the majority of the chemical reactions that occur require energy. The exceptions are those reactions that release energy to provide what is needed by the other reactions.

In general this energy can come from either fats or glucose. When major amounts of energy are required it generally comes from fats. These fats come from your stored fat in adipose tissues. For fine-tuning the amounts of energy they need your cells use the glucose that circulates in your bloodstream. This is obtained either from food or from the breakdown of stored glycogen in your liver.

It is important that the amount of this glucose remains within fairly narrow limits. If your blood sugar level rises too high, as in diabetes, it can cause damage to various tissues. If it falls too low, as in hypoglycaemia, you are deprived of needed energy.

To maintain this normal blood sugar level, several hormones come in to play. When your blood sugar level rises above the normal range, insulin is pumped out from your pancreas and this enables the cells to take up the glucose. The cells that need it for energy use it, your liver takes up any spare and stores it as glycogen; if there is any more left it is converted into fat and stored for later energy needs. When your blood sugar level falls below the normal range, adrenaline is released from your adrenal glands and this stimulates the release of the stored liver glucose so that your blood sugar level can return to normal.

Every time you are stressed your whole body uses glucose, adrenaline is released and liver glycogen is broken down. Stress can eventually lead to adrenal exhaustion. When this happens your blood sugar level will fall and stay down for a prolonged period. During this time you will experience all the symptoms of hypoglycaemia. These can include any of the following:

- fatigue
- headaches
- irritability
- nervousness and tension
- anxiety
- depression
- nervous habits
- insomnia
- mental disturbances
- dizziness
- shaky hands and legs
- weakness
- internal 'shakes'
- tight chest
- extreme hunger
- sugar and other food cravings
- night sweats

During times of stress you need more glucose. However, do not rush out and eat sugar or sugar-rich goods. You may think that eating sugar is the answer to a low blood sugar level, but this is not so. Say you do reach for a chocolate bar, a bag of toffees, a piece of cake or a sweet dessert, what will happen? Your blood sugar level will shoot up, insulin will come out and pump it down, your exhausted adrenals will be unable to stop the fall and you will be back with a low blood sugar level. What is the answer?

The answer is to eat small frequent meals. Eat whole grains rather than refined (white) grains and their products. The former release their starch (and so glucose) into the blood stream slowly over a prolonged period of time whereas the latter release their starch in a rush. Eat highly nutritious and high-fibre foods such as vegetables that also release their energy into the bloodstream slowly. Then turn your attention to your adrenal glands; they need support at this time. You will recall that this means most of the B-group vitamins, especially vitamin B_5 and vitamin C.

Finally, hypoglycaemia can result simply from stress and exhaustion. However, it can also be a symptom of other problems such as nutritional deficiencies, poor diet, malabsorption, excessive consumption of sugars, food and environmental allergies, digestive problems and many others.

Step 13 – Check out those hidden allergies

If you have any of the allergy symptoms discussed here or if you have any reason to suspect you have hidden allergies or food sensitivities, check it out. Have the appropriate tests done and then follow the treatments. Allergies could be the cause of your stress, or they could also result from your stresses.

You can turn many improbable statements into truths if you vary your definitions. If you define cars, as did Henry Ford, as black vehicles on four wheels, you can look at a stretch of motorway, gridlocked with traffic, and blithely declare that there are virtually no cars on the road, happily excluding from your consideration any of the coloured cars.

Medical allergists commonly define allergies as substances to which you have specifically identifiable antibodies. These tend to be the allergens that create obvious symptoms. If you break out in hives every time you eat strawberries or oysters, or choke and have trouble breathing every time you eat peanuts, then these are known and obvious allergens.

However, another type of allergen exists. It includes foods or other substances that activate your white blood cells and set off an inflammatory reaction. Substances that come into this category are usually referred to as 'masked food sensitivities'. For simplicity here we will also refer to them as allergens.

You may have totally unsuspected and hidden food allergies or sensitivities of this type. By definition they are hidden. They do not cause immediate reactions. Instead, they lead to a general malaise, a build-up of repeated symptoms, but symptoms that do not occur every time you are exposed to them. Rather, they build up and become part of an overall problem without an obvious cause.

Almost invariably, if present, they lead to an increased level of stress and tension. In fact, they may be a major cause of your stress. Equally, when you are stressed you are more likely to react to any of these allergens and to suffer symptoms. So to reduce the stress in your life you should check to see whether or not you have such allergies. A simple test can check you out against hundreds of different foods and/or common (food) chemical additives to see if you react allergically.

There is also a simple test you can do yourself at home. It is not infallible but may provide clues. It is based on the fact that many allergens will cause your heart to beat faster and hence your pulse to rise. Measure your resting pulse before eating a test food, then afterwards and at half-hour intervals for the next two hours. If your pulse increases by more than 10 per cent, then you are probably allergic to that food. Make sure that you are resting or you could get a false rise that has more to do with your activity than with allergies. Note, however, that if your pulse does not increase it does not necessarily mean you are not allergic to that food, only that it does not affect your heart rate.

What symptoms may result from allergies? Almost any symptom you can think of could be caused by an allergen. The most obvious ones include:

- headaches
- migraines
- sinus problems
- blocked nose
- excess production of mucus
- blocked ears
- wax in the ears
- glue ear in children
- frequent sneezing
- asthma
- digestive symptoms such as the production of gas, burping and the passing of wind, alternating constipation and diarrhoea
- skin conditions such as eczema and dermatitis
- joint problems such as arthritis and rheumatism

Mental problems that can be caused by allergens include all the symptoms of stress – irritability, tension, anxiety, mood swings, insomnia and a wide range of emotional and behavioural disorders. On top of that, I repeat, almost any symptom could be caused by an allergen. Over the 20 plus years I have been working in this field I have had many such surprises. Patients with diagnosed allergens who have then avoided the indicated foods have lost not only their more obvious allergy symptoms but also a wide range of other symptoms and problems, many of which they had not even thought to mention at the initial consultation.

Step 14 – Tackle candida

Consider the possibility that you are having problems related to the mould organism *Candida albicans*, particularly if you have taken antibiotics or used the oral contraceptive pill. Buy or borrow a book on the subject and consider whether or not the information given there applies to you (e.g., *Overcoming Candida* by Xandria Williams).

Candidiasis used to be a rare problem. Then antibiotics were discovered. Initially they were used with caution but in recent decades they have been dispensed with increasing frequency. In addition to whatever benefits they may provide they alter the nature of the organisms within your digestive tract. *Candida albicans* is present in most people but only forms a tiny percentage of the gut flora and its numbers are held in check. The use of antibiotics allows candida to flourish, become dominant and wreak havoc.

It can also flourish if you do not produce sufficient amounts of stomach acid. (Another reason not to take antacids). This acid is vital for normal digestion and the efficient absorption of nutrients. Unfortunately, a diet lacking sufficient amounts of essential nutrients, including minerals and B-vitamins, leads to a reduced production of acid. The amount of acid you produce can also decrease with age. When the acid output from your stomach into your small intestine decreases, candida is encouraged.

There are many other ways of telling whether or not candidiasis could be part of your problem. The first indication is based on symptoms and many of the books on the subject contain questionnaires. Common symptoms include:

Mental
depression
fatigue or lethargy
feeling drunk
feeling of being drained
feeling spacey or unreal
poor memory and concentration

Digestive
abdominal bloating
abdominal pain
alternating constipation and
　diarrhoea
burping
passing wind

Genital/sexual
impotence
loss of sexual desire
menstrual cramps or irregularities
persistent vaginal burning or
　itching

PMS
prostatitis
vaginal discharge, thrush

Limbs
burning or tingling
muscle aches
numbness
painful or swollen joints

Skin
athlete's foot
fungal infections
jock itch

Others
cravings for sugar, bread, cheese,
wine and beer
erratic vision
spots in front of the eyes

Tests for candida can also be done, for which you will need the advice of a professional. If present, an excess of this organism can lead to many symptoms that mimic stress and also reduce your ability to handle the normal stresses and strains of life.

Self-treatment programmes are described in many books on the subject. Alternatively, get professional advice.

Step 15 – Check your thyroid

You need energy to handle stress and your thyroid gland is instrumental in stimulating your metabolic rate, thus generating both heat and energy. It is estimated that thyroid deficiency, or an underactive thyroid gland, is a commonly unrecognized or misdiagnosed problem. The normal ranges set for the medical tests for blood hormone levels have been selected so that most people are considered to have normal thyroid function. However, some researchers put the true incidence of underactivity as high as 40 per cent and suggest that the 'normal' blood levels are wrongly set.

The best way to tell if your thyroid is working correctly is not to measure your blood hormone levels but to measure your resting temperature, since temperature control is one of the thyroid's jobs. Prepare a thermometer in the evening. Immediately on waking (naturally, not with an alarm clock) and while you are still as relaxed as possible, measure your armpit temperature. It should be above 97.8°F or 36.55°C. If it isn't, you should add kelp to your programme, and if the temperature remains low then a homoeopath should be able to give you the appropriate remedy.

Step 16 – Improve your immune function

Stress and your immune function are inter-related causally in two opposite ways:

a) Stress reduces your immune function and
b) an over-burdened immune system leads to health problems and reduced capacity to handle stress.

There are certain obvious signs of the effect of stress on your health. We know that bereavement or grief can lead to infections such as pneumonia. When you are stressed you are not surprised if you succumb to every infection going. Your resistance is lowered and old problems can flare up.

What happens when you do get a cold or the flu? Of course you become run down and experience the usual symptoms, true. However, you also lose or reduce your capacity to handle stress. Tasks that you do normally and easily when healthy become a stressful burden when your immune system is under pressure. You can't cope.

To boost your immune system:

a) Take at least 2,000 mg of vitamin C a day
b) Take a strong antioxidant supplement
c) Eat several pieces of fresh fruit daily
d) Have a salad of fresh vegetables each day
e) Ensure an adequate protein intake

Step 17 – Manage PMS and the menopause

Premenstrual syndrome (PMS) and the menopause are not diseases. However, the hormonal fluctuations that occur during a monthly cycle or those that occur during the menopause can put a stress on your body that reduces your ability to handle other stresses. By helping your body to handle these changes you can increase your stress-managing capacity.

PMS

Menstruation should be a normal and healthy cycle. Ideally it should be regular – occurring around every 28 days – and pain-free. If it isn't, then you may benefit from professional advice as there are several ways that problems can be corrected naturopathically. However, our main focus here is on the stress-related problems that can occur in the premenstrual period, usually from 0-10 days prior to the period.

PMS has many symptoms; many but not all are mental and emotional, and they are generally subdivided into four groups.

PMSA   irritability, nervous tension, anxiety, allergies
PMSC   hypoglycaemia and sugar cravings
PMTD   depression
PMTH   includes fluid retention and allergies.

⌐∿

Many books have been written on the subject and any naturopath should be able to help you. You may be able to identify your type of PMS yourself and follow the overall guidelines given here and elsewhere in this book as they apply to you. When you have other stresses in your life you do not need the extra problems that PMS can bring for a third or more of the month.

Menopause
Similarly, the menopause is not a disease or illness, despite the way many women rush to their doctor once it occurs. It too should be almost symptomless, other than the cessation of your period itself. However, it is often accompanied by many emotional and mental symptoms including anxiety, irritability and depression. If you are going through 'the change' and not enjoying the experience, then get advice. Naturopaths will have many helpful suggestions.

Programme for PMS/menopause management
Include soya proteins and foods in your diet. They contain many helpful compounds. Buy GM-free soya products. Increase the amount of vegetables in your diet as they contain many of the essential minerals needed at this time. Milk and dairy products are a less useful mineral source; in addition, they may be worsening rather than helping your problem as so many people are allergic to them.

There are many different herbs (black cohosh, liquorice, dong quai, ginseng, wild yam and others) and homoeopathic remedies that can help. The details of a programme that would benefit you will depend on the specific symptoms from which you are suffering and you may need professional advice. A beneficial nutritional programme will generally include evening primrose or borage oils and fish oils, vitamins E, B_3, B_5 and B_6, calcium and magnesium, digestive enzymes and hydrochloric acid.

Step 18 – Love your heart

The connection between stress and heart attacks is almost as standard as the connection between stress and ulcers. If there is a history of heart disease or high blood pressure in your family you should pay particular attention to this step. Again, this is not the place for full details of what you should do, so check books on the subject or get advice. General rules for a good diet apply and make sure you eat fish several times a week.

You should have your blood pressure checked regularly. If it rises do not turn to drug medicines. You would be better advised to put both parts of this book into action even more thoroughly and to eliminate the cause of the problem. There are also several important nutritional steps including ensuring an adequate intake of calcium and magnesium.

By all means check your cholesterol level but it is wise to recall that for 50 per cent of the people who develop a heart problem, their first early-warning sign is death. They often had normal blood pressure and normal cholesterol levels. A more useful blood test is for your homocyteine level. If this is high you should get advice on treatment immediately and reduce your stress and overload.

Step 19 – Mind your back

When stressed you are likely to stress your muscles, to hunch over and to sit and stand in unnatural positions. If your work involves physical stressors it is probable that in your rush to get things done you may lift heavy weights without proper care.

When cross or tense you probably hunch your shoulders and tense the muscles of your neck, leading to longer-term problems in these areas and possibly to headaches and other secondary problems.

To alleviate this problem the first step is to become conscious of it. Make a determined effort to relax all those tense muscles, and before you can do that you have to become conscious of them, so give yourself time each day to check them all out. You will probably be surprised at just how tense you are physically. It's a good idea to have osteopathic check-ups and, if you are so inclined, treating yourself to a weekly massage may be more than just an indulgence.

Check on your activities. Do you hunch your shoulder to hold the phone? This will almost certainly be on one side only and will cause neck problems. Do you frown? Does it help solve the problem? No, of course not, so practise relaxing your forehead – after all, you don't really want all those lines, do you?

Step 20 – Have fun, communicate and recharge your batteries

This step, like part of Step 10, is not nearly so frivolous as it sounds. You can deal with almost any stress if there is a light at the end of the tunnel.

Communication is important, particularly if you are in a relationship as your partner may be an unintended victim of your stress. I frequently advise patients who are part of a couple to put aside one night a week for each other. No matter what else crops up, nothing should interfere with this evening. One week he plans an evening for her, the next week she plans one for him. This way you both have the alternate pleasure of giving and receiving. More importantly, in regard to stress and overload, you know there is a time coming up in the next day or two when you will have time to talk things out together while you are also relaxed and able to do something you enjoy. Just this knowledge in itself can be a help. It also means there is no need to throw out ideas, comments or needs 'on the run' and at inappropriate times. Use this evening for improving your communications and your relationship, away from children and domesticity, as well as for doing something you or your partner enjoy.

If you are not part of a couple it is still important to ensure you have regular fun. You may think you are too busy or too broke to book that theatre ticket, go to that football match, invite friends in or do whatever it is that helps you recharge your batteries. You don't have time *not* to. You will find that doing something to which you have looked forward gives you the energy and initiative to keep going with the stress load you are carrying and may even help you to solve problems and make decisions more easily.

If your need is to have quiet time for yourself, then plan this in too. Make a certain time of day or of the week sacrosanct, yours and yours alone. Go for that quiet walk, take time out to relax at home, listen to music or take up the hobby you've abandoned. Perhaps you've already tried to do these things but then felt guilty, knowing there were a thousand things you should have been doing. Perhaps you've been feeling that with the stress load with which you have to cope it is irresponsible to take time out for yourself. No, it is irresponsible *not* to recharge your batteries from time to time and to keep yourself happy, well and healthy.

The Mini 10-step programme

This is for those without the time, commitment or inclination to make major changes, but who still want to make some improvements and feel some benefit:

1 Buy a top-quality multivitamin and mineral supplement and take one every day.
2 Take a stress formula with extra B-vitamins, vitamin C and relaxing herbs (such as 'Adrenomax' by the author).
3 Remove sugar from your diet and increase your intake of fresh fruit; eat dried fruit if you crave something sweet.
4 Give up coffee, tea and chocolate. Replace them with dandelion coffee, herb teas (particularly chamomile or valerian) or dried fruit and nuts respectively.
5 Change your diet. Reduce the amount of processed foods, increase your consumption of vegetables and salads and buy organic produce whenever possible.
6 Reduce your intake of alcohol. Drink mineral water in a wine glass when eating out – it feels just as elegant.
7 Replace white flour with brown, white pasta with brown and white rice with brown.
8 Allow yourself 10 hours a day of sleep, relaxation and fun.

9 Take regular exercise – you don't have time not to.
10 Consult a naturopath. They can short-track your route to your individual regime for maximum health and relaxation.

Relax – it could be a lot more fun.

Resources

Other books currently available from Xandria Williams

Choosing Health Intentionally £5.99

Learning about, overcoming and dealing with the emotional problems associated with illness.

Choosing Weight Intentionally £5.99

Learning about, overcoming and dealing with the emotional issues around weight problems.

The Four Temperaments £8.99

Learn about your temperament and those of other people; discover the similarities and contrasts and so improve communications and relationships.

Beating the Blues £8.99

You're Not Alone £7.99

Living with Allergies £7.99

Fatigue – the secrets of getting your energy back £7.99

Overcoming Candida £5.99

Liver Detox Plan Ebury Press, 1988 £7.99

Supplements by Xandria Williams

'Liver Detox' - contains the nutrients and herbs recommended the *Liver Detox Plan*.

'AdrenoMax' - a combination of the nutrients and herbs recommended in *From Stress to Success*.

Ordering

The books can be ordered from good bookshops or from Xandria Williams. The supplements can be ordered from Nutri Imports on 0-800-212-742 or from Xandria Williams.

Index

bloating 295, 335, 342
blood clots 275
blood pressure 275, 284, 286, 301, 346
blood sugar 25, 283, 286, 289
   hypoglycaemia 336–9
   mind-body link 292, 304–5
   minerals 321
   toxins 323
boasting 142
body 225, 271–7, 286–309
breakfast 311–14
British Society for Mercury-Free
   Dentistry 326
bronchitis 299
bullying 101–3

cancer 56–7, 300
Candida albicans 7, 296, 305, 323, 341–2
candidiasis 25–6, 296, 305, 335, 341–2
carbohydrates 288–9, 290
cars 223
case studies
   addictions 110–12, 115–16, 118–22
   adoption 87–90
   affirmations 153–6, 158
   anger 116–17
   creating 52–3
   cultural filters 44
   early experiences 74–7
   external stressors 11–17, 27–8
   fear of failure 68–70
   filtering 50–1
   individual filters 45–7
   interpretations 86
   intuition 179–80
   Life Plan 208–9, 217–19, 228–32
   limiting thoughts 61–3
   major worries 173–6
   memories 79–81
   minor worries 168–71
   other people 192–8
   outcomes 130–6
   perfection 243–9

   preferences 112–14
   regression 101–6
   responsibility 139–40
   running a phrase 34–6
   unplanned children 91–2
   willingness to change 124–6
   worst-case scenarios 162–3
cave paintings 148
Caveman Diet 317
challenges 29
chamomile 330
change 13–15, 21, 53–4, 57
   outcomes 129–30
   programming 97
   responsibility 141–2
   thoughts 137–8
   willingness 123–8, 257–8, 266
children 22, 82–97, 148, 185–6
   Life Plan 208–9, 222, 225
   overload 280
   proaction 189–94
   ten-step regime 312
chocolate 327–8, 348
choices 10–11, 58, 139, 180–1
cholesterol 301–2, 346
circumstances 180–1
coffee 326–7, 348
colitis 296
colleagues 222
comfort zone 143
communication 347–8
concentration 305
confidence 21–2, 116, 152, 154, 264–5
confusion 304–5
constipation 297–8, 335, 336, 340, 342
control 57–60
coping strategies 159, 161–4, 261–2, 266,
   282–3
corrections 227–30
courage 143–4
cravings 327, 342, 344
creativity 41–54, 142, 144, 180–2
criticism 21, 23, 235–40